The Autobiography of
Abbie Hoffman

Other Works by the Author

Revolution for the Hell of It
Woodstock Nation
Steal This Book
Vote! (coauthors Jerry Rubin, Ed Sanders)
To america with Love (coauthor Anita Hoffman)
Square Dancing in the Ice Age
Steal This Urine Test (with Jonathan Silvers)
The Best of Abbie Hoffman (edited by Daniel Simon)

The Autobiography of Abbie Hoffman

Introduction by Norman Mailer

with a new afterword by Howard Zinn

Four Walls Eight Windows
New York/London

First Four Walls Eight Windows edition October 2000.

Published in the United States by
Four Walls Eight Windows
39 West 14th Street
New York, NY 10011
http://www.4w8w.com

UK offices:
Four Walls Eight Windows/Turnaround
Unit 3 Olympia Trading Estate
Coburg Road, Wood Green
London N22 67Z

Library of Congress Cataloging-in-Publication Data:
Hoffman, Abbie.
    Autobiography of Abbie Hoffman/Abbie Hoffman; introduction by Norman Mailer.
    p. cm.
    Originally published: New York: Putnam c1980.
    ISBN: 1-56858-197-1
    1. Hoffman, Abbie. 2. Fugitives from justice—United States—Biography. 3. Radicalism—United States. I. Title.
    HV8658.H63 A36   2000
    364.1'31'092—dc21
    [B]   00-021241

Printed in Canada
10 9 8 7 6 5 4 3 2 1

to
ANGEL
my running mate, who led me into the valley of life.

Dear Abbie—
Wait till Jesus gets his
hands on you—you little
bastard.

Anonymous

(My all-time favorite hate letter.)

Contents

Introduction
by Norman Mailer

Abbie is one of the smartest—let us say, one of the quickest—
people I've ever met, and he's probably one of the bravest. In the
land from which he originates, Worcester, Mass., they call it
moxie. He has tons of moxie. He is also one of the funniest people I
ever met. He is also one of the most appealing if you ask for little
order in personality. Abbie has a charisma that must have come out
of an immaculate conception between Fidel Castro and Groucho
Marx. They went into his soul and he came out looking (or at least
he used to look) like an ethnic milkshake—Jewish revolutionary,
Puerto Rican lord, Italian street kid, Black Panther with the old
Afro haircut, even a glint of Irish gunman in the mad, green eyes. I
remember them as yellow-green, like Joe Namath's gypsy green
eyes. Abbie was one of the most incredible-looking people I ever
met. In fact, he wasn't Twentieth century, but Nineteenth. Might
just as well have emerged out of *Oliver Twist*. You could say he
used to look like a chimney sweep. In fact, I don't know what
chimney sweeps looked like, but I always imagined them as
having a manic integrity that glared out of their eyes through all the
soot and darked-up skin. It was the knowledge that they were
doing an essential job that no one else would do. Without them,
everybody in the house would slowly, over the years, suffocate
from the smoke.

If Abbie is a reincarnation—and after you read this book you
will ask: how could he not be?—then chimney sweep is one of his
past lives. It stands out in his karma. It helps to account for why he
is a crazy maniac of a revolutionary, and why, therefore, we can
say that this book is a document, is, indeed, the autobiography of a
bona fide American revolutionary. In fact, as I went through it,
large parts of the sixties lit up like areas of a stage grand enough to
hold an opera company. Of course, we all think we know the
sixties. To people of my generation, and the generation after us,

the sixties is a private decade, a good relative of a decade, the one we believe we know the way we believe we know Humphrey Bogart. I always feel as if I can speak with authority on the sixties, and I never knew anybody my age who didn't feel the same way (whereas try to find someone who gets a light in their eye when they speak of the seventies). Yet reading this work, I came to decide that my piece of the sixties wasn't as large as I thought. If we were going to get into comparisons, Abbie lived it, I observed it; Abbie committed his life, I merely loved the sixties because they gave life to my work.

So I enjoyed reading these pages. I learned from them, as a great many readers will. It filled empty spaces in what I thought was solid knowledge. And it left me with more respect for Abbie than I began with. I had tended to think of him as a clown. A tragic clown after the cocaine bust, and something like a ballsy wonder of a clown in the days when he was making raids on the media, but I never gave him whole credit for being serious. Reading this book lets you in on it. I began to think of Dustin Hoffman's brilliant portrait of Lenny Bruce where, at the end, broken by the courts, we realize that Lenny is enough of a closet believer in the system to throw himself on the fundamental charity of the court—he will try to make the judge believe that under it all, Lenny, too, is a good American, he, too, is doing it for patriotic reasons. So, too, goes the tone of this unique autobiography. Comrades, Abbie is saying, "under my hustle beats a hot Socialist heart. I am really not a nihilist. I am one of you—a believer in progress."

He is serious. Abbie is serious. His thousand jokes are to conceal how serious he is. It makes us uneasy. The literary merits of his book are circumscribed by a lack of ultimate irony. Under his satire beats a somewhat hysterical heart. It could not be otherwise. Given his life, given his immersion in a profound lack of security, in a set of identity crises that would splat most of us like cantaloupes thrown off a truck, it is prodigious that he is now neither dead or demented. He has to have a monumental will. Yet it is part of the civilized trap of literature that an incredible life is not enough. The survivor must rise to heights of irony as well. This is not Abbie's forte. His heart beats too fiercely. He cares too much. He still loves himself too much. All the same, we need not quibble. We have here a document of a remarkable man. In an age of contracting horizons, we do well to count our blessings. How odd that by now, Abbie is one of them. Our own holy ghost of the Left. Salud!

Commence Prayer

My sister once told me this story. Twelve years ago she was on an airplane headed for New York. It was a routine flight until the pilot realized the landing gear refused to engage. He asked ground control for instructions as the plane circled the landing field. The runway was coated with a foamy cushion; fire trucks and ambulances moved into position.

Meanwhile the passengers were told of each maneuver in that cheery, right stuff voice pilots manage to affect so well. Stewardesses glided about the cabin calming folks. Passengers were directed to countereffect the initial jolt by placing their heads between their knees and grabbing their ankles just before the moment of impact.

Suddenly the pilot announced over the intercom: "We are beginning our final descent. At this moment, in accordance with International Aviation Codes established at Geneva, it is my obligation to inform you that if you believe in God you should commence prayer."

There are some things about society you have absolutely no way of discovering unless you're in a crisis. As it happened, the belly landing went without a hitch. No one was injured in the slightest. The next day I called the airlines and asked about the prayer rule. No one would volunteer any information on the subject. It was strictly "no comment."

I could see their side. There are lots of secret rules by which power maintains itself. Only when you challenge it, force the crisis, do you discover the true nature of society. And only at the time it chooses to teach you.

Occasionally you can use your intellect to guess at the plan, but in general the secrets of power are taught in darkened police cells, back alleys, and on the street. I learned them there. And I think cops learn them there too. Like those airplane passengers we all learned them just before the possibility of the final descent.

Here Comes Trouble

I was born November 30, 1936, on the top floor of a three-decker wooden tenement house—its style of architecture unique to Worcester, Massachusetts. At the end of the block was the Harrington-Richardson Arms Company, one of America's famous gun factories, at the other end, Beaver Brook Park, home of the Barnum and Bailey Circus for one week every summer. Me and the birth-control pill were just about the most celebrated things ever to come out of Worcester. At one time, most folks up there wished the pill had come first.

Our family lived there three years. I don't remember much: the primal scream shouted over the crib railing into the darkness while Mama enjoyed mah-jongg with the girls or Papa played gin rummy chomping on an unlit Cuban cigar. If I made a noise, someone would say, "There's trouble." Family mythology insists that as early as one month of age I could lift myself with my hands and feet, doing inverted push-ups for anyone who cared to watch. I've carried the image a long time. Me, lying on my parents' bed, showing off for all the relatives. Thus is destiny for the first-born son of the first-born son of a Jewish family.

We moved just before the war "to get the Jews" broke out. A short move up Chandler Street to Geneva. The new place was a private dark brown house with a porch and a huge back yard. My father drove a battered black De Soto sedan. He worked nearby as a druggist in Uncle Kanef's drugstore. I remember the drugstore. There are hundreds of photos showing me standing in its doorway—like Monet's Rouen Cathedral, each slightly different.

My mother was a secretary before she got married. She met my father in the Recreational Bowling Alley down on Main Street. My father bowled in a league. My mother fell in love with him because he wore a clean white shirt every Friday night. Since my father never spoke of intimate things, I have no idea why he married

Mama. It could have been for her looks, for her superb penmanship, or for love. Perhaps nobody knows why their parents married. The reasons hidden in the back of the bureau drawer along with the prophylactics.

For them my life had been pretty much the ultimate in Jewish nightmares. I used to see everything as a struggle with my father, just transferred to various institutions. Psychoanalysts encourage us to see things that way. In the past years, I felt the war was over between us and tried to make peace, but he had too many heart attacks and down deep was crushed by the pain of life. We both tried at times to patch things up. He died three weeks after I went underground.

Once during the surrealist phase of my life—money burnings, Pentagon levitations, and other revolutionary highjinks, a local reporter managed to pull off an interview with him. "He was such a bright student," my father said. "He could have been somebody, a doctor or a professor—now we have to read the papers to see which jail he's in." The article struck a popular nerve and appeared in hundreds of newspapers. In New York, the *Post* carried the story with the headline "Oh Dad, Poor Dad, Abbie's Heart Belongs to DADA." My father got a lot of "me-too" letters from parents all over the country.

His son's notoriety must have confused my father. It is, after all, a type of success. Judges asked him for my autograph. FBI agents leaped out of the bushes and took photos of him and made sure the customers knew who his son was. He never approved of what I was doing but never (to use a gentile expression) disowned me. I remember him in his later years. Despite the personal successes, like becoming national president of his businessmen's club, he went out bitter. He loved prime-time America, but Watergate shattered his tube. It was a personal blow, as if what his children had been saying all those years had suddenly been proven true. He felt old and cheated. There was no reason to hang on to life.

In formulating struggle with society I always stressed its personal aspects. Our public and private relationships constantly intersected. Once at the Miami conventions, during negotiations with the city council, I explained, "If your police force messes one lock of my curly hair, my father's never coming down here again." I was talking of generations, speaking figuratively. A councilman answered, "I *know* your father and he'll still come down. He loves the beach!"

With hindsight, I wish I had been kinder to Papa. When I was little we often went fishing together. Getting up at the crack of dawn, lowering worms over the side of an old rowboat, grateful for any-size fish. We fished on the lake with the longest name in the dictionary. Fifty-seven letters, the Indian translation of which means, "You fish on your side of the lake, I'll fish on my side of the lake, and no one will fish in the middle." The last time I saw Dad, when I was living on Long Island, I took him out deep-sea fishing for big ones, returning the favor. The trip didn't work though. Ma got seasick and Dad kept yelling at my kids not to sit on the edge of the boat. My final image of him is shouting, "No!" The fishing expedition flopped, as did all the other attempts at reestablishing communication. I tried in lots of ways. I always kept one suit and tie in the back of the closet. The funeral suit. Hippie or no hippie, I would wear it to Temple Emanuel on that day he died: My fugitive flight began in the suit. I wrote him that night—"Hey, I know what you're going through pa, now that I have kids of my own. Parental love's the only real charity going. It never comes back. A one-way street. In what way should your son be different from all other sons?"

The Whole World's Wrong and You're Right!

I resented my father for not fighting in World War II. He had a private war to fight, supporting his parents and us; still a 4-F father was not someone you bragged about in a time when all heroes were "over there." It was total war even for us kids. We had to go on paper drives, roll the tin foil from chewing-gum wrappers into silver balls, plant victory gardens in Beaver Brook Park, and on weekends volunteer to turn screws in little portable ironing boards that supposedly accompanied soldiers into battle. (Thirty years later, I was to learn that victory gardens weren't much help, the tin foil balls were never used for anything, and what the hell were soldiers going to do with little portable ironing boards storming the beaches of Normandy? I guess all that stuff mattered though in terms of "keeping the home fires burning.")

My father specialized in figuring out how to get meat without ration stamps. Family first. He helped me score Fleer's Double BubbleGum, which was hard to get during the war years. The best bubble gum the world ever produced. It came wrapped like salt-water kisses with a comic strip inside. You could chew it all day, blow bubbles bigger than your head, seal the seam with your teeth, and take the whole thing out of your mouth like a huge pink lung. You could put it in a glass of water at night on the side of your bed and next day it was as good as new. One piece could last the whole week if you treated it right. For some reason after the war, all bubble gum deteriorated, even Fleer's. It may have something to do with the proliferation of plastics. Who knows?

Right after the war ended, Uncle Kanef died and totally read my father, Johnnie, out of the will. Goodbye drugstore. Johnnie struck out on his own and gave birth to the Worcester Medical Supply Company—a firm catering to the needs of doctors and hospitals. He pushed bedpans, Band-Aids, and barbiturates in bulk. A middleman, who carried home each night the great anxiety that the big drug companies would "go direct," rendering him instantly expendable. He traveled a great deal throughout his territory, and many of his life experiences are reflected in Miller's *Death of a Salesman*, which as a result has always been my favorite American play.

For a long time, the store was the place Mama called when I "acted up." I got punished for acting up. I'm never sure how hard he whipped me. Your classic macho stand-off, I think of it as one long, continuous, raging battle, with me refusing to cry and him huffing and puffing. After a few years, I learned that dungarees absorbed all the whammy out of a whipping.

One thing that really upset him was my not eating everything on my plate. Often I was banished to my room upstairs without any supper. I'd go days without eating. What no one ever knew was that I had already squirreled a secret cache of Devil Dogs, Tootsie Rolls, and soda for these occasions. I used the same fake-out much later in life while doing time in the Cook County Jail—I was never more than half-a-martyr.

He was prone to admonishing me with clichés while scowling and pointing with his outstretched index finger. "The Whole World's Wrong and You're Right!" was one of his favorites. "That's right," I'd answer, conceding not an inch.

I decided very early in life to fight back by developing asthma, one of the all-time great psychosomatic weapons. Supposedly it's related to choking of infantile tears, and some psychoanalyst had success with patients who he had recall childhood experiences while peeling onions. My parents often had to cancel hotel reservations at the beach when I came down with an attack. Making the rounds of specialists was a monthly routine. My favorite was an old German duck in Boston with a heavy accent and a pickled baby in a bottle. He'd stretch me out and stick little needles in my back, charging a "pretty penny" for all this fancy pricking. He always came up with a list of things I wasn't supposed to eat or be near. A typical list read like this:

The Patient Should Refrain From:
eggs, butter, milk, grains of all types including bread, cereals, and pastries, poultry, and all sharp seasoning. Also he is to stay away from all animals with hair, feathers, ragweed, daisies, dandelions, and drafts. All dust should be removed from his room daily.

This is the first set of written laws I can remember ignoring. Nonetheless, after the age of eleven, I discovered other weapons. Asthma and I parted ways.

I was a bowling maniac. It was nothing for me to bowl twenty-five strings a day. I was a Duncan yo-yo champ at eleven. Could do a one-and-a-half somersault off a diving board and scramble like a rabbit on the basketball court. Played knock-down guts football. Was captain of my tennis team in college. If you saw me on the tennis court you'd say "there's one aggressive go-getter." My coach, Bud Collins, has since gone on to become the Walter

Hell Unleashed, 1943. (My father
wrote this caption on the original
photo.)

Nuclear Family Quiz: Can
you identify the people in
this family portrait? Two
Uncle Sams, upper left rear
(pick rich one). The oldest
living Kanefsky-Shapoz-
nikoff, cousin Cynthia, my
first date; Mother; Papa; the
kid thrown over the wall at
Auschwitz; the nurse, the
one with the lobotomy;
Uncle Al; Aunt Ruthie, the
ragpicker; the unmarried
aunt. And finally, why is
everyone smiling?

Anna Kanefsky, bar mitzvah boy with watch, and Morris Shapoznikoff.

Cronkite of tennis. I used to down a bottle of honey and wrestle my ass off for the Brandeis wrestling squad. I stank though. I can throw a curve ball underhand with a softball. Whip it in there with some steam too. (The craziest softball team I ever played for was just that. A bunch of crazies. When I worked at Worcester State Hospital we had a team of patients and staff that played in a league along with barrooms and metal shops. We'd get beat sometimes 42-1. Scores like that. The first baseman was a catatonic-schizophrenic. You'd scoop up a grounder, wing it at him, and sometimes he'd forget to put his glove up and the ball would just zonk him in the chest or head. The second baseman was this sixteen-year-old kid who set fire to his own house. If you hit him a high pop-up, he'd start circling around like an airplane flying on one wing. The left fielder was prone to dizzy spells. There were four staffers and five patients, and all the patients were on massive doses of Librium and Thorazine. As a rule, the mental patients lacked speed on the basepaths.)

I never took anything as seriously as sports. I used to roller skate every Friday night. Slooping and sliding with a girl, trying to cop a feel, while the organist played "Peg o' My Heart." I even played golf. General Douglas MacArthur said, "Sports make the guardians of our nation strong." I studied America by playing its games and seeing its movies. Until college, the closest I came to reading about Western civilization was Classic Comics.

I'm a certified member of the North American Underwater Instructors Association and consider scuba diving the future sport of the Aquarian Age. I have been in the caverns off the coast of Isla de Mujeres where the sharks go to sleep and get high. Philippe Cousteau, who unfortunately just died, took me out to play with the whales and listen to them talk. Off the coast of Honduras, I went 275 feet down—my depth gauge lied. I was alone and running out of air. All around was nothing but blue, the most brilliant blue I've ever seen—and I was not sure which blue went down or which blue went up. Today I'm staring out at the sea off the coast of Captiva. There is sunken treasure out there and huge sea cows that sing like mermaids.

Bowling and pool were strictly for money. Cash up front. When I was rambling around college towns inciting folks to riot, back in the sixties, I'd kill an hour or two hustling pool in the student centers. As well as I can remember, only a cowgirl in Flagstaff outhustled me. Played a lot of poker. Used to take on this leader of a car-theft ring, head to head, when I was fourteen. I'd bet on anything: cards, ballgames, bowling, horses. I did okay, but really I'm not the hustler I pretend to be. I've lost my share. There was just too much that couldn't be won by hustling. Despite a common opinion, I'm only half-a-hustler. Half-a-martyr; half-a-hustler.

Mama Tried

Mama was a real nice mama. She understood and forgave a lot. Closed the door real quick when she caught me jerkin' off and never said nothing. Stood by me in the sixties and would have come to Chicago or other trials, but Dad wouldn't allow it. She knew I was a "banditle" when I was thirteen and the cops came to the house looking for someone who was going around changing the number plates on the neighbors' cars. Mama shooed them away. I could make her laugh and she me. She had a sense of humor. When I started shouting that kids should kill their parents for the revolution, she thought that was pretty funny, since most parents at one time or another wished they'd never brought their kids into the world either. Merle Haggard must have had us in mind when he sang, "I got only me to blame, 'cause Mama tried."

In her era, women had their place. If she had a good idea or ambition it was quickly dismissed as "female frivolity." She was kind and generous, and as I said always shooed the cops away. Now that Papa's gone, she walks the widow's lonely night, struggling to make a new life. She's seventy-four years old and fighting. We're very proud of Mama. She sends me toothbrushes, wooden picks, and dental floss twice a year by secret underground couriers with a note saying: "Your teeth are very important."

Halloween was a week-long celebration around our neighborhood. We used it to get even with nasty neighbors. We'd shovel dog shit into a bag. Leave it on the stoop. Set it on fire. Ring the bell. And wait for someone to come out, stamp on the flames, and come up with a shoe full of kaka. We had BB-gun wars and fights with snowballs we'd store in the freezer for days, making them hard as rocks. We'd sled down steep streets playing chicken with cars that crossed May Street. We would build tree houses in the woods, paint our faces like Indians, and make mock raids on the richer Zenith Drive family houses. We would catch snakes and put them in teachers' desks. Later I defined Yippie time as "Valentine days and Halloween nights."

I went to the best grammar school in the city. I scored A's in all the subjects but consistently flunked conduct. Actually I began majoring in sexual fantasy pretty early in life. See, there was this blond, Roxanne, in the third grade, and . . .

Family Forever

Jack's my younger brother. Not an easy thing. If we were building a tree hut and the hammer fell, Jack's head was always somewhere beneath, waiting. If I was swinging a golf club driving golf balls into yonder neighbors' windows, for some reason Jack always managed to straighten the tee at the right moment to get a whack.

Jack took on dad's business and made it grow. He's active in liberal politics. He's lost a lot of business because of my reputation, and told them all to stick it. Once he earned a state award for work with the mentally retarded, but the committee felt it wouldn't look right for the governor to shake hands with the brother of—and changed its mind. Jack is more than my brother—he is my friend.

I have a little sister. Phyllis was really cute. When she was four years old, the paper took a photo of her listening to the globe with a stethoscope (from Dad's store) to see if the world was going to end soon, as some scientists were predicting. I guess they were wrong.

Phyllis fell in love and married a guy who's this big honcho in the Mexican government. The Mexicans call her Elena because there are no Phyllises in Latin America.

I liked my Aunt Ruthie. Her husband, Uncle Al, was a pain in the ass though: he said hello by grabbing you in a hammer lock, and it really hurt. Phyllis used to kick him in the shins every time and say things like "You bastard, cut that shit out." Which was not the way, of course, to open a family Passover meal. Family meals with twenty or thirty people were common.

When I was into hypnosis, my Auntie Ruthie had a minor operation on her arm and for some reason it refused to move afterward. As the first family member to have made it to college, it was assumed I had access to secret cures. On a Friday night, all the relatives huddled outside the door listening, while inside Sophomore Svengali hypnotized Aunt Ruthie. Zonk: in twenty seconds she goes into this deep trance and starts moving her hand freely while talking all this deep psycho stuff. Here I am—monkeying with a relative's cerebral cortex while Papa bangs on the door yelling, "How's it going in there, already?" She came out of the trance okay and didn't remember anything. Anyway, the hand was okay a week later. (I got real good at hypnosis, especially self-hypnosis, which I found useful in the same way others utilized Yoga mind control.)

Then there was Aunt Sara and Uncle Lou who took care of my *bubbie* when my *zaddie* died. Died in my arms mumbling ancient Hebraic chants, leaving me his entire estate which totaled sixty-four dollars. My grandmother is a rock. She just celebrated her ninety-eighth birthday and comes from a town in Russia that hasn't even existed for sixty-five years. Once she called my brother to her bedside and asked him to tell me that her brother had been a leading Bolshevik in the Russian Revolution and had been killed by czarist troops. Apparently she had guarded this secret with ghetto silence for over half a century and now that I was underground wanted me to know. I took it as a great compliment because she dismissed all my *mishigas* with a scowl and a wave of her arm. At least I think that was her attitude. Jews survive on ambiguous gestures. Dismissal could have been acceptance. Or both. She told me recently that she would live until I was "free." "I am free," I answered.

Now Mama's side is extra exciting: First there's Aunt Rose. She was the first woman accepted to Middlesex Medical College (which later became Brandeis University). The experience produced a lot of tension topped with real tragedy. One of my mother's brothers was killed in a car accident returning from Boston where he had gone to buy a diamond ring for his bride-to-be. Aunt Rose flipped out. She wound up in seclusion at Worcester State Hospital, which was a real horror in the forties. (Later when I worked there as a psychologist in the early sixties I used to visit the old facilities: cages, padded cells, ice-water baths, dungeons. God, I used to think, my aunt went through this hellhole.) Finally doctors persuaded the family to let them do a frontal lobotomy. They stuck a scalpel straight up her eyeball sockets to the top of her head and wiggled it back and forth, severing the lobe connections. I remember when she came out of the hospital, wearing a wig, mumbling *non sequiturs* and eating everything in sight. All us kids were scared shitless.

Then there's my uncle "Schmully." He took over his father's wrecking business in Clinton, twenty miles between Worcester and nowhere. Just before he entered the service he guessed soldiers would be shaving a lot for parades and that razor blades were a good investment. He bought two thousand shares of Gillette stock at two dollars per. That was in 1940. Schmully had country smarts.

Rumor insisted there was lots of money buried out there under some rock in Clinton. I really liked Schmully. He didn't talk much, but he sort of huffed this cynical "hun hun!" at all new-fangled notions. He was a Jew accepted and liked in the most redneck Polish-Irish town imaginable. They even made him head of the American Legion Post. He had a pink Cadillac and an old black Labrador retriever and everyone thought he'd die a bachelor. One day, however, he showed up with this snazzy dame with flaming red hair and a thick Irish brogue and announced they were getting married. Well the family didn't exactly start throwing *mazeltovs* around. Marrying a *goy* was equal to getting pregnant before marriage or going bankrupt. It was worse, even, and Jinny was the shicksiest *shicksah* you could imagine. I liked the whole thing. They were in love and showed it—unlike my other relatives, who hid their affections.

The family was not without its celebrities. At one extreme

branch of my father's family tree was a lady named Frieda Lipshitz who changed her name to Georgia Gibbs and became famous in the fifties. Georgia did a female Pat Boone number, ripping off black rhythm-and-blues songs banned from the radio. She cleaned up the lyrics and scored with several hit records. On my mother's side, there's my cousin Sydney Schanberg, who won a Pulitzer Prize for his excellent reporting of the war in Southeast Asia. He's now metropolitan editor for *The New York Times* and rising. Everyone's proud of Sydney.

Origins of the International Jewish Conspiracy

The original family name is Shapoznikoff. My grandfather's brother stole identity papers from a German named Hoffman and fled to America around 1900. When my grandfather arrived at Ellis Island, shortly thereafter, the customs man read the note which said "Deliver Shapoznikoff to Hoffman" and dubbed my grandfather *Hoffman* as well.

We are part of the Ashkenazi branch of Hebrews who migrated, via Persia and the Orient, to Russia, finally settling in the Ukraine somewhere near Kiev. "We lived in the woods," explains my grandmother. "They would not allow Jews to enter the city." Grandfather's family, like hers, also fought in the revolution and many history books describe the heroics of one possible relative, General Shapoznikoff, a free-spirited patriot eventually executed by Stalin.

Despite these traces of Bolshevik blood, I was far from a red-diaper baby. Indeed my father internalized America's anti-red phobia and never spoke of family history. If he had any politics they were Republican conservative. Of course, all politics were secondary to business and religion. I came into this world acutely aware of being Jewish and am sure I'll go out that way.

Judaism has never been so much a religion to me as a noble history and a cluster of stereotypes. Big noses, curly hair, and departed foreskins were all worthy of celebration. Jewish identity, self-awareness, and the acculturation process let you know very early in life that you were put on earth to make choices.

Jews, especially first-born male Jews, have to make a big choice very quickly in life whether to go for the money or to go for broke. It is the great genetic gamble we've all been granted. Wiseguys who go around saying things like "Workers of the world unite," or "Every guy wants to screw his mother," or "E = mc²," obviously choose to go for broke. It's the greatest Jewish tradition, but unfortunately most take the other road and aim for the upper-middle class of whatever society they find themselves in at any given moment. Most are "better" Americans, just as fifty years ago they were "better" Germans. They keep their noses clean and never get drunk.

Intellectual arrogance and moral indignation grow out of the ghetto history. For five thousand years, Jews always had the opportunity to rebel against authority, because for five thousand years there was always someone trying to break their backs. And yet most Jews, aware of having been chosen, back off from this inevitable clash with society. They forsake destiny and choose instead the gelt and assimilation. Constantly, however, the drive for money is obstructed by the ethical ambiguities of Jewish teachings. It's this and it's that. Neither here nor there. An ideal attitude for producing intellectual curiosity and humor. An attitude often necessary for survival, but an attitude shrouded in "Jewish guilt," destined to end in unhappiness.

In Worcester, as the forties became the fifties, it seemed the entire Jewish community had chosen to survive by assimilation. Great psychological dilemmas revolved around religious traditions at odds with the desire to be accepted. Our family was plagued with Talmudic riddles—What's our stand on kosher bacon? On mixing milk with meat? Was chocolate-covered matzo legit, or a mockery? How could something that tasted as good as lobster be *"trefe"* (forbidden)?

Slowly, my parents got sucked into the social melting pot, where they were to simmer uncomfortably for the next thirty years. Having opted for a life in mainstream America, it became very difficult, even hypocritical, for them to try and push any strict code of tradition down our throats. We were often exposed to scenes like this: "Now kids, remember those nice people the Silvermans. Well, they're not Silvermans anymore. They are now the Sills. Be nice."

Deep down I'm sure we felt our parents' generation was a bunch of cop-outs. Six million dead and except for the Warsaw ghetto hardly a bullet fired in resistance! I remember being very young and on our way to a family vacation in New Hampshire. I turned over the hotel brochure I was practice-reading and spotted a curious little announcement. I read it aloud to the whole car. "Hey everybody, what does 'Christian Clientele Only' mean?" Everyone turned Protestant white. "Johnnie, they accepted our reservation! Didn't they know?" My parents wanted desperately to avoid a scene. "Avoiding a scene" was a very common expression then. Over there, six million Jews were avoiding a scene, and on the home front on a beautiful fall day in the mountains of New Hampshire my father made a U-turn and we headed for another hotel. I was angry enough to muster up an asthma attack.

It wasn't all their fault, of course. Like everyone else, I tried to "pass" loads of times if the odds were too high. On the school bus, I faked bowing my head when we passed Blessed Sacrament Church, afraid the Irish kids would throw my books out the window if I didn't. Once or twice I even crossed myself before jumping into the YMCA pool, fully conscious of what the C stood for. There's a thin line between "avoiding a scene" and "using your head," another popular Jewish expression. But in *Gentleman's Agreement* Gregory Peck had played the hotel rejection scene better than Papa. You can guess at the confusion of the period.

During the assimilation/anti-assimilation debate raging in the community, I was shuttled back and forth between the Orthodox yeshiva after school on weekdays and the Reform Temple Emanuel on weekends. It was getting me pretty mixed up. Eventually tefillin and Torah lessons gave way to dancing classes and discourses (in English) on the nature of life and how good things were in America. The temple, but three blocks from my house and directly across the street from my grammar school, was a large brick structure about as religiously stimulating as a Ramada Inn. And like the Ramada Inn, it specialized in the family trade and seemed on more familiar terms with tax shelters and parking ordinances than with the Almighty. The rabbi, a shy little fellow, was given to lofty rhetoric but slow to oppose a Jewish petition aimed at excluding a black dentist from purchasing a house on nearby Flagg Street. Once, when I asked, the rabbi told me that people like Norman Mailer and Philip Roth gave Jews a bad name. The rabbi was not exactly one of your go-for-brokers. When he grew too old, he was farmed-out to a minor-league temple in New Mexico.

Our congregation grew so large that the board, of which my father was a member, hired on an additional rabbi who gave peppier sermons. Handsome and young, his name was Alex Schindler. Today he's the country's leading rabbi, the one who tells the President to send more planes to Israel. It took both rabbis to bar mitzvah me into manhood.

The social scene revolving around the temple was a whirlwind of fashion and gossip. Classes spilled into parties and clumsy attempts at dating as the pack formed. I was smart, popular, and accepted. But for some reason I got quickly bored with the fox trot and dressing up for receptions. I started drifting down to the corner of June and Chandler streets, hanging out with the likes of Squeekie McGovern, Paduzzi, and the notorious Foster brothers. We shot craps in alleyways, smoked like chimneys, wolf-packed the neighborhood at night, and frequented downtown pool halls and bowling alleys. At thirteen, a part of me had already begun to drop out of the mainstream.

By this time I had been channeled into Seaver Prep, a city-run ghetto for brains. We studied erotic subjects like Latin and algebra. Right before graduation, I had an attack of appendicitis and was rushed to the hospital just in the nick. I went from the hospital to graduation exercises, limping across the stage. I got a standing ovation, tying the applause for the school's only Negro. In the fall, I'd be shipped off to high school, and the fifties were about to begin.

A Teenager in the Fifties: Jewish Grease

We spent the summer in Onset on Cape Cod. A place I would spend most of my teenage vacations. Onset wasn't the Cape Cod of the Kennedy compound or the intellectual retreat of Provincetown. Cape Cod extends from the body of Massachusetts out into the Atlantic like Arnold Schwarzenegger's arm. The *real* Cape is out where the fist sits in Hyannisport. Onset was the little pit the other side of the elbow where all the sweat collects.

There were teenagers from Worcester and from a host of tough, working-class suburbs around Boston. Places like Chelsea, Everett, Dorchester, and Roxbury. While the Kennedys down the road were sculling in the bays, we were playing rough beach games like buck-buck, where two gangs would take turns jumping on each other. Salt water held sand on your inner thighs, and when you came down you were supposed to scrape your legs hard against your opponent's bare back. Drawing blood if you could.

My friend Bert had a bronze Ford convertible with tiger-skin upholstery and glass-pack mufflers that made the engine sound like a machine gun. He was very cool, Bert was. Had a special driving style, curved around the steering wheel like a cobra with his right hand on the gearshift ready to scrub out at the drop of a dare. The Dorchester boys were already into pegged pants, D.A.'s, and leather jackets with slots sewn inside for stilettos.

We'd do a lot of booze and end up at the wrestling matches. Once we rumbled with Chuck O'Brien's gang from Fall River, and I got thrown off the railing to the ground ten feet below. Just like in the cowboy pictures.

I went steady with little Suzie from Everett. I was nuts about her. I even painted my black leather Roll-O-Flex skates with dayglo silver paint that said "I Love Suzie." She was the best dancer I ever went with. We did strange horny dances that had

names like the Roxbury Mule, the Chelsea Slouch, and the Ginney
Crawl: some real sexy where the guy would dip on his knees up
close to the gal and run his hand from her ankle slowly up to
her. . . . well, it depended. One ritual went like this: The guy
would say, "I'm an Oldsmobile," and start up real slow. The girl
would say "Red light." After a few more car models, he'd say he
was an ambulance and when she'd yell out, "Red light," thigh
high, he'd just say, "Ambulances don't stop for red lights, baby,"
and grab her crotch. It was a lot of giggles.

We all had a favorite book called *The Hoods*, which I keep
trying to find again. With all due apologies to Puzo, it was *the* great
Mafia novel and it served as our instruction book for manliness.
Macho meant walking barefoot on the hot concrete streets, cruising alone at night through Irish turf, finger-fucking in the movie
theater, and being able to spit through the crack in your two front
teeth. We played chicken with cars and gambled on everything.

I brought my summer on the beach back to the city. When high
school began, I was grease. A smart hood. Jewish grease.
Chicken-fat pomade.

Classical High School, like all high schools, was not a place you
went to learn anything. Like grammar school, it was a place you
spent time having more sexual fantasies and bitching about the
regulations. Regulations went like this: No smoking within two
blocks of the school; no D.A.'s permitted; no pegged pants less
than thirteen inches at the cuff (they measured!); garrison belts
were verboten, as were belts made from chains.

I got straight A's in U.S. history and never learned there had
been a depression, race revolts, Indian massacres, people like
Sacco and Vanzetti or the Rosenbergs, or that blacks were getting
lynched in America.

This is how Shakespeare was taught: Everyone had a book
called *Hamlet* in front of them. You read five lines and the person
in back of you read five. Shakespeare round-robin. While one
person read, everyone but the next reader slept. Poor Hamlet, what
a way to die—five lines at a time by me, then Paduzzi, then Skinny
Alice, then Jocko Mahoney. (Jocko, by the way, grew up and
became an FBI agent. He parlayed his schooldays into a career
explaining me to the rest of the bureau.)

Nationally, people were saying things like "What's good for General Motors is good for America," "The only good Red is a dead Red," and "Pepsi puts more bounce in the ounce." The last was the only political slogan to reach me directly. All I knew about politics was that Eisenhower was president and that he played golf in the high eighties. It was all I was supposed to know. There was a war on in Korea. I remember only that the yellow bellies fought dirty by having so little regard for life they would rush us in waves of human flesh, trying to exhaust our boys' ammunition until they succeeded in overrunning a hill. Did you ever hear of such a dirty way to fight?

Also I remember going all the way to Saint Nicholas Arena in New York, where Alan "Moondog" Freed was throwing a big party for the Drifters' Clyde McPhatter, who had just been drafted. Moondog gave him a gold watch inscribed "To the greatest *Earth-Angel* of them all—from his fans." And then they sang that song again and "God Bless America" and I passed out from too much gin and my buddies Charlies and Hack had to drag me back to the hotel, me dry heaving all the way across New York.

Once in Mister Cravetti's math class I cracked a joke. Cravetti went tapioca. He ran up the aisle, yanked me out of the chair, and dragged me to the principal's office. The principal was a snobby geezer named Fenton.

"Hoffman," he wheezed, "you seem to be having some adjustment problems here at Classical. Smoking in the toilets, carving on desks, joking in class, and look at how you dress, what the heck is that shirt called?"

"This, sir, is a Billy Eckstein pink-on-pink. Neat huh? I had to go all the way to Sam's in Lynn to get one."

I stared up at a sea of frowns.

It was along about this time that I met my first culture hero: Herbie Gamberg. He was small, wiry, with blond hair and a hook nose. Herbie played real guts football. A real scrapper and smart as the dickens. He was doing time at a new institution called Brandeis, and he came back to the neighborhood with a load of foreign ideas, dropping names like Nietzsche, Freud, and Albert Camoo. Herbie and I got into a discussion about God after a basketball game. He converted me to an atheist in the locker room. I thought about it for days and wrote a lengthy treatise questioning the concept of a Supreme Being. Not exactly prime Spinoza, it was nonetheless from the heart and head.

After an English class, I passed the twenty-page document up to the teacher, Mr. Brooks. It wasn't even a term paper, just an extracurricular dissertation; a pure inquest into deep waters. I was very proud. Next day Brooksie calls me to stay after class. He starts off slow, arguing some of the philosophical points, with me respectfully rebutting. Just as I'm making a subtle argument about reward and punishment, he calls me a "little communist bastard" and grabs me by my Billy Eckstein collar. Rrripppp!

"You ripped my fuckin' shirt! I went all the way to Sam's in Lynn . . ." I scream. Meanwhile Brooksie, who was hard-of-hearing, starts tearing up my paper and hurling the confetti at me. In return, I turn over his desk and tackle him. Pretty soon other teachers are on the scene and one says, "This is curtains for you, Hoffie." And it was. Mama made a lot of trips to intercede, but I was sixteen now, and legally the state could absolve itself of all responsibility for my education.

It's not to be found in the *Guinness Book of Records,* but I was the only Jew in the history of Classical High School to be expelled. I sent it in on my *Who's Who in America* form, but they X'd it out with all the other really important data.

About a week later, an event happened that really socked Worcester on the map, or rather almost socked it right off. It was June 9, 1953; 5:20 P.M. I was talking long distance to Suzie when an operator cut in and said, "I must interrupt this call. We are having a tornado and the police are trying to reach your father."

Dad was away so responsibility passed to the eldest son. The chief of police called, telling me to open the store immediately and begin supplying plasma and other necessities to the Red Cross stations. At the store, I was met by a Red Cross volunteer. Outside the sky was pitch black. Giant hailstones streaked by. I called New York suppliers and a whole chain of activity was set in motion. Through the night I rushed plasma at high speed to the suburbs. Seeing huge areas flattened. Trees smashed into houses. Rooftops torn off. A bus bent in two wrapped around a telephone pole. Bloodied bodies crawling out the windows. The radio said winds had hit three hundred miles per hour. It was a war zone. We lugged plasma into tents, climbing over dead bodies and people screaming. I worked the entire night. One hundred and twenty people were killed. It was one of the worst tornadoes in the country's history. The following day I helped search the rubble for bodies. I reached down a hole and my arm came up covered in blood. Disaster tested me. I liked the challenge.

That summer was cruising season. I had a sweet little '52 Ford. We cruised the downtown streets looking for broads. I'd do the talking. We'd get some booze, head to the drive-in, and make out like crazy, "busting a few rubbers" now and then.

Once I picked up this curly-haired sweetheart named Dixie. We went out lots of times till once she got really plastered and barfed all over my father's Roadmaster. Twenty years later I got a message from Sonny Barger, head of the Hell's Angels, "Tell Abbie, Dixie was my girlfriend too." It took me a while to recall it all, but sure enough Dixie was a biker moll and Sonny was head of a biker pack outside Worcester. He's doing time now. Heavy time.

I played the role of high-school dropout to the hilt—putting in days in the pool hall. Sometimes we'd take in the track or get into three-day poker games. I had a huge wardrobe of clothes. At one time I had seven pairs of shoes, all suede except for one pair of blue alligators. Weekends I'd race down to Everett and take Suzie dancing.

Suzie had a load of boyfriends. Once she showed me a bracelet with five high-school rings on it. Suzie was great in the sack. I wasn't really jealous since we lived so far apart. Once on her doorstep a fellow suitor jumped out of the bushes. He was a tall, skinny kid and before I knew it he pulled out a switchblade and stabbed me in the thigh. I kicked him in the crotch and he doubled over—a few good whacks and he fell down. Suzie was screaming. It was 2:00 A.M.

She sneaked me into her basement and wrapped my wounds with Kotex. I hitched back to Worcester. Next day, Doc Argoff stitched me up and told me had it been a half-inch deeper I could have bled to death. He asked me how I got it, because you have to report knife wounds to the police. "I got it shaving," I said, and he laughed. I guess we both saw the same movies. I was proud of the scars. So was Suzie.

From Bum to College Boy

Naturally my parents were not enthusiastic about my career as a bum. My father had a friend, a rung-and-a-half up the social ladder, whose son went to a private school. From there, everyone got into "the college of his choice." So the following year, D.A., pegged pants, and all, I enrolled in Worcester Academy to finish out my high-school years.

The Jewish barrier had been cracked and Yids were pouring into the place like the eleventh plague, much to the chagrin of the old Yankee traditionalists. Every day we had to go to chapel, and Headmaster Piper would give us one of those rousing Calvinist sermons on the ethics of "hard work." Then we'd all rise and sing a hymn while Mrs. Piper piped the organ. My favorite hymn was "Onward Christian Soldiers." You know, the part that goes "With the cross of Jesus, going as to war," Jewish kids weren't supposed to say the name of Christ out loud, so we all had to sing "with the cross of Hum Hum, going as to war." I did a two-year stretch at Worcester Academy, and by the second year Hum Hum was giving Jesus a run for his money.

The academy was upset when I told them I liked the idea of going to Brandeis University. It was only seven years old, and the academy wanted ivy-covered walls for its protégés. They presented such rational arguments against Brandeis that I fell in love with the place.

So one day in the fall of '55, my parents drove me and a huge black trunk down the new Mass Pike and onto the rolling green hills of Brandeis. There was a lot of parental hugging and kissing before Papa drove off. Until the day he died, he always blamed Brandeis for my corruption. Be it divorce, dope, hippies, or *schvartzes,* he always ended up cursing Brandeis. "If it hadn't been for Brandeis . . ." he used to mumble in a pained litany.

Fraternities were not allowed at Brandeis, but frat humor prevailed. The second day on campus, I was asked if I'd like to fuck a townie named Louise. She gave big discounts and fucked all the willing freshmen during orientation week. I was told to show up at a side entrance to the Castle, this honest-to-goodness castle sitting high on one of Brandeis's hills. At 2:00 A.M., I was ushered into the bathroom and told to quickly take off my clothes. Across the hall was the luscious Louise. Once in a while someone would come out saying, "God, fantastic!" etc. Then it was my turn. My guide opened the door and murmured, "Louise, here's a nice young man up from Worcester, who's heard so many things about you."

"Oh, no more please, my back is so sore," murmured Louise. "Be a good sport," said my guide. "All right . . . but leave the lights out," she agreed.

The door closed. As she rolled around in the bed and murmured, my cock got harder. "Have you ever fucked before, sonny?"

"Where are you, Louise?" I called. Groping for Louise, I tripped and fell into a group of bodies.

Surprise! Surprise! Lights exploded. The room was filled with thirty guys, including one who had played Louise. It was all clean Animal House fun. I was one of the boys now. There was only one problem. I couldn't stand "the boys," and, at first, I didn't know what I was doing at Brandeis. I came thinking I wanted to be a doctor. The only people my father admired were doctors, unless of course, they didn't pay their bills. So when it came time to sign up for courses, I went "pre-med," electing chem and math.

Brandeis was an unusual school at that time. It had embarked on a massive building program and all around were sprouting modern lecture halls, museums, dormitories, and libraries. Brandeis had an enormous edifice complex. Its proud centerpiece was the three chapels, designed to resemble open Bibles. One for the Catholics. One for the Protestants. And one for the Chosen People. The thirty-foot-high gray stone Bibles had been calibrated to within an exact millimeter of the same height. How's that for ecumenical equality? Every building had the name of a rich Jewish family attached to it. Even trees had plaques. There was a big bronze statue of Louis Brandeis on one of the hills, and when it came time for the unveiling, Eleanor Roosevelt, who taught there, pulled a sheet off our namesake. It looked like the good Justice had cut loose with a gigantic fart, sending his robes billowing in the wind.

Brandeis was lucky. In 1953, when Joe McCarthy brought his traveling witch hunt to Boston, he terrorized every school but Brandeis. He was afraid of being labeled anti-Semitic. As a result, the best professors from a host of other institutions fled to Brandeis. People like Herbert Marcuse, Frank Manuel, Louis Coser, Irving Howe, Max Lerner, Leo Bronstein, Abraham Maslow, Philip Rahv. Brandeis, for its size, had the most exciting faculty in the world. In my freshman year alone there was Leonard Bernstein for music and Eleanor Roosevelt for foreign affairs.

I had one of the greats right off. A one-legged giant named Frank Manuel, who had lost his limb in the Spanish Civil War. His course was the History of Ideas. I gobbled up everything he offered. Most of the other students, kids from New York, seemed used to this interchange of ideas, and familiar with names like Descartes and Rousseau. I was a comparative hick. Every new idea hit like a thunderclap.

Once when I thought I had nailed a contradiction in the last words of Jesus, based on the New Testament gospels, Dr. Manuel offered me a deep insight. "Abbie, my boy," he said, hunching over his crutches, "don't you understand? Nobody knows. People wrote those books years after the Crucifixion, and they've been changed with each upheaval in the church. History is made up. It's all made up. Nothing but *Grimm's Fairy Tales.*" God, he was beautiful. I was awed by his raw intellect. Gripped by the novelty of the liberal arts, I wound up cutting chem and math classes.

That summer when I told my father I was majoring in psychology he was a bit disappointed. "That and ten cents will get you on the subway." (Which was funny because the MTA had just jumped its fare—promoting a popular song by the Kingston Trio about poor old Charlie who got trapped riding forever beneath the streets of Boston. You needed fifteen cents.)

I had a summer job as a grinder in a defense factory. The work required security clearance from the FBI. I manned the swing shift on the assembly line. Horribly exhausting and dangerous work, my hands were continually getting cut. Years later I would be instrumental in organizing a series of demonstrations and lawsuits against the plant for racial discrimination. Two guys I had worked with on the line tipped me off that a goon had been hired to beat me up.

That was my first experience with your basic "proletariat class." Every time I hear the phrase I recall those days and the workers trapped on the swing shift, stuck in the pits, sucking up oil into their lungs, punching time cards for the Boss. Every time I hear the word *capitalist* I see the face of the plant owner, Robert G. Stoddard, one of America's great Yankee imperialists and for years my hometown enemy number one.

When I returned to Brandeis in the fall I still played poker and hit the track on weekends. I met a guy called Red Bell, a race-track tipster at Suffolk Downs who ran a delicatessen as a sideline. One night, my roommate, Manny, and I got the idea that the students needed some nighttime food. We made a deal with Red, and each night we picked up a hundred submarine sandwiches (a.k.a. heroes, clubs, po-boys, wedges, grinders) and carted them from dorm to dorm yelling, "Get your subs, red-hot subs!" It was a terrific success. In 1972 when I spoke at Brandeis, the students wanted to know if it was true that I was the first submarine-sandwich man. It was true.

Other changes were taking place. For example, it was over with Suzie and me. I had become a stranger in the world of hoods. Goodbye suede shoes and bebop clothes. Goodbye hot rod. Goodbye Suzie Q.

I wrote a paper on the Studs Lonigan trilogy as seen through the eyes of a pool hustler. It provided a nice transition from the street world of the hood to the introspective world of late-fifties academia. The quest for identity became paramount. "What" became replaced by "why." (Later, of course, I came across a pill that let you experience the entire fifties internal trip in just eight hours.) My teachers were tops in their fields. Herbert Marcuse, America's most brilliant Marxist. Maury Stein, a young, inspirational critic of mass culture. Paul Radin, whose studies of the

Winnebago Indians are classics in anthropology. Arch-liberal Max Lerner, ever willing to alibi America's shortcomings. An incredible pillar of scholasticism, Kurt Goldstein—one of the pioneers of gestalt psychology. There was a witty, sarcastic genius with an Alfa-Romeo named Philip Rieff and a crafty old codger named James Klee who slipped off each summer to score mushrooms in Mexico.

Most of all, I loved Professor Abe Maslow. I took every class he gave and spent long evenings with him and his family. There was something about his humanistic psychology (considered radical at the time) that I found exhilarating amidst the general pessimism that pervaded Western thought. A hundred years of examining the dark side of human experience, chiefly because of the influence of Darwin and Freud, would be set in perspective by Maslow's insights regarding healthy motivation. His growth psychology, the postulation of love and creativity as driving needs, and the idea of self-actualization, gave birth to a new generation of mind probers. Maslow is the legitimate father of the human-potential movement currently cashing in on his ideas. A worthy bearer of the name Abraham.

Maslovian theory laid a solid foundation for launching the optimism of the sixties. Existential, altruistic, and up-beat, his teachings became my personal code. (Realizing the anti-intellectual character of American life, I always claimed I got my ideas by watching television. That was of course a put-on, nobody ever learned much watching television. I studied with the greatest gurus of the fifties.)

Maslow, a true pioneer, was far from a social radical. His models for self-actualization were easy traditional good guys— Eleanor Roosevelt, Albert Einstein. He backed off from revolutionary struggle, believing that change came from influencing the top echelon of society. Toward the end of his life, during the Vietnam War, he spent time holding sensitivity sessions with Pentagon generals. He reasoned that by reducing sexual repression he could limit their aggression. I disagreed, as did his daughter Ellen. He probably just allowed them to kill with less guilt. Still I've found everything Maslow wrote applicable to modern revolutionary struggle in America, especially when corrected by Marcuse's class analysis.

Marcuse and Maslow, by the way, could never find it in themselves to say a decent word about each other. It doesn't take a great deal of insight to see the entire sixties (myself included) as the synthesis of these two teachers.

Maslow introduced me to a great many humanists—Aldous Huxley, Carl Rogers, Harry Harlow, Erich Fromm, Erik Erikson, Gordon Alport, and a most unusual fellow named D. T. Suzuki. Suzuki introduced Zen Buddhism and made it comprehensible to Westerners. He really played the part. At least ninety, he traveled with a twenty-year-old mistress—beautiful Miss Lotus Blossom, with gleaming black hair down to her tail bone. He wore a hearing aid that, strangely, he turned on only when he was talking. A great actor, he would ask for a glass of water, drink it, and say, "Only when you come to learn the water drank *me*, will you understand Zen." Hard-boiled students gave him "thumbs down," but I loved the act. Suzuki was grandmaster of the put-on, and Zen, like Judaism, uses satire as a form of teaching. Zen teaching, by the way, can be summarized in the Yin-Yang. The student trains to recognize instantaneously the complementary opposite of each utterance or thought. Although its method is grounded in universal truth, practiced alone Zen produces a certain amorality (seen positively as tolerance). The existential concept of "will" should be applied, I think, so that truth, like art or engineering, can better serve the moral imperative. Look to the East by seeing the West. You are here to make a better world.

By my sophomore year I had already become semi-"bo." "Bo" meant bohemian—as in desert boots, dungarees, and never combing your hair. Beer bashes gave way to illuminations over espresso in dark cellars. Folk concerts were big and Pete Seeger loved as one who almost single-handedly resisted. However, politics at the time meant student riots at M.I.T. because the food was bad. Fights over dorm regulations such as whether sophomore girls could have boys in dorm rooms. . . . They couldn't, but junior girls could.

Now I wasn't a total bo. Because of a limited attention span, I never became totally anything. America's speeded-up cultural transitions (fads) all became my own, but transitions should not be confused with conversions. I never felt I rejected any of my past. Ever.

Brandeis had a football team which was about as incongruous as
nuns at a cockfight. The school had something to prove. Not only
did Jews have brains, but they could tough it out as real men on the
gridiron. The fact that the school's football players were mostly
imported dumb goys didn't seem to matter. The earth mover
behind the team was Bennie Friedman, athletic director and chief
fund raiser. The football team was Bennie's baby.

As captain of the tennis team I had dealings with Bennie. So
when a committee to abolish football was founded, I was chosen to
negotiate the idea with Coach Friedman. Bennie was a bronzed,
dapper, senior-citizen ad for White Horse Scotch and I was this
unshaven bo with a green book bag. We were in the musty-sock-
smelling catacombs under the Shapiro Athletic Center. Bennie
took me into his office and pointed out every trophy he'd won. I
complained that the football team was using 75 percent of the
sports budget and it wasn't fair. Bennie folded his manicured
hands behind his head, leaned back in his swivel chair, and said,
"Sonny, you know the two greatest things that ever happened in
this history of the Jewish people?" I thought for a while and gave
up. "Well, I'll tell you. The first was when the Jews got up an
army and walloped the living shit out of the British, and the second
was when I made All-American twice at Michigan State." I
tiptoed out of the room while Bennie stared at the ceiling, murmuring about the big game with Michigan.

Sex was cut short just before going all the way. Dope was
nonexistent. Politics were minimal, and Brandeis, even at that,
was considered "avant garde." Avant garde! The other campuses
must have been real numb-numb joints!

My parents paid tuition, but I hustled most of my own money
gambling, and I made a steady eighty bucks a week peddling
sandwiches in the dorms. I had extra for distractions.

My first real distraction was a beautiful '55 streamlined, fiber-
glass, supercharged Corvette, which I painted a golden bronze
never seen before. It was the first and best model Corvette with the
wire-mesh headlight covers and swooping-fin rear end. It was such
a flash that my girlfriend Sheila was uptight about riding in it. Its
bronze twenty-four-coat lacquer glaring off our gray sweatshirts

and all. I racked it up a few times racing. When it got wounded it didn't dent, it ripped. It attracted too many cops though, and later I traded it for a small, quieter Volkswagen and a future filled with fewer speeding tickets.

My second distraction came in my junior year. I decided to tour Europe on my own the summer of '58. This was a big step, and I was really up for it. Three days after finals I boarded Pan Am out of Logan Airport and headed for London. I had a scruffy old duffel bag stuffed with drip-drys, a copy of *$5 a Day*, and about eight hundred in cash. Flights lasted fifteen hours or more then, heightening the drama of sunrise off the coast of Ireland's green and fertile etcetera. Zoom! it's touchdown, Shannon, Ireland. Adventure. Tingles of anticipation. Gas up. Roaring into the sky and soon we're taxiing up the runway of London's Heathrow Airport. My nose is frozen to the window.

"Look at that will ya!" They're driving on the left side of the road, just like people said. Everything's so different. The hotel is all crystal and brass. Tradition haunts the stairwell.

In Soho, a shapely blond lady with that pinky-white British skin and a missing tooth approaches me. "How'd ya lake to git inta something narce n wum, luv?" Her eyes flickering like machine-gun flack. "Would you like a drink, missie?" says I, playing a little cockney on my vocals. "Oh you American ar yu?" "Right. I'm from New York, name's Fred," I say. "I'm Brenda. Cost you two quid for a quick toss." My heart was pounding away. I never had been with a whore before, never mind a *foreign* whore, Jesus, who knew what you could get. She leaned over and stuck her wet tongue in my ear. "I think I'll try the quick toss, if you don't mind."

She steers me around a few corners and up to a cab stand. Seems she knows one of the cabbies and soon me and Brenda's piling into the back seat and the shiny black cab starts up. "Put this tube on." She was talking about the condom (a.k.a. rubber, safe, bag, balloon). "Where are we going?" "We're here, laddie. This is where it's happnin'. We do it in the cab." Old Brenda hoists her skirts above her waist and after a few clumsy thrusts, one of which lands me scrambling on the floor, I manage to enter her. Our body rhythms are overshadowed by the taxi's more passionate throbs.

Soon the driver's thumping on the partition and shouting encouragement. "Shake a leg, ain't got all night you know." Somehow it ended.

When I withdrew she reached and pulled the tube from my shriveling cock. "I needs it for my next," she said. "The good kind, they are. You gets twelve customers on a tube, sumtimes more."

America was the only country that actually *disposed* disposables.

Then it was off to Paris. France was in the midst of losing the Algerian War. The government had collapsed and Charles de Gaulle had been summoned from his country farm to salvage what remained. He was to enter Paris the day I arrived. There were a million Frenchmen waving banners on the Champs Elysées. A group of students, linked arm in arm, marched up the broad sidewalk singing, "Allon son, fon de la patri-e-yah . . . la jour de gloray t'arrivay . . ." It was the only French song I knew besides "Frère Jacques" . . . and I joined the procession singing lustily. On the third "March-on!" this wave of club-swinging gendarmes swooped down on us, trapping students beneath their capes and pounding them to the ground. The whole area came alive with swarming, shoving students. I got clubbed to the ground, staggered up and ran, following racing bodies. My ribs ached. We headed for the Métro entrance. People were being pushed to the side. Everyone was screaming. Somehow I got shoved into a subway car, the doors shut, and we sped off to safety.

It was my first political demonstration. My first beating by police. To this day I have no idea what the marching and clubbing was about. I've been back to Paris since, and two times have somehow ended up in demonstrations that were trashed by police. Paris spotted the troublemaker in me even before I did.

I bought a used motorcycle and headed south to Pamplona. It was the third day of fiesta and the streets were packed with Harvard students guzzling wine out of sheepskin botas. Here and there were Basque *campesinos* with sweatshirts that said things like KICK ME I'M A SCHMOO and HARVARD UNIVERSITY. Everyone roamed the plazas looking for Hemingway. The Pamplona chamber of commerce annually started the "Hemingway's here" rumor as soon as the first bulls charged down the streets.

Pamplona was a brawling street party with round-the-clock dancing, drinking, swearing, bullfights, fireworks, and bull runs. It was a constant battle to stay awake. I got one terrific scar on my right palm when a bull trapped me in a corner and I ripped my hand scampering over a barricade. I witnessed my first bullfights seeing the great Ortega work the cape, and although it's not fashionable around the counterculture, I've always liked bullfights. It's an art that makes perfect sense. Any artist worth anything tempts the horns of Death (whether it be physical, spiritual, or social). On the last day of fiesta, me and the motorcycle staggered down the Pyrenees and headed for Madrid. Halfway there, blazing sun beating down on my bare back, rounding a mountain curve going sixty, the front wheel skidded on a soft shoulder. The next thing I knew I was tobogganing down the road on my stomach. Pavement tore into my flesh and ripped my clothes. The motorcycle crashed into the mountainside, baggage flying all over. I tumbled over and over, coming to rest on my back. Pants in tatters, body bloody raw, sun burning my eyes, each breath painful agony. An invisible weight pressed against my chest.

I lay there for an hour convinced I was dying, when on the horizon I hallucinated a group of women with earthen jars perched on their heads. They floated toward me, and when they started swabbing my wounds, hallucination became reality. I found myself mumbling Spanish words I didn't even know. Soon a truck showed up. The bike was loaded aboard and I, trembling in shock, was wrapped in blankets and driven to the town hospital.

The town was Salinas and the hospital was a bare room over the main tavern. A guy plucked a guitar in the corner. A señorita propped a cigarette between my lips and the doctor dusted my raw flesh with sulfur powder. I was in Hemingway Heaven surrounded by singing angelitos.

Later, I was wrapped in bandages and loaded aboard the train bound for Madrid. I woke up the next day in the English-American Hospital on the outskirts of Madrid, where a doctor explained they had to shoot me with morphine in order to cut the sulfurized bandages off my skin and that I was a very, very, lucky young man.

After a few days I was released, and much to everyone's surprise including my own, I boarded the still battered motorcycle and headed for Barcelona, city of rebels. Fortunately, wounds have always healed quickly. (I do, however, have enough scars to fill two FBI wanted posters.) Machoooo Man!

From Barcelona back to Boston. Traveling alone, abroad, honed my instincts for survival in the foreign land of Underground.

Castro at Harvard Stadium

Back from Europe, I buckled down to finish at Brandeis and make it into some classy graduate school. I moved in with two older seniors. One a former army lieutenant on scholarship who fixed cars, studied hard, and fucked more undergraduates than anyone, with the possible exception of a history professor I had known. While we were roomies, his mother, a woman from Iowa in her seventies, performed the Classic American Suicide. She lived by the side of the then great Interstate Route 40 which straight arrowed its way through the Midwest cornfields—for hundreds and hundreds of three-lane-blacktop miles. One night, she moved her rocking chair off the front porch and set it in one of the blind dips the highway made. The cars clipped by at eighty miles an hour. Zip-zip-zap. Goodbye old woman—Goodbye America. Whistler's Mother by Jackson Pollock—Splash!

My roommate left school on special leave. He returned for spring semester and graduated. He's probably in the CIA now sucking gimlets in Burma.

My other roomie was one of the few blacks on campus. He stuttered and talked at night to his dead mother. Jim Anderson was his name. He had written an opera at age ten, and six or seven other compositions by the time Leonard Bernstein discovered him and channeled him off to Brandeis. Jim was probably a genius. Did you make it big, Jim? Where are you now? I sense he's strung out

Ralph Norman.

Brandeis University
wrestling team, 1958–59.

Worcester (Massachusetts) *Telegram & Gazette.*

Sheila, Amy, Andy, Abbie: 1964.

on America's back wards. If I were a black genius, I think I'd go crazy and get locked up somewhere.

My last year at Brandeis was spent "rounding out" my academic personality. Doing the sort of things that look good on a graduate-school résumé. Chairman of the Film Society, president of the Psychology Club, and captain of the tennis team. Several visiting lecturers made an impression on me. Erik Erikson describing doing psychoanalysis in the U.S. with an English vocabulary of under five hundred words. Dorothy Day vividly re-creating the soup lines outside her Bowery mission, the *Catholic Worker*. And Martin Luther King, Jr., reporting on the successful bus boycott in Montgomery, Alabama.

The best speaker I ever heard was not on campus but across the Charles River at Harvard Stadium. It was in March of 1959. Eighty thousand of us cheered ourselves hoarse, screaming, "VIVA!" "VIVA!" The speaker Señor Fidel Castro: young and flashing in his green army fatigues. Tall and bearded, at thirty he could have been one of our younger professors, and here he was International Champ of Liberty; Guerrilla Fighter Extraordinaire. A real hero. He spoke in Spanish, exhorting us to answer the call of the oppressed. Back in Cuba, he began translating the "call of the oppressed" into expropriation of U.S. interests and public trials of Batista's torturers. The American press quickly lost its momentary fascination with guerrilla heroes, but I did not succumb to their influence.

I went back to playing tennis and studying hypnosis, extrasensory perception and other subjects not generally favored by graduate schools. The prestigious, exotic University of California invited me aboard and I wired my acceptance. Later I learned they were impressed by my grades in learning theory and experimental psychology. It was a good thing they didn't inquire further. In learning theory, my dissertation was on witchcraft. In experimental, while all the other students were dutifully recording galvanic skin responses and prodding rats with electric jolts, I was studying ESP under simulated stress conditions. They were expecting a potential B. F. Skinner, and I was halfway down the road to becoming Uri Geller. The mysteries in a chem lab just didn't seem to compare with communicating with your belly button and trying to crack the cosmic recipe.

Brandeis was a spawning ground for intellectual heavies. Marty Peretz, now editor-owner of the *New Republic,* was the class Kissinger, hated, but respected, by all of us. Steve Berger, the class politician, carried through his career in New York City. Lettie Cottin-Pogrebin, an editor at *Ms,* was then making history as Brandeis's first cheerleader. Lettie was the type of student who, just before an exam began, raised her hand and asked if neatness counted. Class of '59, the future is in your hands. My classmates reached out and grabbed it with gusto.

Berkeley and the Birth of the Sixties

The University of California lets you know it's there. If you approach it walking up Telegraph Avenue, you pass through huge Sather Gate when entering the campus. Driving up University Avenue, you mount a gradual incline for two or three miles until you press against huge stone walls. Coming down from the magnificent pine forests in back of the campus, you are drawn magnetically to the huge elliptical stadium and the omnipresent bell tower, the Campanile.

We are the largest University in the world. We have 14 Nobel Prize winners (6 mcre than Harvard). We are NCAA champions in basketball and 6 other sports. We have an Atomic Radiation Laboratory. We have gigantic gymnasiums, gigantic hospitals, a gigantic computerized administration system. We have classes with more students than the entire enrollment of the schools you have just come from.

A sprawling impersonal megalopolis of the mind. The "Multiversity" as President Clark Kerr later called it. On registration day we stood in line four hours to receive IBM cards for each class. Five years later an anonymous student was to scrawl a legendary slogan across one of those very cards: I AM A STUDENT—DO NOT BEND, FOLD, OR MUTILATE.

Cal was huge all right. I taught child psychology as a teaching assistant in the home economics department. There were sixteen hundred students in the class. The largest class was rumored to be freshman biology with five thousand students. I looked for the class one day and got lost. There was a chess game played between two facing dormitories with one window for each square. On Band Day, six thousand musicians covered the football field led by a conductor on a fifty-foot tower. They played "Battle Hymn of the Republic" while ten thousand special students in the stands held up cards forming "Niagara Falls." At the count of three everyone wiggled and the falls were made to shimmer and shake. One student went four years through U.C., graduating in 1960 with honors. After graduation, a campus fraternity confessed that the student was their mascot—a six-year-old Chow dog.

Walter Tolman was a figurehead in the psychology department and too old to really teach. You could, however, visit him in his study, and many graduate students did. He was a hero not only for his brilliant career as a psychologist, but because he had led the battle to abolish loyalty oaths. The heavies of the department were Krech and Crutchfield, who had written the most popular introductory-psych textbook in the country. Krech spent most of his time in the radiation lab, bombarding rats' brains with gamma rays, while Crutchfield struggled desperately to bring them back to normal. Together they scored multimillion-dollar grants.

Off-campus became my classroom. I got a small furnished place on Channing Way and counted my funds. Three hundred bucks. Just barely enough to feed the Volks till Xmas. I needed a hustle bad.

"Hey man," said my buddy Nick in the locker room after grueling three-on-three basketball. "If you're going home for Christmas you better get a ticket now."

"How's that?"

"Well, by November everything's booked solid. Fuck yeah,

there's probably eight thousand students here from the East. Then you figure in Stanford and State and you can guess at the jam-up.''

Wheels were turning. The BO-RAH Travel Club was forming. Something for everyone. Bohemians and Rah-rahs. One big fat plane, some stationery, and maybe . . . just maybe . . .

The officials at United Airlines were downright hospitable. Over free dinner at Top of the Mark they threw out figures related to fuel costs, landing fees, insurance. Halfway through the baked Alaska they quoted a price. My god, I could make eight grand, save students forty bucks on a ticket, and get a free ride home and back to boot! We shook hands, and I promised to make a down payment in a month. Three full days were spent in the registration office copying addresses of students from New York. I composed a letter and did a mailing over the weekend. Membership applications poured in. A success! But . . .

United called a week later to say they had to cancel out. They referred me to a non-schedo company, Trans-Ocean Airways, which gladly agreed to the charter. The plane ended up flying zig-zag across the country—forced to land only where it could get clearance. The flight took eighteen hours, but everyone seemed to have a good time. There was a continuous crap game in the aisle and folks got too drunk to notice how long it took. For years I kept getting inquiries about the club.

All around there were strange rumblings. In time I started dropping into political discussions sponsored by a group called SLATE. Across the Bay in North Beach, Ginsberg, Ferlinghetti, Corso, and Rexroth could be heard shouting angry poems at the dawn. On February 1, 1960, students staged nationwide demonstrations boycotting Woolworth's for its racist policies. In Greensboro, North Carolina, black students were being stuffed into jails for trying to get BLT sandwiches at a lunch counter. Nikita Khrushchev found the can-can scenes in *Irma la Douce* pornographic, was refused admittance to Disneyland, and got a rousing reception from hundreds of thousands of people as he rode through the streets of San Francisco.

There was a successful battle to get Harry Bridges, controversial leader of the Longshoremen's Union, allowed on the campus. A U.S. Army general's son went on a fast protesting ROTC. His

Pentagon Papa showed up in an air force super jet to talk him out of it. Father didn't succeed.

Three months before, as a student guidance counselor, I cautioned a freshman with screwy radical ideas against dropping out of school. Marty Kenner was his name. Now I was sitting on the porch of his crowded den listening. On and on he passionately explained about capitalists this and capitalists that. He said the U.S. government was evil and mentioned a group called the CIA.

"The CIA," I interrupted. "What the hell is that?"

"They kill people Eisenhower and John Foster Dulles don't like. They overthrew the *elected* governments of Guatemala and Iran. They are trying every day to kill Castro," Marty explained.

"Come on Marty, let's be serious. Dulles okay, but Ike . . . he'd never hurt a fly." I was skeptical, but I listened. It wasn't the words so much as the excitement in his voice. Besides, outside it was raining hard, so tennis was out. I wasn't even sure such a group like the CIA existed. A few days later, Gary Powers was shot down in a spy plane over Russia. Now we all knew.

The sixties had indeed arrived. It was March, and one could feel the rush of a new spring in the air. But before there was spring, there was spring vacation. Sheila was coming west to visit.

Sheila and I started going together two years before. Off again, on again, we seemed to grow closer three thousand miles apart. She was a petite, olive-skinned "bo" with mysterious green eyes. Eyes so attractive that people would stop her in public and remark about them. Her exquisitely carved face never seemed to sit right on a body she carried awkwardly. She was a bookworm. A grind. We spent hours in libraries and attended symphony concerts. She was a pretty good artist. But unfortunately one who continually looked back, never finishing paintings. A feminist before her time with sharp views and a sharp tongue. Even playing the dating game we had our battles. Looking back, I could scarcely say I was in love with Sheila or she with me. There was mutual stimulation though, and then, as now, we respected each other as worthy opponents in some eternal struggle of the sexes. It should also be noted that Sheila was—something not uncommon at the time—a virgin.

Leaving all this aside, I missed her and had made enough on the travel club to send her a ticket to Cal.

She arrived with a broken foot and I carried her from the Redwood Forest, to the hills of Sausalito, and finally to the rugged cliffs of Big Sur. In a cabin nestled there among spruce trees, we bedded down. What a night! Sterling Hayden, who had just kidnapped his own kid from his former wife and disappeared, was in the next bungalow and everyone knew it. Somehow our pillow ended up on the gas heater and a small fire broke out. Amidst all the excitement, I managed to, uh—she managed to—due to divine intervention and a faulty rubber, she got knocked up.

Sheila returned to complete her degree at Brandeis, and I buckled down at Berkeley. Back East, in Sheila's belly, nature was slowly but persistently working its ever-lovin' course.

During the first days of May, 1960, two generation-shaking events happened within a week. I was a witness to events that were to mold my consciousness forever. On May 1, a group of us caravaned out to San Raphael to stand silent vigil outside the walls of San Quentin Penitentiary. Inside a man in a cage on death row was eating his last meal. He was a thin, short, dark-haired fellow, with a rather large nose, and he bore some resemblance to Danny Thomas. Although there was only circumstantial evidence and no eye witnesses, he was accused and found guilty of being "the Flashlight Rapist" in a sensational 1948 trial. Seems he, or someone, surprised women at night by shining a flashlight in their eyes and ordering them to suck cock. Caryl Chessman was found guilty of the crimes and sentenced to die in the gas chamber. Since the trial he had fought a twelve-year battle with the first whiff of death. He had written several popular books and managed to stay the executioner's hand longer than anyone in history. In doing so, he had become a symbol for the battle against capital punishment. Tonight was his eleventh hour.

Throughout the world people gathered outside U.S. embassies. The only person who could spare his life—Edmund "Pat" Brown —sat in the governor's mansion and issued a statement: "Although I personally am opposed to capital punishment, the laws of the state of California must be obeyed. My hands are tied."

The newspapers and radios were blasting appeals for Chessman's life. It was a foggy drizzle of a night. A few hundred stood vigil, Shirley MacLaine and Marlon Brando among them. The warden came out and served coffee and doughnuts. He made a short speech through a megaphone explaining that he, *too*, was opposed to capital punishment. It was still drizzling the next morning when he reappeared and announced that at 10:10 Caryl Chessman had succumbed peacefully as per the laws of the state of California and how everyone had done all they could to save his life and may God rest his soul. Amen. The rain had blurred the ink on the picket signs. Around me people were in tears. Someone moaned, ''No! No!'' as if he had been wounded. No one shouted. No one threw a rock.

Dazed, we piled into cars and headed back to Berkeley in silence. ''How does that work?'' someone asked of no one in particular. ''In a democracy, I mean, no one wants to see him die and the state kills him?'' There was silence.

Ten days later the House Un-American Activities Committee opened hearings into alleged subversive activity in the Bay Area. The hearings at the Federal Building in downtown San Francisco were open to the public. Only ''the public'' turned out to be friends of the committee. Admittance was by a white card distributed by local American Legion halls and DAR groups. Stacked galleries for public pillorying. It was the last of the great anticommie roadshows designed to beef up the Cold War, get some good schoolteachers fired and warn the nation about the ever present *Red Menace*. J. Edgar Hoover wanted to keep his job and his boys had nothing better to do, crime in America having been solved, I mean.

For a week the papers had been filled with notices advising HUAC to stay out of town. Advertisements signed by the National Council of Churches, by a thousand university professors, by nearly every labor union in the area were prominent, and still the hearing was to happen on schedule. Unaware of the secret pass system, students waited from dawn for the hearing doors to open. When they did, only to admit a selected few, the crowd surged forward, chanting, ''Down with HUAC! Down with HUAC!'' There was no stopping us.

It is customary when traveling abroad to say, ''San Francisco is the best city in the U.S.'' I've heard people who've never even been to San Francisco say that. They should have been there on Bloody Friday that week in May 1960.

There was an elite special force of riot police called the goon squad. Each member stood six feet or better, in solid black leather, crowned by a white crash helmet with a plexiglass visor. Each carried a club. There were water-hose teams. Some had a device called the "knee bender." You hooked it around a person's wrist and turned it once. The person fell to his knees in pain. A second turn broke the bone. The force of the water hoses drove people smashing into plate-glass windows. Students were clubbed to the ground, thrown off balconies, and kicked in the face. A pregnant woman was thrown down a flight of stairs. All around there was panic. Things like this had happened in Japan when riot police waded into snake-dancing protesters, but those were just television news images. Now it was real and scary.

I was separated from those I came with. People ran into stores. The tall black-leather shapes pursued, swinging their sticks. Sirens wailed all around. Screams filled the air. I ran through the side streets toward the theater district.

Four blocks from the riot, everything was as it always was. The passengers debarked from the cable car and helped the ticket man make the turn-around and climb back up Powell Street. Old men waited for the triple-bill movies on Market Street to open. No one seemed aware that the century's most turbulent decade had just begun.

David Rogers entered graduate school with me. We shared two classes and occasionally studied together. An intense guy, he began his career in psychology to find out more about himself and change the world. The laboratory maze was a wandering corridor of emptiness. Gamma-ray machines fried his brains. One week before exams he walked out on the Oakland Bay Bridge and leaped to his death. They found Dave's camera on the railing. Objective scientist to the end, he had set the timer to catch his own agony in flight. Back in his apartment, the authorities discovered all his psychology books shredded. Woodworth and Schlossberg, the 1,600-page tome of experimental psych, had been stuffed in the toilet.

A day later Sheila called and said the rabbit had died, the report was positive. "I'll be there in a week, we can get married," I said.

"We can get what?" she shouted. "I've got to graduate next week!"

"Then we'll get an abortion."

"It's too late. Besides I'm scared."

"Hang on, I'll be there."

It took three hours to pack and three days to arrive. The U.S. was one long blurred highway. Berkeley back to Boston. I drove the last fifteen hundred miles straight, gulping No-Doz and coffee dinners.

A truck driver from Memphis had showed me a good trick for staying awake. You pinch the top of your nose bone, squeeze, and massage up and down real fast. The radio's blaring tornado warnings near Waco, Texas. The announcer is urging drivers to slow down and keep a sharp lookout for twisters. It is 3:00 A.M. in the morning. I begin to rub my nose, fast. "Luck be a lady tonight. . . . Luck be a lady tonight. . . ."

Faulty Rubber, Failed Marriage

"It must have been that night on Big Sur. What are we going to do?" Her eyes brimmed with tears.

"Look, Sheila, I passed this exam and I've got a job lined up at Worcester State Hospital. We'll get by. We should get married." Like most of our generation, we had no place to turn for advice. No columns. No books. No clinics. Certainly not our parents. Nowhere.

We sat in a rabbi's study somewhere in Rhode Island.

"Now, Sheila, you must be a good Jewish wife. In time you'll have Jewish children, and you'll have to set a fine example," he pontificated. In time, we thought, in five months! We both rolled our eyes in impatient disgust.

The rabbi cleared his throat and continued, "There is no greater calling in life than to be a Jewish mother." Sheila was on her feet, enraged at his impersonality. I thought she was going to slug him. He droned on, "These days people consider it modern . . ." The door slammed. I followed her to the car.

We were the first couple married in the fancy new temple in Warwick, Rhode Island. The groom wore a white tuxedo. The bridesmaid cried. Manny, the best man, fumbled for the ring. My father got drunk and cursed Brandeis. A blue-haired yenta I'd never met kept squeezing me between her enormous tits, wailing how old everybody was getting. There were acres of food surrounding a yellow swan carved out of oleomargarine. (Butter would have de-kosherized the event. It was a meat wedding.) We danced the hora over and over. Someone fell into the punch fountain. People kept stuffing envelopes in my pockets and whacking me on the back. "You gotta really be hung," gestured Uncle Al, placing his left wrist in the crook of his right elbow, swinging his arm up and down. "The kid's got a schlong like an elephant. Hey, the kid's got a schlong like an elephant!" he announced.

Sheila and I got lost on the way to our honeymoon and ended up in a semi-abandoned hotel. She spent the night throwing up while I read *Love without Fear*. She doesn't close the bathroom door, I kept thinking. What am I doing here? We're strangers. No we're not. She's my wife. Shouldn't she close the door? What should I do when it's my turn to go? I'll hold it in. Hold it in? You could be married for fifty or sixty years. How are you going to hold it in that long, schmuck? What are you ashamed of, she's now your wife?

God, there were so many things to work out. I didn't know how to be married. As it turned out, she didn't know how to be married either. She would say she did. And I would say she didn't. Silence. "I do!" "You don't!" "I do." Exhaustion. Door slamming. Slugging matches. She threw a dish at me and chipped a bone in my elbow. I once got her head under a pillow and squeezed, squeezed, squeezed.

The marriage was a shambles. Both of us tried for six years to slug our way out of it. Unfulfilled in separate lives, we couldn't maintain any joint venture. Later, when it was over and I had entered into a real love relationship, I spent nights wondering how it had happened. Unwilling to accept "the times" as candidate for villain, I was always haunted by my continuing sense of guilt and failure. But maybe there was just too much crowded in: constant movement, pregnancies, abortions, careers floundering, and a multitude of activities. We had fundamentally different approaches to life. She collected. I threw out. She ate slow. I ate fast. I was reckless. She was cautious. Be it movies, books, music, art, or drugs, we disagreed. Only on politics did we agree. That only seemed to make things worse. We ended up having marital spats on the picket line.

Andrew Michael Hoffman was born during an ice storm on the last day of 1960. "Happy New Year," announced the doctor, "you just got yourself a six-hundred-dollar tax deduction!" After his birth we started experimenting with various contraceptive foams and diaphragms. A year later she missed two periods in a row, threw up a few times, and I drove the urine sample down to the lab. Somewhere in the universe another rabbit died, and the next day a technician beamed, "Congratulations."

My father had over five hundred doctors for clients, and I suppose one among them did abortions, but my father was not a person I could ask. Possibly local friends knew, but I couldn't bring myself to ask them either. Abortion, along with cancer and halitosis, were things better kept private. I rang up a college friend who had gotten an abortion from a physician in Queens. For six hundred dollars the doctor would do it on a day's notice.

"Well, that settles it," I told Sheila. "We have an appointment Friday. Patty will go with you." We closed out the thousand dollars in our bank account, got a weekend babysitter, and drove to New York.

Patty and Sheila were to be picked up on a street corner in Manhattan and driven to the doctor's secret clinic. I waited anxiously at a friend's.

"Damn it!" Sheila exclaimed. "We waited until nine-thirty and no one showed."

"They don't even answer the phone. Something's wrong," added Patty.

At midnight, when the *Daily News* hit the stands, we knew. Read all about it! Read all about it!

QUEENS ABORTIONIST KILLS VICTIM
Chops Body in Pieces and Flushes It Down Toilet

"Oh my god, it's him!" shouted Patty. "That's his house in the picture."

The article described how his patient had died and he had tried to dispose of the evidence. It appeared to the authorities that he had fled to Cuba. The following day the doctor filled pages of copy. He had performed thousands of abortions. The girl was shown in her graduation photo next to the "bloodstained toilet." The *News* made a big deal about Communist Cuba being a sanctuary for abortionists.

After an experience like that, you don't shop around. We drove back to Worcester in silence. Seven months later, Amy was born. I wasn't present. We were already legally separated, only to try again the following year.

Two years later, I made a trip to the same laboratory. Another rabbit was offed and again it was confirmed that Sheila was pregnant. She was on the pill, no less. Neither rubbers, foam, nor the pill had stayed. . . .

Five days a week at midnight, a plane lifted off the runway from Kennedy Airport and headed south to Puerto Rico. It was nicknamed "the abortion flight." On Labor Day weekend not that many tourists headed for the Caribbean. Aside from the pilot and copilot, I was the only male on board. Half the passengers were in tears. The other half held the Kleenex boxes in their laps.

In Puerto Rico I began by calling gynecologists listed in the Yellow Pages. Luckily most spoke English. Unluckily none would have any part of this. No matter what excuse I gave, they insisted that Puerto Rico was a Catholic country and it was illegal. Frantically I started taking cabs to Old San Juan and back to the hotel district. "No wanna bebe—needa bueno doctor," I explained. "I know doctor," a cabbie offered after prodding. He drove into the barrio and made a phone call. Someone in the interior of the island would do it for two hundred and fifty dollars; the driver wanted fifty bucks to take us there and back. I agreed.

We drove over roads that were crowded with people, horses, burros, and cattle. Pigs and chickens scattered when we passed through small villages. There were acres of pineapple and bananas being harvested. It was midday and blistering hot. Sheila gulped tranquilizers.

To middle-class New Englanders, a doctor's office in the in-

terior of Puerto Rico presented something of a cultural shock.
Chairs with ripped upholstery. Dusty floors. Bare tables with
chipped paint. Light bulbs without fixtures. "There's a sterilizer
over there," I said, trying to cheer Sheila up. The driver fetched
the doctor from somewhere down the street and he appeared. A
round, jolly chap dressed all in white with a long, stained, white
apron. At that period we couldn't help but flash on the "butcher"
image, since that's generally how the press referred to abortionists. He had a good manner, though, and even encouraged me
to assist in the operation.

Sheila stretched out on the table. He shaved her and poured a
bottle of Phisohex over her stomach and thighs. Adjusting her legs
in stirrups, he announced he was ready to begin. I held her and
mopped her brow. He poked and prodded in "there" with long
instruments. From working in my father's store, I knew these
instruments were foreign to the average American doctor's office.
I was sure they were illegal—like switchblades and fireworks.
After five minutes of prodding, he pulled out a bloody hunk of
tissue. "Eso es!", he exclaimed.

I realized it was done and all right. "It's over, Sheila."

She bled all the way back to the hotel and throughout the night.
We used up two boxes of Kotex. I spent an hour trying to clean the
blood off the sheets, not wanting the hotel to think a murder had
been committed. Right-to-lifers I guess would say one had. Sheila
was fine though.

One Flew into the
Cuckoo's Nest

Work at the Worcester State Hospital was pretty casual. You came
a little late and left early. Most of my job consisted of testing
patients. I worked with Rorschachs, MMPI's, the WAIS,
Stanford-Binets, TAT's, and a host of other tests. For a while I
worked in the admissions office.

Despite my friend R. D. Laing's belief in the myth of madness, many of the patients were whacked out of their skulls. A farmer about to give birth to John Kennedy's next child. A woman who had rented a hotel room the Easter before and had thrown three kids out the window. A guy who got tired of having to pay his wife for sex. (One night when she kept screaming, "Hurry up and come," he reached down and strangled her.) A woman who felt her skin peeling off each time she washed. An air swallower. There's a weirdo for you. Air swallowers gulp air to get high. It puffs up their stomachs to the point where some even burst. Swallowers have died from overdoses of air. (Maybe we should make it illegal.) There were two Jesuses and one Joe Stalin. But the majority of patients were simply old people who got put away because they were too much of a problem at home. Probably half their disoriented behavior was related to being institutionalized.

By then strait jackets and padded cells for the most part had been replaced by tranquilizers and television. The place was understaffed. What few psychiatrists there were barely spoke English.

State mental hospitals are an ugly realization of what lies at the end of the road. High-school classes should be taken on tours of the back wards. After a while the sheer hopeless oppression of the place either numbed your humane impulses or drove you out.

I lasted three years. At the beginning, I had planned to return to school, but as the kids arrived this became impossible. Besides, I was fast developing a view that making things better one patient at a time was not good enough. After listening to hundreds of patients, I was convinced the problem lay out there. Beyond the walls.

Making Outrage Contagious

In the fall of 1960, I was invited over to Clark University to watch a movie that had been creating quite a stir on campuses. *Operation Abolition* was a documentary made by the House Un-American

Activities Committee. The film proposed that the students, workers, and teachers who protested HUAC had been duped by a handful of Communist agitators. I doubted more than a handful of the protesters had ever heard of the "ring leaders" being labeled as "ruthless, cunning enemies of our system" by the southern congressman narrating the film. I got so angry I jammed a pencil point into my hand.

During the question period, I rose to challenge the film's traveling lecturer, Fulton Lewis, Jr., 3rd. I announced right off that I had been in the riots and rattled off a number of inconsistencies in the movie. Lewis, son of the famous right-wing radio commentator and staff worker for the committee, kept trying to shut me up. A goon squad from Holy Cross started yelling, "Pinko! Pinko!" The Clark students rallied though. "Let him speak!" "Let him speak!" The atmosphere got pretty tense. The formality of a standard campus lecture broke down in a swirling mass of catcalls and shouts. And there I was standing at my seat, now in the aisle, pointing my finger, waving my arms. I had never spoken in public before. I was totally possessed. The rush of being in the center of commotion, armed with conviction. I recognized I had an ability to make outrage contagious.

Next day I received a call from a Mr. Todd, head of the local ACLU chapter. Would I tour Massachusetts with the film as the chapter's representative? I quickly agreed.

I opened in Orange, a small town in central Massachusetts noted for its annual parachute-jumping contests. The Unitarian Church was host. The first five rows were packed with American Legionnaires. They wore blue canoe hats and clutched tiny American flags in their hands. The rest of the seats were filled with farmers.

Lights out.

The audience sat silently for the next hour as swarming protesters dissolved into mid-shots of congressmen warning against the Communist Conspiracy. When it ended, the minister introduced me as a representative of the American Civil Liberties Union, from Woostah (we all talk that way). I rose and walked to the front. Stage center. I stood face to face with the American Legion platoon.

Hi folks. I've never in my life given a speech before but I happened to see this movie the otha night and really got angry. See, I was there last May in San Francisco and I was mad when this here politician called me a "dupe." I never met a Communist yet and I doubt I'm gonna meet one here tonight [uneasy laughter]. But one thing I learned growin' up here in Massachusetts, you just say right out what's on your mind. That's what Paul Revere and his friends did. Now, uh, the ACLU has documented one hundred and forty-two factual errors in this film. Did you see that fat lady bouncing down the stairs? Everyone always laughs at that scene. She's a pregnant woman and when she got to the bottom a policeman kicked her. Did you see that scene of Mr. Brown, the Communist? That was filmed a year before in another city and spliced into the movie. Did you notice the congressman who remarked about the Communists wanting to impose a dictatorship in this country? He comes from a district in Louisiana where more than half the people are Negroes. No Negro has been allowed to vote in that district for ninety years. Every two years he receives ninety-six percent of the votes. Khrushchev only gets ninety-four percent! The only question we have to ask ourselves is why us taxpayers have to foot the bill for this junk!

There was a short silence, and the legionnaires began. "By the way, sir, do you believe in God?" For half an hour they continued. I was asked if I'd let my daughter marry a Negro, if the ACLU was a Communist front, and other sticklers. Finally one of the farmers in the back spoke up, "I don't know, I think this here fellah's got a good point." And he starts to list some mistakes he's spotted in the film. He's not the only one speaking up. Jesus! The Farmer-Labor Party rises from the dust! I got all tingly inside.

I fell in love with America that night. Cornfields. Town meetings. Niagara Falls. Hot dogs. Parades. Red Sox double headers. America was built by people who wanted to change things. It was founded on strong principles. I saw myself as a Son of Liberty, riding through the night, sounding the alarm.

Duddy Meets the Avant Garde

After I toured for the ACLU, I enrolled in a night course at
Brandeis on the history of the movies. The teacher was a great old
pioneer of movies, Arthur Mayer. People have commented from
time to time that I live my life as a movie. Obviously, from the title
of this book, I don't disagree even if I'm unsure what they mean.
This course flamed my love of movies.

After Mayer's course I decided to bring cinema to Worcester.
One day, while riding by an abandoned theater that I regularly
attended as a child, I got a notion to reopen it showing what we
pretentiously called art films. On investigation, it turned out the
theater was owned by Duddy's Cadillac City, across the street.
The owner agreed to the plan.

I had known Duddy for several years. Everyone in Worcester
knew him. He was the prototype of the fast-talking, checkered-
jacket, cigar-chomping, used-car salesman. A grammar-school
dropout, by the age of thirty-five he had built a used-car empire
from scratch. Everyone said he was a gangster, but then everyone
says that about all Italians. "There's people behind him," my
father, somewhat jealously, warned me.

He was far from a gangster, but he talked like one. A neat
staccato gutter speech straight out of *Guys and Dolls*. We took a
shine to each other right away, coming from such different worlds.
I was "da professah" in Duddy's eyes, and he asked all sorts of
questions about life. "Which o' deez paintins yo like professah,"
he'd ask, trying to select one for his office. I gave a cultured little
critique, and Duddy would look at me askance. "Maybe . . . I
tink dey wuz dun by the same blind faggot," he'd opine. Riding
into Boston to bargain for films, we'd get into long sexual discussions. "Nah, you ain't eaten pussy has ya? How can ya get pass de
smell? Sneezin' in da suitcase, I mean."

Duddy had some offbeat insights about the American economic system. In the lobby of the Park Arts Theater we sold popcorn and had a classy library of film books. One day I saw Duddy fingering one of the books. "Hey, how much we make on a book?" he queried.

"Forty percent," I shot back.

"*Forty percent!*" he exploded. "Can you beat dat shit? We make five hunnerd percent ona lousy bag of popcorn ana no good forty ona book. A *book!* A *book*, damn it," he repeated. Books were holy sacraments to Duddy. He told me he had never read a single book in his life. "I tink the Communists oughta run dis country. Imagine five hunnerd fuckin' percent on a lousy baga popcorn and peanuts ona book." He shook his head.

Every day at 5 o'clock, I'd grab a sandwich and head to the theater. On the way I'd pick up the films at the bus station. I opened and closed the theater, kept all the books, arranged the marquee, bought the films, the candy, the books, the tickets, cleaning supplies. I paid the help and devised the advertising campaign. In addition, I put out a monthly bulletin with a lengthy review of each film, modeled after the one Pauline Kael wrote for the Studio Guild in Berkeley. After four months of total exhaustion from working seven days a week at two jobs, I decided to pack it in. Duddy couldn't have agreed more. We were ten thousand dollars in the red. "We shoulda gone straight into da popcorn bizness." He grinned.

After the first month of movies, I wanted to have the world premiere of a film. I had read that the titular head of the underground film world, Jonas Mekas, and his brother Adolpho had made an experimental movie called *Guns of the Trees*, which no one would exhibit. I decided to invite them up to Worcester. A week later, six denizens from New York's mysterious Greenwich Village showed up at the theater. Most of them wore old army clothes with high riding boots and six-foot woolly scarves. Adolpho sported a bushy black beard and a floor-length navy overcoat and huge boots. He looked like a jolly singer of country ballads but had a manner more like that of Eric von Stroheim, in *Sunset Boulevard*. Jonas dressed totally in sepia, matching the color of his skin and long stringy hair. His face came to a point in front, and he moved like a bloodhound on the scent. He spoke in a heavy Lithuanian accent without moving his lips. I couldn't wait to introduce them to Duddy.

Guns of the Trees began.

After fifteen minutes I found it close to impossible to follow— an endless swirl of sunlight cascading through the branches of trees interspersed with naked people running backward through a cabbage patch. Not even a priest urinating on a bank managed to hold my interest. I was more interested in getting Duddy's appraisal of this celluloid weirdness. Once when the screen went stark white following a piercing air raid siren, Duddy, thinking the film had broken, shouted up to Mike in the projection booth. He just got through shouting when on came the naked people running backward through the cabbage patch again. Finally it was over.

"Well, whaddya think, Duddy?"

"I dun know, I guess it wuz pretty good."

"Pretty good! What was it about?" I asked.

"Dat's a good question, but at least it wuz in English, not like doz uddah two you had by dat Bergerman guy," he replied.

I copped out and convinced him Worcester wasn't ready. Later I faked and told the Mekases it was Duddy's decision.

Once we were about to show a mildly controversial movie called *The Mark*, with Rod Steiger and Stuart Whitman. It was billed as a story of homosexual love. I was invited to tape a radio talk show on the aims and objectives of the theater. When the show was over, the host took me aside and said he doubted they could use the show. "How come?" I asked.

"There are certain subjects taboo around here. Homosexuality is one."

"Homosexuality!" I shouted. "I just mentioned that it was the theme of *The Mark*. I couldn't say it was a cowboy movie, could I?"

"Yes, I know, but we wouldn't want to encourage young people to see a movie like that."

Sure enough, the radio show was censored. The newspaper (which owned the station) changed the ad mat announcing the movie. It read, "*The Mark* Is in 5 Simple Words: A Story of

Love." I stared in amazement at the notice. Five words, my foot. It was only four! They had airbrushed the word HOMOSEXUAL. I called up the business manager to complain. "But 'homosexual' isn't a dirty word. It's like 'toothpick' or 'strawberry,' " I argued.

"This just happens to be the policy of our department," he answered. "We're a family newspaper."

Strange as it might seem, that's the way it was way back in 1961. Later this same newspaper used the same "family newspaper" argument with me when they refused to print photos of racial beatings in the Southern civil rights movement. Do you think the word "family" used in this context means a denial of the truth?

Kindergarten for Organizers

The following spring I bounced from art to politics. H. Stuart Hughes, the co-chairman of SANE (Committee for a Sane Nuclear Policy) and professor of political science at Harvard, announced he was running for the vacated seat of Senator Leverett Saltonstall. More important, he announced he was running as an independent on a strong anti-military-spending budget. An antimilitary platform placed Hughes well beyond the liberalism of the time, at least Kennedy liberalism. (John Kennedy, too many people are prone to forget, campaigned as a hawk, wanting to close the make-belive missile gap.)

From all over the U.S., organizers poured into the small office in Cambridge. We went all over the state in an effort to collect 146,000 voter signatures to place Hughes's name on the ballot. I was in charge of the signature drive for central and western Massachusetts. We would organize caravans of volunteers to sweep through cities and towns, gathering names. Armed with voter lists, we knocked on doors, stood in shopping plazas, and manned tables on busy street corners. We usually slept in the basement of a sympathetic church.

It was exhilarating. There is no better way to learn the skill of organizing than canvassing door to door. If you stick to it, you can't help but develop into a good organizer. The people force you to become convincing—and the more varied the people you meet, the better you get.

Confounding the experts, we succeeded. Hughes would be on the ballot along with one of the Lodge boys and young brother Teddy Kennedy. From the onset there was never a doubt as to the outcome. Not in Massachusetts. However, most of us realized we were educating ourselves about the realities of the political process.

Strategy sessions sharpened our instincts. *I. F. Stone's Weekly*, the *National Guardian*, *The Realist*, and a host of small magazines were avidly read and discussed. Civil-rights organizers gave us buttons and literature, and we in turn passed them on. Everyone sang the songs of the southern movement. We learned about fund-raising teas, bake sales, car washes, press conferences, concerts. We negotiated across tables with union leaders, incumbent politicians, and city editors. It was an honest, worthy campaign, and by October the polls showed a respectable 15–20 percent of the vote going to Hughes. Enough to undercut Teddy and establish a power base in the state. Then the roof collapsed. It almost collapsed on the whole world.

Spy planes criss-crossing Cuba had discovered missile bases under construction. Furthermore, Russian ships were speeding toward Havana. On board were nuclear delivery systems.

People crowded into bars to watch Adlai Stevenson display aerial photos on television. The national guard was mobilized. People emptied their savings accounts. Schools held daily air raid drills. The radio blared directions from civil-defense officials on "what to do in the event of a nuclear attack." Rational scientists said things like "Be sure to shield your eyes from the first flash of an atomic blast." Many people were convinced the end was at hand. There were already thousands of people walled up in fallout shelters.

Everyone connected with our campaign rushed to Cambridge. Hughes was being pressed hard for a statement. Finally he went along with the staff and attacked Kennedy's brinksmanship. At that time, in any Senate race it would have been considered foolhardy to take such a position. In Massachusetts, going against John Kennedy was close to heresy. The day after the statement, the press took off its gloves and the name-calling began. The "thoughtful, serious professor" became the "Russian puppet from Harvard." The campaign was torpedoed. Even so, many of the best organizers of the sixties cut their eyeteeth on the Hughes campaign. Hughes went on to become more conservative, but it was our generation's first taste of national organizing. Many of those who worked in the campaign fanned out across the country via Students for a Democratic Society, the Student Nonviolent Coordinating Committee, or the scads of local ad hoc groups that made the sixties. Boston's always been a good place to get things moving in the right direction.

Boston to Broadway

On a trip to secure entertainers for a Hughes benefit, I had paid a visit to Arthur Mayer and asked if he could make some introductions to movie people in New York. The vice-president of Walter Reade Theaters decided I had potential and enthusiasm, and that fall I started my apprenticeship.

I was assistant manager at the DeMille Theater on Times Square. When I was young, Times Square was my Mecca. The lady billboard that blew Camel smoke rings. The Bonds waterfall with nude Adam and Eve statues twenty feet high. The huge theater marquees. Mr. Peanut walked these mean streets. Religious hustlers worked each corner as swarms of tourists descended from buses. It was said that if you stood at 42nd Street and Seventh Avenue long enough everyone you ever knew in your life would at one time or another walk past.

The corner stand gave me free hot dogs and piña coladas. I discovered the Luxor Baths on 47th Street where, after a hard day's work, the Jewish garment-district merchants gathered for a steaming shvitz bath and a dip in the pool. There were the Broadway plays if you liked that sort of stuff. But more important, there were movie theaters. Acres upon acres of movie theaters.

After a month I was named manager of the Baronet-Coronet Theater on Third Avenue, opposite Bloomingdale's. They were just completing construction, and I was to be the first to run the twin theaters.

The theaters were to be Walter Reade's showpieces, so all stops were pulled out. Aside from Hilly Elkin, Walter Reade, Jr., had the most garish taste of any rich person I've ever met. Strictly Miami Modern, the Baronet-Coronet sparkled brighter than a Woolworth's jewelry case a week before Mother's Day. The lobby glittered with gold lamé. The ushers were decked out in gold jackets. There was even gold glitter embedded in the sidewalk.

My job, at first, was to put together the staff and bribe building and fire inspectors to ensure we could open on time. It was shockingly up front. Not a single city official who entered the construction area turned down a bribe. When I journeyed down to Foley Square to obtain permits I always carried three or four sealed envelopes, paperclipped to the application. I was shown how to shake hands with a fire inspector while palming him a hundred-dollar bill. Four thousand in graft passed through my hands. It was listed as "gratuities" in the daily report. Live and learn.

Walter Reade, Jr., was a towering man. He had rosy cheeks, black hair that waved back and up, like a row of new balcony seats, and shiny Italian shoes. He always wore a red carnation in his buttonhole and a shit-eatin' grin on his face. A windmill of faked exuberance.

Junior wanted a real classy opening. The movie was some phony French ballet and the star, Ludmilla Tcherina was on hand. The "Lady in White" she was called, as white was the only color she wore. Hence five thousand white roses filled the lobby. We ordered cases of champagne. Paintings on loan from museums lined the wall. Two spotlights criss-crossed the sky above Third Avenue. Frantically, we swept and polished right up to the moment when Junior would step out of his limousine and whisk the Lady in White along the red carpet stretched across the golden-glitter sidewalk and into the bright theater.

Soon the sparkling lobby was crowded with celebrities and reporters. Junior was beaming. "Hoffman, don't you think it's time we showed off our *piece de résistance*?'' he instructed. This was a special curtain of hot air blown by huge underground fans through a grating at the entranceway. It prevented unwanted cold air from entering.

I gave the signal to one of the engineers and a switch was thrown. *Oh my God!* Someone had forgotten to clean the construction dirt from the air ducts. Billows of soot rolled like waves into the lobby. People dropped their champagne glasses and ran, shrieking, up the escalator. "Fire!'' screamed some idiot. Lady in White turned gray and fainted. I ran to the basement and threw off the switch.

The Lady in White went back to France. Junior went on a cruise. I got fired and returned to all-night poker games on the West Side. Years later I read that Junior skied off a trail at St. Moritz and disappeared into an avalanche. I could picture him zooming down the mountain slope in a white tuxedo until all you could see was the red carnation.

My Last Job

I went back up to Cambridge to see Sheila. Somehow we would try again. Neither of us were ecstatic, we just didn't see any alternative given the fact that separation cost more than staying together.

Reconciliation meant getting a job. I shined my Florsheims, had a résumé printed, and made the rounds of the employment agencies. Westwood Pharmaceuticals, out of Buffalo, was looking for a detail man to work central and western Massachusetts. I was offered what seemed like a huge amount of money, bonuses, green-stamp incentives, expense account, and best of all, free use of a Chevy Impala.

A week later we packed up the gear and kids and headed back down the Mass Pike to Worcester. Bert, the regional sales manager, and I sat in a hotel room for a week while he "broke me in.'' He read me word by word a two-hundred-page salesman's hand-

book. Bert was a nice enough guy. He had worked his way up:
"No Jew ever got this high," he confided to me. A traveling
salesman for twenty-five years, he was strictly all company and
thought of nothing but boosting sales figures.

He summed up the art of salesmanship in a single word:
"KISS, buddy-boy, KISS. That's the solution. Keep-It-Sim-
ple-Stupid." He taught me the tricks of the trade: how to get
by a stand-offish secretary, how to capture the doctor's attention
and how to make a rehearsed pitch sound spontaneous.

The detail man on the road links the doctor to the drug industry.
The company tells the detail man what cures, the detail man tells
the doctor. Medical treatment begins in the corporation sales
department, not in the doctor's office.

Actually, most doctors don't even want to hear from cures.
They want long-term treatment plans and ten-month regimens.
They love chronic repeaters, like psoriasis and arthritis. Half the
patients in any waiting room are hypochondriacs. Our company
specialized in dermatologicals. No one really knew much about
the skin, so it was a great moneymaker. I once put the question
squarely to Bert, "Hey, do any of these products *cure* anything?"
He searched for an answer we could both live with. "Nothing we
sell is going to kill anyone."

That was a drug company's dream—temporary relief and no
malpractice suits.

It took me two months to get the feel of my territory. By the third
month, Bert was back to check on my progress. Blessed with
souped-up adrenal glands, the gift of gab, and chutzpah, I had all
the makings of a first-class Willy Loman.

Every salesman cheats a little. It's programmed into the system.
After six months, I decided to cheat *a lot*. I sold samples, fudged
expense accounts, and cheated on the time. I ended up working
about ten hours a week: after two years even that became unbearable. For some mysterious reason, sales went steadily up and I
earned three raises.

The job lasted three years. I started to believe that nobody with a
suit and tie worked in America. Not only was I ripping off the
company in the traditional way, but Westwood, a right-wing
corporation, was unwittingly underwriting a civil-rights or-

ganizer. For as soon as the sales manager left, off came the suit and tie, out went the samples, and out of the garage sped the shiny Impala to the nearest sit-in or rent strike. In the next three years I would lick six hundred thousand stamps for mailings.

Like so many others, I would spend long nights cranking out leaflets. I would be beaten and thrown in jail. I would march and speak at rallies, organize rent strikes, and disrupt school-board meetings. Through direct action I trained myself to become a social activist. One of thousands, learning on their own. Dwight MacDonald once made an interesting comment to me about the sixties. "What ever possessed you people?" he observed. "The notion of acting out your ideas defies the intellectual tradition." Whichever way Dwight meant that, he was right.

Hometown Ghetto Education

In 1959 I had voted twice for John Kennedy. By absentee ballot and also in Berkeley. Inspired by him, I had even tried to enlist in the Peace Corps. Being Catholic, Kennedy had fought an underdog's battle. Coming after Eisenhower, he was spring following winter. Kennedy heated our passion for change, and when he was killed that chilly day in November we mourned. Kennedy often lied to our generation, but nevertheless he made us believe we could change the course of history. Inspiration can come from strange and unusual places. In the early sixties, we thought we were responding to Kennedy's inaugural call to do what we could for our country. His death left a chasm between president and people that might never be bridged.

The National Association for the Advancement of Colored People was about as archaic as the name sounds. Worcester had a typical chapter. Each week members gathered in the chapel of a downtown Negro church. There would be Bible readings and gospel songs. Then someone would suggest used clothes or books to be sent to a southern church or would give a heated speech about equality ending with a lame motion to send a telegram to the president. If a newcomer asked what could be done about the jailings in the South or local discrimination, the person was politely ruled out of order. Sister Martha would strike a few notes on the piano and everyone would rise, join hands, and sing "Shall We Gather at the River." Coffee and pastry followed.

After two meetings I decided to take over the chapter. I wasn't the only one thinking along those lines.

In successful Irish families that spawn politicians and police chiefs, there is always a spot reserved for one devoted young man to enter the priesthood. Through him the entire family gains salvation and is henceforth free to manipulate stocks, invest in real estate, and plot takeovers of wards and counties. The Gilguns were such a family in Massachusetts, and since Bernie, one of the younger brothers, didn't show an early desire to go for the throat in worldly matters, he was shuffled off to the seminary as the family's ambassador to heaven. Father Gilgun took Pope John XXIII at his word and, with an ecumenical passion, a fiery temper, and a bottle, set forth to challenge the dogma of the church and the strait jacket of the old order. Aside from Malcolm X, he was the best movement orator I ever heard. Perhaps he was better than Malcolm, for his head was not crammed with an abundance of fact; his passion went straight from heart to tongue. When he spoke, his white ruddy face flushed blood red as he rocked back and forth on his small black shoes, building a cadence. His eyes rolled upward as he searched the heavens for answers to questions he would hurl into the sky. Pulling with his arms outstretched as if he were climbing a rope to God's very door, he would intone: "Lord is it not *our* blood running in the streets of Birmingham tonight? Do not the cattle prods burn *our* skin? Do not the dogs of Bull Connor tear *our* flesh? Guide us O Lord for we are not afraid." "We shall not . . . We shall not be moved. . . ." he would sing. Later, backstage, so to speak, he gave me a jab in the arm and a leprechaun wink. "I really slipped it to Jesus, eh buddy?"

D'Army Bailey was black and angry. He had been thrown out of the University of Louisiana for civil-rights activities. He went out the back door while the lynch mob was coming through the front. Clark University offered him a scholarship and he headed north.

An Irish priest, a Jewish salesman, and a hungry black law student. We were the perfect American Trinity. The three of us would meet before each meeting and plan our campaign. D'Army learned *Roberts' Rules of Order*, I developed a knack for publicity, Gilgun marshaled the local flock. One night, instead of the usual twenty-five members, two hundred people anted up two bucks and packed the pews. When the good Reverend signaled for some old church gospel, someone shouted, "How 'bout 'This Little Light of Mine'?" Before anyone knew it, rows of young people were clapping, stomping their feet, and belting out: "This little light of mine, I'm gonna let it shine, Oh Lord. . . ."

There was something about singing freedom songs in a black church, stomping on the wooden floor, smiling, gearing up your courage, that summoned a spirit never to be recaptured. At least not for me. Those years, 1963–1965, were filled with the cry of a movement at its purest moment. People who had never sung a note in their lives gained perfect pitch overnight. People ventured into the streets, faced down police dogs, endured beatings, and grew stronger. The war against racial inequality was by no means won, but legal segregation was defeated. That it was. It was accomplished by people like those in the pews that night. Knowing I was one of them feels very good now.

Within months we became known as the most militant NAACP chapter in the country. There were persistent visits from the national office, and once we were threatened with disenfranchisement. The old guard got money from rich do-gooders but we had the troops and the will. If the structure of the NAACP became too cumbersome, we moved outside it, using only its name and mantle for respectability. We established a CORE chapter and a local neighborhood-action council.

We set up landlords for discrimination suits and picketed stores that refused to hire Negroes. We taught black people how to lie at job interviews just like all the white people did. Ironically for me, our toughest battle was against the defense plant where I had once worked.

The plant was owned by Worcester's robber-baron, Robert

Stoddard, controller of the city's media, rabid antiunionist and arch conservative. Stoddard was also one of the largest Goldwater-for-President backers and a national founder of the John Birch Society. The plant could not be cracked without a fight. The figures were incredible (especially in a time when the governor's mother was walking picket lines and going to jail in Florida) but Wyman-Gordon had thirty-six hundred employees, only thirty-three of whom were black—thirty-two of the thirty-three were janitors, and the thirty-third was the janitors' straw boss.

Whites entered the plant as janitors and passed on; only the blacks remained to pick up the shit. We proceeded secretly. In previous years, union organizers had been run out of town, and I was certain I'd lose my job or worse. Once, as we campaigned for equal jobs, the personnel manager called me up. "We know you're behind this trouble. How can you do this? We gave you a job," he insisted. My father called next, "Why *them*, of all people? They're my best customers!" he shouted into the phone.

In a small community organizing is very different than in a huge city like New York. The local paper prints your address and background. A dead skunk on the door, a threatening phone call are common occurrences. Organizing in the place you were raised personalizes the experience. In your hometown there is nowhere to hide. When we picketed, guys I'd shot pool with would drift out of the pool hall to eyeball me. Nigger agitators were hated, but there was someone they bowled with marching and singing those darkie songs. "How come you fallin' in with this bunch a lunatics, Abbs?" they asked, following me along the picket line. I tried to change their minds.

There was nothing abstract about Worcester. Picture this: The picket lines at Wyman-Gordon have failed to effect a policy change. The protesters decide to crawl under a diesel truck to prevent it from entering the factory. The oversize tires tower over us and grease smudges our shirts. On the street you can hear paddy wagons arriving and some workmen screaming: "Jungle bunnies, commie bastards— Go home to Russia!" Through the din comes the voice of the plant's personnel manager. He's leaning under the truck shouting, "Abbie, your father's here and wants to have a word with you. Could you come out for a second?"

"Don't go," D'Army insists, grabbing my arm.

"I gotta, D'Army, I just gotta. My pa's got a bum heart. They're his best customers. I don't know what to do. Save me a place, I'll be right back." I duck out and sneak past the hecklers.

"Okay! Okay!" says my father. "So it's what you believe in. But do you have to get your shirt so dirty?"

We sat in FBI offices protesting nonenforcement of the new Civil Rights Act. We chartered a bus and took black kids on a tour of the rich community, pointing out the mansions of the big industrialists. We published a newspaper. In the black community itself, we set up daycare centers and held voter-registration drives. A community hangout, Prospect House, was founded and then, as now, served as the organizing hub. We went to funerals and bailed neighborhood people out of jail.

I was surprised to discover that most of the whites in the local movement were Catholics. Descendants of the early Christians who fled to the catacombs outside of Rome. These were the people who would have fought the Inquisition or donned the yellow star of oppression. Spartacus, Bonhoffer, Teilhard de Chardin, and Pope John XXIII were heroes. They identified with the worker-priest movement in France, the revolutionary priests and nuns in Latin America, and attempts to break the conservative hierarchy of the church.

It was in this community that Sheila, the kids, and I found ourselves most comfortable. On Passovers we celebrated as did the early practitioners. We bathed each other's feet at the holy meal, adding civil-rights songs to Bible readings. Once a week there were communal feasts, and we observed obscure holy days such as Pentecostals when we would march through the woods with banners and flowers. Joyous celebrators of life, they convinced me Jesus wasn't too bad a guy after all. (One should remember the life of Jesus was far more radical than those who founded the Church could ever afford to let on. "Disciples are," as Alan Watts reminds us, "those who got an A in the course but missed the whole point!")

On the edge of the black ghetto we opened a storefront and held weekly lectures. A small forgotten ghetto, shoved up against a new freeway, slowly organized. The skills and the ways of city politics were learned on the street. At the time, there was no school in the country to which you could go to learn the trade. Aside from the great organizer Saul Alinsky and possibly Martin Luther King, Jr., few teachers could be found, even as models. Instead America offered only resistance. Later, when I, as well as others, marched on Washington or Chicago, we carried with us the lesson that the local power structures had fought us tooth and nail—that racism was ingrained in the system. We also realized that the lesson came in spite of our formal education. (My critique of democracy begins and ends with this point. Kids must be educated to *disrespect* authority or else democracy is a farce.)

Going South

As our local movement broadened its base of participation and as I traveled to Boston in the course of my job, I mingled with civil-rights workers who shuttled back and forth from the South to centers of support in the North. Bob and Dottie Zellner were such a couple. The first whites to enter Mississippi as freedom workers for the young Student Nonviolent Coordinating Committee. Hard working and dedicated, they typified the new breed of activist. The southern rural struggle based on the highest of moral principles—equality—inspired a decade of protest.

Everywhere I went I solicited funds and volunteers for the upcoming Summer of Freedom in Mississippi. The Zellners had no trouble enlisting me as a SNCC worker early in 1964.

I made a short trip to Jackson, the state capital, to confer on strategy. SNCC had drafted plans to challenge the all-white delegation to the Democratic Convention in Atlantic City.

The stories I learned in the South now seem like ancient history, like the stories of the pyramids or the Napoleonic Wars, but this was the mid-1960s and they were real. As real as NO COLORED SERVED HERE signs and two drinking fountains, one a foot lower than the other. Wall, Mississippi had a barrel where a Negro was supposed to stick his head when he felt like laughing. Even in the state capital a black was to step aside on the sidewalk when a white wished to pass. You knew you were entering the black community when the pavement ended. Children clustered on the stoops of wooden shacks. Some wore hand-me-down T-shirts with holes, the smaller ones had no clothes at all. The diet of greens, grits, and occasionally pig feet and entrails produced anemia in three-quarters of the people. ("Soul" food's romantic image deliberately obscures the lack of dietary nutriments.) By puberty most had rotten teeth. Tuberculosis, trichinosis, and other diseases begged for treatment. Generally the whole family slept in the same room, often in the same bed. There were only two people who made a decent living in a rural black community. The man who stuck you in the ground—the undertaker—and the one who got you from there to heaven's door—the preacher. Except for a very few places along the Gulf—such as Gulfport or Biloxi—this was the order of things. In every conceivable way of measuring poverty, Mississippi was to be found at the bottom of the list.

In June, before the influx of students began, a field worker greatly admired by us, named Michael Schwerner; a college volunteer, Andrew Goodman; and a local organizer, James Chaney, drove out to a town called Philadelphia in the northeast corner of the state to investigate the burning of a church. They did not return. Their burned-out station wagon was discovered in a ditch. A month later their bodies were found in thirteen feet of newly poured concrete. Before they had been shot, they had been whipped to death with chains. Every bone in their bodies had been crushed. Their crime probably was they had all been riding in the front seat. In Mississippi, even in private cars, the custom was for blacks to ride in the back. And in Mississippi, the custom was the law. While they were searching for the three, several unaccounted-for black bodies were found in the swamps and rivers. Some had been burned, others castrated. Most black families I met in the South had a relative who had been murdered by white people.

We held a march in Jackson. Three thousand were arrested and herded into a field. Chalk lines were drawn on the ground to signify the cells of a makeshift jail. As soon as I was released I flew north. Few organizers chose to stand trial in the Deep South during that period. If there was a good lawyer available, such as Charles

Morgan or Billy Kunstler, you might chance a trial, but the general policy was to give a false name, jump bail, and move on. The following year I would be arrested four more times in Mississippi and Georgia.

Often civil-rights workers were "fed" to the other prisoners. The sheriff would promise a bottle and a little time off if the other prisoners made you "feel comfortable." Once I had a noose dangled before my face by a redneck deputy who said I had run a red light in Yazoo City. Yazoo City had no traffic lights at the time. When I pointed that out, I was busted for insulting an officer. Throughout all this, I had the feeling I was learning American civics for the first time.

Being Right Is Not Enough: The Convention of 1964

I arrived early in Atlantic City. We lined up churches and camp fields for sleeping and local committees to do the cooking. Soon busloads of troops were pouring into town. Directing operations were a tough breed of self-taught organizers, not seen in this country since the heyday of union activity in the thirties. Cleve Sellers, the Zellners, Doris Rube Robinson, Julius Lester, Elizabeth Sutherland, Stokely Carmichael, Dale Smith, George Ware, Ivanhoe Donaldson. Names now mostly lost in the broad sweep of historical overviews. For me, this was the largest gathering of heroes since the signing of the Declaration of Independence.

And then there was Mendy Samstein. Mendy was my inspiration. We had been close friends at Brandeis. He had gone on to Atlantic Union in Georgia, and under the influence of Howard Zinn had become the most trusted white organizer in SNCC. When the Black Power crunch came in 1966 and whites were asked to leave, Mendy drifted away, broken-hearted. He had survived two bombings and worked the toughest communities. But when the power shuffle that occurs in every left-wing organization began, he couldn't handle the emotional strain.

So many good minds smashed on the rocks of factionalism! A movement organizer has a life expectancy of about two years. Even the best get plowed under. The pressures are enormous, rewards few. Last I heard, Mendy was a cab driver in New York.

Mario Savio put in his two years. He and Mendy worked in the McComb operation, eighty miles south of Jackson. Later Mario returned to Berkeley to lead the biggest student movement in the country's history. Fame crippled him, robbed him of the solitude his soul thrived on, and drove him out of the movement. Everyone who gained fame on an antielitist premise had his measure of guilt to overcome. Mario couldn't hold it together.

Bob Moses was the best of the best organizers. In looks, he was deceptively anonymous. The ubiquitous bib overalls, lighter blue denim shirt, and sneakers. He had copper-colored skin and steel-rimmed glasses. He rarely spoke, and when he did—always in the most serious, gentle tone—everyone listened, for he had the blue-print for victory in his head. We imitated his low-key style of organizing, even his patterns of speech. He was the only negotiator who could easily move between dirt-poor rural blacks and high-level White House officials. His organizing methods became the very definition of "participatory democracy." So admired, he was called the "Moses of Mississippi," but he, too, lost the battle with fame. Soon after Atlantic City, he changed his name and dropped from sight.

In politics being morally right is not good enough. We learned that in Atlantic City. Fannie Lou Hamer was a militant grass-roots leader and symbol of the challenge to the all-white delegation. In a church hall, she detailed how sheriff's men sat on her head and held her feet while others whipped her for trying to vote. For hour after hour, others told stories of beatings for trying to register. On the boardwalks we rallied around the clock. In hotel rooms we met with Democratic delegates from our home states. The mayor of Worcester pledged me his support to the Freedom Delegation. When we tabulated the votes we had more than enough. We were going to win! We had become the darlings of the convention. Delegates gave us passes, took us to dinner, stuffed money in our pockets, and begged for buttons. The old-line southerners were scared. We weren't slugging it out in some vine-covered swamp but on Yankee turf in the glare of world publicity. If the Mississippi regulars got booted, southern power brokers announced they would bolt the party. Lyndon Johnson told Hubert Humphrey that if he wanted to be vice-president he better work something out, and quick. As the arms got twisted and the patronage dangled, our support gave out. I never forgave Humphrey for the spineless role he played. The freedom delegates were offered observer status and allowed to sit at the back of the hall but not to participate. It was called "the back-of-the-bus compromise." Only Medgar Evers, Aaron Henry, and the older NAACPers were happy. SNCC was furious. Moses was completely wrecked. He had come close to working a miracle and felt he had failed. The press and party politicians complimented us on a historic victory but we wanted more. Much more.

Return to the South

When I returned to Mississippi the following summer, things were already falling apart. Atlantic City had split our ranks. There were those who still believed righteousness was enough. But a growing number of black organizers guided by Malcolm X and Frantz Fanon had run out of cheeks to turn. SNCC was soon to find it impossible to keep preachers' children like Julian Bond and John Lewis together with militants such as Stokely Carmichael and Rap Brown. And, of course, there was the difficult problem of the white organizers.

I worked in a freedom school in McComb. One day some people carried in a casket to show the students. Inside was Robert Shaw, the first community black killed in Vietnam. None of the kids wanted to talk about it. They were sharpening their internal hatred. It was difficult for a middle-class white to understand their resignation in the face of death. That was the moment I most felt the separation between myself and those I wanted to organize. It was an emotional chasm no amount of good feelings could overcome.

At the freedom school we taught U.S. history, history of the civil-rights movement, arithmetic, and reading. Role playing was often used, as the kids loved to act. We'd construct educational dramas. A day at the U.N. with kids as delegates, a courtroom scene, a town-hall meeting. Like *all* school systems, we propagandized.

The Ku Klux Klan was so strong they once held a rally in the middle of Route 80. Cars had to by-pass the meeting on side roads. It was hard to believe your eyes, but there they were: two hundred white sheets, flaming cross and all. Fifteen years ago, the Klan was no outmoded joke. A faceless nightmare, they were furnished by the police with a list of our license-plate numbers, and they patrolled the borders of each black community, gunning for organizers. "Coon huntin'," the local whites called it. I had several 100-m.p.h. chase scenes on narrow dirt roads, racing from one ghetto town to the next, knees vibrating out of control with fear.

Our major local campaign that summer was against the McComb Holiday Inn. Black maids, paid forty-nine cents an hour, decided to go on strike and needed our support. Daily picket lines were scenes of vicious Klan beatings. Once I was thrown to the curb and kicked repeatedly. An FBI agent leaned over and asked sarcastically if my civil rights had been violated. No one got arrested except SNCC workers.

After McComb, I moved on to Americus, Georgia, a stone's throw from Jimmy Carter's ranch house. SNCC had an alliance with Martin Luther King's Southern Christian Leadership Conference to carry on an intense voter-registration drive. Reverend Jan Selby, also from Worcester, and I were secretly housed in a woodshed belonging to a black school teacher. Every day we marched, got arrested, bailed out, marched, and got arrested again. Andy Young was, as I recall, project director for the Americus campaign. Vagabond agitators, we crisscrossed trails as demonstrators headed for Selma. Little by little, the South changed and the COLORED ONLY barriers came down.

All of us who worked there had ambivalent feelings about the southern whites. The ones who overcame their racial hatred were terrific humans. As one told me: "There's just two things we hate down here, bigots and niggers." At least they didn't hide behind

false words and absentee landlordism. Two months later, when
SNCC moved into the northern ghettos, liberal support evap-
orated. The up-front viciousness of the southern experience
proved small potatoes when compared with the institutionalized
violence of northern racism.

The Hometown Stomp-in

By the fall of 1965, in addition to our civil-rights activities, most of
us had begun to work against the widening war in Vietnam. It was
the time of teach-ins, and debates raged throughout the country. In
Washington, Ernest Gruening and Wayne Morse were the only
two senators who voted against Johnson's Gulf of Tonkin resolu-
tion. They were called mavericks and treated as hysterical freaks
by the media. Of course, everything they said was accurate.
Johnson and the CIA fabricated the incident. Morse and Gruening
were prophets ahead of their time. (Morse and I used to corre-
spond. When I last saw Gruening, during the Ellsberg trial in Los
Angeles, he took me aside in the corridor and proceeded to talk
about the evils of multinational corporations. He felt the military
would try to assume power within my lifetime. I can still feel his
frail hand on my arm. He was more than ninety at the time, and still
fighting a system he considered unjust. It's surprising how many
people at the top of our society fear a military coup. Walter
Cronkite, for example, is another one.)

Two senators, a baby doctor, a few professors, a couple of nuns,
some students, and the traditional pacifist groups made up the
early antiwar movement. Opposing your government's foreign
policy at a time of war has never been a popular idea. In Worcester
we announced the city's first antiwar march ever. Two hundred
and fifty demonstrators walked from the courthouse to the city
hall. Few had protested in public before. The night before they had
had to search their hearts. What mattered in life: a job, the church,
the community, or the need to act on one's moral convictions?

For a week, organizers had been receiving threats. A bomb was found on someone's porch. A hammer and sickle were smeared on the door of a bookstore. I used my southern training to teach nonviolent defense: one team would play the role of aggressors, shouting taunts and spitting; the other team would be taught temper control. If knocked down, they were to curl into the fetal position and crawl quickly to a wall or curbstone, gaining more protection for the back. Cardboard signs could be used as shields. Eyeglasses and jewelry were discouraged—a violent yank of an earring could rip an ear lobe. Men wore jock straps or cups. People were taught how to dissipate violence by diverting attacks on fellow marchers. Above all, no one was to panic or strike back. The best protection was a cool head, because all around would be chaos. Nonviolence never meant acceptance of injury. Great physical and psychological training were required.

We began our march in front of Worcester's Court Hall, right under a rather peculiar legend chiseled in the granite: *Obedience To Law Is Liberty*. There were ten parade marshals, of whom I was one. A young minister named Elmer Sterner and Father Gilgun led the procession, carrying olive branches in their hands. As I handed signs to people we would embrace or pass kind words. This was not a faceless outpouring of tens of thousands, these were my close friends. We celebrated holidays together and shared bad news. Slowly, silently, we began the ten-block march that would bring us to city hall. We felt tiny and few.

After some blocks, we began to notice three cars following us. Now they sped forward. "Watch out!" Boys jumped out and started hurling eggs. A few struck home and the cars sped off. At the next intersection we saw the police holding back angry crowds, with American flags bobbing up and down. The chants grew louder and louder. "Traitors!" "Traitors!" We marched on our side of the police, they on theirs. The mob broke the lines and attacked our column. "Get that Commie priest! He's holding the Viet Cong symbol" (the olive branch). They grabbed Gilgun, tore his priest clothes, and pummeled him to the ground. Someone with an American flag on a long pole charged at the minister. He was pinned against a storefront, a blood-crazed lunatic bayoneting him with a golden eagle. A Holy Cross student got smashed in the face, cut to the bone with brass knuckles. Other marchers got pelted with rocks and fists and spit. All the signs were torn and trampled on. Anger vented, the attackers ran. People helped each other up, brushed each other off, and we moved forward. Gilgun, clothes torn, white collar unfastened and jutting into the air, started singing, "We shall overcome. We shall overcome some day." Everyone sang softly.

To die at that moment, I thought, might not have been so bad. Like the Christians being eaten by the lions, singing and all. Like in *Quo Vadis*. People have for years asked me how come I wanted to be a martyr. I always wasted energy explaining how I didn't. Inside I kept saying, Is that the worst way to end up?

We finally made it to city hall and began our rotating circle. To picket in America you have to keep moving. It's illegal to stand still. There were now two thousand hecklers standing around us, crowding on the city-hall staircases. John Gerassi, a movement expert on foreign affairs, was standing on top of a sound truck, giving a speech, arguing with the crowd. Occasionally missiles would pierce the air. Aside from a few slashed tires and broken windows, we survived our initiation. We were not alone. In hundreds of similar scenes across the country, opposition to the Vietnam War was growing.

The CIA Turned Me On to LSD

Shortly after the demonstration, I got a call from Manny, my college roommate. He was now an army psychologist, working on secret LSD experiments with soldiers (recently it was revealed that these experiments were CIA-funded), and he wanted to know if I was interested in trying some. "Sure," I replied. I had never even tried marijuana, but I heard talk about LSD at Maslow's house. At Berkeley, I had lined up at the Langley Porter Clinic for two hours hoping to be a subject in an LSD experiment, but the quota was filled. They paid volunteers one hundred and fifty dollars to take it then!

I talked it over with my old friend Marty Carey, an artist who had just put together a pop art show and seemed to know something about the strange world of drugs. Marty got all excited at the prospect of my impending trip and offered his loft. I promised to get him some if it worked out. This was just about the time a *Life* magazine cover story was touting LSD as the new wonder drug that would end aggression. I've always maintained that Henry Luce did much more to popularize acid than Timothy Leary. Years later I met Clare Boothe Luce at the Republican convention in Miami. She did not disagree with this opinion. America's version of the Dragon Lady caressed my arm, fluttered her eyes and cooed, "We wouldn't want everyone doing too too much of a good thing." What a royal bitch!

Saturday morning, visitors bearing small packages showed up at the house. Manny quickly ran down general instructions and suggested we take the LSD right away. Then he unwrapped a wad of tin foil, and three sugar cubes tumbled out like gambling dice. We drove downtown to Marty's loft. Thoughtfully Marty had thrown pillows around and set up a stereo.

Say what you want about the CIA, but they sure had damn good acid. All the colors from Marty's gorgeous paintings began swirling around the room. Time danced in space. I talked continuously. When the others didn't want to hear, I picked up the phone and called God—collect. We had a nice chat. The Virgin Mary swept down from a cloud in the ceiling and I think we. . . . I'm not sure, but we petted a little. She was really nice. I rolled on the floor laughing hysterically. I experienced erotic laughter, whatever that is. Once I took our buddy Ira's pen and wrote, "I was burned on the silver rim of space." It took on meanings beyond meanings.

After four hours, someone said, "Hungry." I went alone to get lunch. Sitting in a diner around the corner, I noticed that the short order cook had left one of the gas jets on without striking the match. Un-oh! Something wrong here. Better not panic, everyone. Atomic bomb mushroom clouds were billowing in my head. "What'll it be, bub?" said the guy with the funny white hat.

"Right, let's see. . . . three ham and cheese, two BLTs, a hamburger with everything, two milkshakes, four Cokes, and better add a tunafish salad too."

"Now let's see," he said. "That'll be four tunafish, two ham and egg, five BLTs, four hamburgers, three malteds and a Coke."

"That's right," I agreed. "Do you have any mushroom clouds?"

"No, we ain't got mushroom but I can whip up a cheese omelet," he casually said.

"Right," I said.

Twenty-six lives later he appeared out of the back room with three huge brown bags stuffed with food. I paid the bill and somehow managed to steer everything back to the loft. "Let's see now, who ordered the pickle-and-mushroom bomb?"

Acid produced this manic sense of energy and I had to be active. I went to the bowling alley, walked the streets, and took a taxi to the house. That night I was scheduled to give a speech in a movement disco at a church.

Father Gonyor eyed me strangely. "Your speech was getting pretty flowery there. What's all the jazz about trailways of life and byways of bliss? You trying to be Allen Ginsberg or somebody, hunh? hunh? hunh?" he jabbed.

The next day Ira rolled some marijuana cigarettes. Three puffs and I was back rolling with the Virgin Mary on the rug. This time I scored.

The following week, Marty and I smoked grass every night. His wife Susan smoked, but Sheila wouldn't. Marriages have busted over this alone. When we exhausted the grass, Susan suggested we grind the seeds and put them in jam. We ate four pot-seed-and-strawberry-jam crackers but with no effect. "Let's get some more," Marty urged. I sent Manny a telegram asking for more LSD. He rang up. "You can't send a telegram like that!" he shouted into the phone.

"But you said it was legal," I answered sheepishly.

"It is, but this is a secret government project. Only a few people on the base even know it's going on."

"Gee, I'm sorry."

"Oh, I guess it's okay," he said. "The telegram said LBD anyway. I'll see what I can do." A week later a manila package arrived from Maryland. Marty and I divided up the contents. I've been a "head" ever since.

That first acid trip had an intense effect on me. A few months later I was fired from my job. It was obvious to anyone that I wasn't exactly putting my shoulder to the wheel of Westwood Pharmaceuticals. I was convinced by now the gods and a benevolent computer had arranged the monthly survival checks. The axe fell in the spring of '66 at the start of the company's annual "big acne season."

Out of Work—Free at Last

The new district manager, a Goldwater Lutheran, took me to dinner. It was at one of those PG-rated restaurants in Springfield, the kind where they wrap your baked potato in tin foil and serve what people consider "a nice relish tray."

"Now, Hoffman," the manager began, "who's kidding who? Your territory's falling apart. You haven't seen some of these doctors in months. I think there's been some *goofing around* up here in Massachusetts! What do you say?"

Seeing the writing in the sky, I quickly ordered an extra dessert on the company.

"Well," I offered weakly, "maybe it's spring fever."

"*Spring fever?* Did you study those sales figures?" He took a sip of his coffee, polished the chair with his bottom, and spoke. "Hoffman, let's be frank," he intoned, and halfway into my second pecan pie, I was fired.

Once all the finer details had been spelled out, it was agreed we'd drive to Worcester in the morning, load my samples into the Impala, and turn over the keys. Then Jack insisted we go out and "hang one on." I just assumed it was company policy to get salesmen bombed after they were fired, so they would be too weak to plot some act of vengeance. Big corporations, I knew, had psychologists map out the strategy of firing.

By our third drink, the conversation loosened up. "Hoffman, there's a certain *spunk* about you I really admire."

"Jack, that's damn white of you."

"Yes, you could have been one of our top salesmen. Tell me, now that it's over, what was it you didn't like?"

"It wasn't what I didn't like, Jack. The thing is, I like black folks!"

He peered over his horn-rims. "I know all you New England boys are pretty liberal, but what the hell do colored people have to do with it?"

"Jack, you know State Street here in Springfield? About a year ago I was dragged off the street there by two fat cops when I sat down and blocked traffic with some people. . . ." For the next hour he sat wall-eyed while I told him what I'd been doing with my life and Westwood's Impala for the past two years. Mississippi, LSD, everything but the rip-off of samples, expense accounts, and company time.

When I finished, he just sat there nodding. "Spunk, damn it, I was right, you got spunk. Oh sure, I'm a rock-ribbed conservative, but I've watched you people on TV; and what I always tell my wife—now don't you go blabbing this—I say those people got *spunk*. Spunk's what's missing in America these days."

It was my turn to be stunned.

The next day we drove back to Worcester, very friendly. I had already sold off most of the samples, so there wasn't much loading to do. "Why don't you keep the unopened cases for your personal use?" Jack suggested. I thanked him and we shook hands in parting.

The aquamarine Impala left a faint line of blue exhaust as it headed down Hadwen Road. Jobless but free, I was left standing on the lawn, with a jar of Fostex Acne Cream in each hand.

How to Talk Good

It was the end of March. Thomas Adams, a descendant of John and Samuel Adams, was about to enter the Democratic primary for senator. There was something noble in his character, shown in his determination to campaign against the Vietnam War.

I agreed to a staff position with Adams. He knew I had kids, and he offered me personal financial support. He also agreed to let me keep my affiliation with SNCC.

SNCC was now under the leadership of Stokely Carmichael, a veteran organizer out of Lowndes County, Alabama, who had vowed to move the struggle north. "We don't wanna sing no more songs, we want power. Black power!" The Watts riots and the new militancy had eroded liberal support. SNCC was being accused of igniting one uprising after another. People were predicting the proverbial "long hot summer," and I wanted Adams's assurance he wouldn't attack SNCC.

Adams thought it over and went me one better. "Why don't you ask Mr. Carmichael if he'd share a platform with me. Why, I'd be honored." Thomas Adams, a sober Yankee pinkface, wore his principles well. One of the few "patriots" his forebears would be proud of, carrying on a tradition that had fought the Revolution and helped build the Underground Railroad.

Stokely was a spellbinding orator. Through gestures and intonation, he articulated the rage of a movement that had seen too many dead, too many beaten, and too little progress. He mastered southern lingo to express his university-learned ideas—"We is SNCC all right but we ain't students no more and you know somethin' we ain't *nonviolent* either."

I studied him hard that night. The year before he had published a brilliant paper on the speech of rural Mississippi blacks. To teach it as faulty English, he argued, was a racial slur, which bred a sense of inferiority at the onset of public education. The paper triggered ideas in my head. I, too, wanted to develop my own style of speech. I wanted to abandon my university rhythms and manner. My whole education taught me to lecture in a way foreign to my innate feelings about activism. Yes, I knew how to present rational arguments, to carefully research positions, to allow "on the one hand this, on the other hand that"—the false equilibrium of ideas—to use a vocabulary as rolled and steamed as a Tudor lawn. Remain aloof from the subject, the university taught me, for only from that high unemotional plateau could one glimpse the truth. It was reasonable and rational. But to whom? The established power, of course.

McLuhan wrote in *Classroom without Walls* that those who draw a distinction between education and entertainment don't know the first thing about either. He meant entertainment not only in the sense of comedy, but of the grander theater of emotion. The successful drug company I'd worked for spent most of its budget on advertising. If *our* goals were ending injustice and stopping an imperialist war, and if we believed in those goals with the certainty with which big companies back *their* product, couldn't we concentrate some attention on our presentation? If we were the TV generation, wasn't there a way of speaking that evoked visual images, rather than spewing forth dead words in rhythmic, religious procession that bounced off dulled eardrums and dissipated into empty space? Wasn't there a way of destroying the boundary between audience and speaker? To let people experience *feelings* as well as thoughts? Above all, to get people to *act*? Could revolutionaries afford to speak the King's English?

Just as rock musicians study blues and soul music for inspiration, I built my style of verbal riffing on Stokely's spoken R & B. Without realizing it, Stokely was one of the formulators of hippie dialect.

Two months later, at the Newport Folk Festival, we were to meet again under strange circumstances.

Festivals for Fun and Protest

Is there anyone who doesn't like festivals? In the early fifties, George Wein got the idea and the permission to hold the Newport Jazz Festival. I attended the first and almost every one thereafter. At the '65 festival, Bob Dylan put on his black leather jacket, plugged in his guitar (horrors!), and sang "Mr. Tambourine Man," electrified. Half the audience booed, half cheered. (Ever the faddist, I cheered.)

Dylan's conversion to rock got all the ink, but another incident struck me as more revealing. Len Chandler, a black folk singer, did an antiwar song, and everyone around me joined in. When the song was over, he gave a three-sentence rap about how he opposed Johnson's war. People booed (Len, not the war). *The same people who sang along booed him for saying what the words of his song implied.* Strange, eh?

When I returned to Newport a year later, an incident occurred that helped me see festivals as organizing tools. During that year I had been stuffing the back seat of the Impala with handcrafts made by the Poor People's Corporation in Mississippi. PPC was a network of rural cooperatives making an assortment of leather and cloth goods. Warehoused in downtown Jackson, Mississippi, the goods were mostly sold through a mailing list of supporters. I started getting stores in New England to stock the products, and I was working out details for wholesaling in the North. A small idea about co-ops for the poor had grown into a fairly ambitious program employing four hundred people, a combination of survival and protest economics.

So when I went to Newport that year, I helped put up a display booth to publicize the project. We set up near the entranceway, carnival style. It looked real down-home, with dolls strung across the top, leather handbags and clothes on display, and a phonograph playing songs from the southern movement.

Stokely, Cleve Sellers, George Ware, and the SNCC Freedom Singers were around to get support from performers. Julius Lester, a SNCC worker and folk singer, was one of the emcees. Every night we'd go off in the bushes and get a little ripped on funny cigarettes.

One night, Ellen Maslow, Martha Kocel, and I were closing up shop when out of the blue—so to speak—these coppers who had been drinking too much charged the stand and began ripping it apart. Stokely, Cleve, and the others had just arrived to take us to a party, and the cops started swarming all over us. Night sticks were flying. "Fuck this shit!" yelled a voice of reason, and we all ran down a dark pathway with these drunken racist cops chasing us. I got knocked down by two brutes, and all I could think of was ditching the weed, which I finally managed to shove under a rock.

We were all rounded up and arrested for disturbing the peace. God, were we pissed—but we weren't the only ones. Julius Lester found out what happened and organized a meeting of the singers. They told George Wein that if things weren't set right the whole concert was off—finished. Crowds were gathering outside the jail. The charges were quickly dropped, but that wasn't enough for Stokely. We immediately went back to the spot where the fracas had occurred. The drunken cops, faces red, helmets glowing under the spotlights, were still in a phalanx, clubs in hand.

Wein asked Stokely what he wanted and he shouted, "I want that fat fucking prick of a cop hung by the balls." The batons warmed up; you could hear the cops grinding their teeth and feel Wein sweating through his shirt. Jesus Christ, I thought, here we go again. But Stokely knew we had some power. Besides, he was very brave.

The trouble was, because of the darkness, none of us could identify any of the attackers. Wein conferred with the chief of police, who offered to line up the entire Newport police force the next morning. None of us could believe the offer. Retribution? The police were actually going to line up for us!

We were up all night trying to figure this out. Everyone wanted to play the scene for all it was worth. Sure enough, at ten the next morning, the Newport Police Department lined up at attention. We marched by them and proceeded to sniff breaths and ask individual cops to shout things like "You nigger bastard!" It was one of the strangest incidents I've ever seen in the movement. Later, there were hearings; nothing happened to the police, of course. I can't recall any time it ever did.

This might have been the last time whites were beaten by police in the civil rights movement. Next year I was back at Newport with some friends. We got busted for handing obscene poems to nuns. George Wein bailed us out and later fixed the charges. "Hoffman," he said, "you're worse than Carmichael."

Adams lost the primary, and I lost the divorce hearing. Sheila got the house, the kids, the books, and the lawn mower. I got two suitcases filled with clothes and my candlepin bowling balls, which weren't going to be much help in New York. Down there they obscenely stuck their fingers in the ball. I gave the balls to my friend Paul, and headed for New York and big-time protest. I felt an inner calling. Not exactly like Joan of Arc, more like a kid shortstop being called up to the majors.

Liberty House

In New York, I shared an apartment on the Lower East Side with a young guy named Howie. We paid forty-nine dollars a month for a three-room railroad flat with a thirty-degree tilt to the west. It was over on Avenue C and 11th Street, where even the subways are afraid to venture. Howie was a Marxist going to medical school, learning skills he could take with him when he joined the guerrillas in the mountains of Bolivia. Living where we did was good practice for him. Avenue C was halfway to South America.

We were the only ones in the building who didn't speak Spanish. The neighbors slept six to a room, made do without heat or hot water, and often (contrary to the American myth) went to bed hungry at night. Rats picked at the improvised garbage dump at the rear of the building. Across the street, junkies lined up on stoops, waiting for the dealer. Children played ball in a maze of overflowing trash cans. The entire block had been condemned, if not officially by the city then certainly by the society at large.

It was a long way from the cottage and picket fence I'd left behind, but I was ecstatic as only one possessed by missionary vision can be. I was here to open a store, in fact a chain of stores, a people's K-Mart, to sell the goods from the Mississippi co-ops. All I had was eight hundred in cash, a check for fifteen hundred to compensate for damages at the festival, and the name we'd chosen—Liberty House.

After days of tramping the streets, scouting for a location, I came across a double storefront in the West Village. It needed total restoration, but its location was good. We borrowed money and raided the back of Macy's for furniture. I lived in the store, scraping floors, plastering walls, and painting.

Soon it was open and flourishing. A dozen volunteers worked there. However, relations with SNCC were strained. New faces ran the office in New York. That winter, there was a national conference at which all whites were purged from the organization. I blew up and wrote an attack on Stokely and black power. Despite racism, most of the nation's poor were still white, and as activists we had to always try and frame the struggle in class terms. Black nationalism, I argued, was a retreat. I went on to catalogue personal affronts that had been directed at white comrades, especially women.

The *Village Voice* printed the piece, giving it full play, and requested a follow-up story. I was quickly turning into the darling of the New York liberals, as I embodied their hope for an integrated civil-rights movement.

Something was awry, though. The praise was coming from quarters I mistrusted. Other white organizers patiently explained the significance of black power. I was given Fanon to read. I started to visit Julius Lester more and more for guidance. A month later, Stokely and I were together at SNCC pioneer George Brown's house in Washington. He ribbed me about the piece, and I joked with him about an ad executive who asked if I could get Stokely Carmichael to pose in "tasteful" ads for a new synthetic black clothing material, with the caption "Black is Beautiful." Only in America we all agreed.

Stokely and others advised me to turn over Liberty House to black management and organize around ending the war in Vietnam. In the spring of 1967 I took his advice.

Some Voices of Guidance

Ending involvement with SNCC and civil-rights activities by no means meant walking away from the movement. Help was needed in the mushrooming antiwar committees.

A community of full-time organizers was evolving around a loft at 5 Beekman Street—people like A. J. Muste, Dave Dellinger, Barbara Deming, and David McReynolds. I respected their pacifist beliefs, but something in their approach jarred my American heartland upbringing. I practiced nonviolence as a *tactic*, but was far from a follower of Gandhi. Confrontation always demanded surprise and uncertainty. By saying "If you punch me in the face, I'll turn the other cheek," you could often get hurt more than if you kept a threat of returning the blows. While Gandhi was fasting in jail, guerrillas blew up trains throughout India. When Martin Luther King, Jr., prayed, blacks rioted, and armed groups formed in the ghettos. Violence and the threat of violence have a good track record when it comes to changing the minds of people in power.

Pacifism could never sound convincing to workers who knew the labor movement's history. Yet it was foolhardy at the time to advocate any strategy that went beyond the nonviolent stance of the antiwar movement. Besides, its base lay in churches and universities; for five years now, they had been my stomping grounds, and I knew what strategies and language to employ there.

In the East Village new turf was opening up. Young runaway kids were flocking to the streets—longhaired, broke, on dope. There were thousands of them already; "hippies," the papers were beginning to call them. People were transforming themselves into living demonstrations of the struggle against bureaucracy. There was work to be done on the street, but I'd like to interrupt our story to briefly mention some influential thinkers at the time.

I have always found Norman Mailer fascinating as a thinker. I first encountered him in the last days of the fifties, swaggering like some tousle-haired Hebraic James Dean—seated on a podium, belting scotch from a bottle, and firing out insults and insights like body punches at a Brandeis audience. Wailing out at technocracy, craving for some primitive intellectual engagement, he lambasted the institutions of learning and culture. Exhorting the crowd to fan out from the hallowed grounds of academe, he predicted a New Age would be born in the gutters and back streets of America's bohemian underworld.

He saw America as the spawning ground for a new musician, a new poet, even a new politician, all heavily influenced by black culture—hip to drugs and sex, educated on a new set of principles. He codified this vision in an illuminating essay called "The White Negro." A cultural manifesto calling for youth rebellion as well as an analysis of the society's pathology, it struck a resonant chord in the heart beneath my leather jacket.

In *An American Dream*, in his articles on the heavyweight fights, in his agonizing over sexual identity, Mailer became a yardstick to continually measure my own thought. *Armies of the Night* is still the best book about sixties protest.

I recall one brilliant speech Mailer delivered at a Berkeley antiwar rally, circa '65, in which he portrayed the U.S. role in Southeast Asia as an extension of Johnson's Texas-rancher mentality. A wickedly accurate satire of Johnson at his most vulgar. Mailer showed how you can focus protest sentiment effectively by aiming not at the decisions themselves but at the gut of those who make them. He ended that speech with a call for national vilification of Johnson, suggesting we turn all photos of LBJ upside down—a sort of politics-by-disrespect.

At midpoint in the sixties, Herbert Marcuse published another important essay, called "Repressive Tolerance." In it, he successfully demolished the myth of the U.S. as the free marketplace of ideas. By oversaturation, the ruling class maintained its control over the minds of the people. Free speech meant a great deal when the founding fathers drew up the constitution—now, however, the *distribution* of speech was of paramount importance. The constitution had been passed from hand to hand, but how could radical concepts be exchanged *now*? It wasn't enough to leaflet on street corners when three networks maintained a nonstop thought barrage directed at millions. The implication of Marcuse was clear: to publicize radical ideas, you needed prime-time access. No one would volunteer the space. It would have to be stolen.

Marcuse was, with the exception of Maslow, the teacher who had the greatest impact on me. I studied with him at Brandeis, and later attended his lectures at the University of California. In the spring of '67, I saw him speaking—of all places—at the Fillmore East. There he was, this statuesque, white-haired seventy-year-old European Marxist scholar, following the Group Image acid-rock band onto the stage, accompanied by the thunderous foot-stomping cheers of America's most stoned-out, anti-intellectual generation.

In *Eros and Civilization* and *One-Dimensional Man*, Marcuse had managed to bridge the gap between Marx and Freud and in one mighty intellectual effort make their thinking relevant to the post-industrial age. He recognized alienation from one's labor as the chief illness of our time. But instead of fixing the blame for the anxiety, the sense of dread, in some primeval battle of fathers and sons (Freud) or a netherworld of the devil (the church), Marcuse put the blame on the competitive economic system. Capitalism forced man to *perform* rather than *experience* pleasure. Sexuality was repressed in order to create manpower hours. Thus, while all his contemporaries were scolding the young for their excesses in politics, sex, and drugs, Marcuse alone cheered us on. For to him the hippie ethic or "polymorphous perversity," as he termed it, was both a return to the origins of health and a push forward to a society in which alienation and repression could be contained.

"De only proper response to dis von-dimensional machine of destruction can be total and complete rrrrrrefusal!" cried the philosopher, standing on the Fillmore stage. The joint went crazy. Ben Motherfucker, leader of the Lower East Side's most nefarious street gang, spat on the floor, raised his fist, and exalaimed, "Dat cat's duh only fuckin' brain worth listnin' to in de cuntree!"

Marcuse allied with the strangest of bedfellows—the Mother-fuckers.

Another key thinker at this time was the Canadian Marshall McLuhan. *Understanding Media* became a guide for comprehending the electronic world. I wasn't sure I understood McLuhan any more than I did Marcuse, but his thinking made me focus on those flashing psychedelic news images that instantaneously seemed to penetrate our fantasy world. "This is reality," TV said. "Seeing is believing." Magic really. Through teleportation one could transport oneself bodily into the homes of strangers.

America has more television sets than toilets. I began to study those little picture tubes. If the means of production were the underpinnings of industrial society, then the means of communication served that function in a cybernetic world. And, if labor was the essential ingredient for production, then information was that ingredient for mass communication. A modern revolutionary group headed for the television station, *not* for the factory. It concentrated its energy on infiltrating and changing the image system. I suppose like cave people we have returned to ikons and symbols for idea identification.

But information was more than a news show: it was punches on an IBM card, scratches on magnetic tape, music, sex, family, schools, fashions, architecture. Information was culture, and change in society would come when the information changed. We would make what was irrelevant relevant. What was outrageous, commonplace. Like freaked-out Wobblies, we would build a new culture smack-dab in the burned-out shell of the old dinosaur.

There were other writers of importance. Paul Goodman's greatest contribution was his dissection of the mass educational system. He urged us to smash the barrier between classroom and society. More than a theoretician, Goodman would help build (with hammer and nails on the Lower East Side) the counterinstitutions to come. Robert Theobold, a new-age economist, crossed the barrier of academia to write in the underground press. That summer he was to hint:

> The only way out of the dilemma of our society is to say that in the short run, everyone is entitled to a guaranteed income, and then very rapidly move into a society in which you simply go into a store and take what you want.

This seemingly utopian vision was shared by someone quite different from Theobold. Fidel Castro had stated on several occasions that the goal of the Cuban Revolution was the abolition of money. Fraternal barter was seen by both Theobold and Castro as the economic basis of humanism. In Cuba, on the Isle of Pines, Castro was to welcome the youth movement's idealism by inaugurating a moneyless society.

This chapter would not be complete (it isn't anyway) without mention of one more crucial thinker. C. Wright Mills had kept his hand on the plow throughout the difficult fifties. His book, *The Power Elite*, remains, two decades later, the best indictment of the new, corporate ruling class. In it he traced the history of those who run America, destroying the myth of "leaders rising out of the masses." If Mills did not invent the concept of the "New Left," he certainly popularized it. In an essay called "The New Left," he uncannily predicted the changing revolutionary strategy. Realizing that rapprochement between organized labor and capitalism had stymied traditional working-class struggle, he advocated an attack on the "cultural apparatus" to be led by the young. Much of the so-called New Left seemed to overlook this important essay while still honoring Mills.

I did not.

The blending of all these ideas, filtered through the experience of everyday life, was the theoretical basis of what was to come. Halfway into the decade, the word *revolution* slowly crept into our vocabulary. And it wasn't thinkers that we sought out, it was doers. The time for study had passed. We no longer felt the need to justify decisions in intellectual terms.

Here Come the Hippies

At the turn of the century, New York's Lower East Side had welcomed my grandparents. Jews running from cultural repression in the Old Country flooded the gateway to the New World. Now 1967 was upon us, and once again waves of immigrants poured into the dilapidated, five-story walk-ups that pressed tightly against the teeming streets. They came not by sea, but from within America, and throughout that spring they thronged to the tenements of the Lower East Side as many as five thousand a week, sleeping on mattresses, ten to a flat.

The hippies came, hitching out of Kansas. Backpacking down from Maine. Jolting along in beat-up buses covered with dayglo sunrises. They had few belongings: a war surplus jacket, a tape recorder with some scratchy cassettes, a hash pipe, maybe some forged I.D. They adopted new names like "Groovy" and "Ladyfinger," and buried their past beneath masses of straggly hair and ill-fitting clothes.

Like my grandparents before, they were fleeing cultural repression. Schools that demanded they cut their hair. Churches preaching false rhetoric. Draft boards ordering them to fight in a senseless war. The world of "plastics" later captured in *The Graduate*. An older generation that had weathered the depression taught the ethics of scarcity while young people saw around them nothing but abundance. Hardly the children of a depression, the hippies came almost fleeing the "good life."

Nobody understood what their parents were talking about anymore. The family came to be perceived as the chief enforcer in a fraudulent society: clearly Father *didn't* know best. When my forebears came to the Lower East Side the first thing they did was figure out how to bring their relatives over; the new immigrants were more concerned with keeping the family far away, and they formed a fugitive colony, on the run from parents and the bounty hunters sent to track them down.

Most of the runaways were not the spoiled offspring of the nouveau riche, contrary to the media cliché, but poor rural teenagers who came to New York because there was nothing doing in their hometowns. They were uneducated and stoned, easy prey for sadists and pimps who set up crash pads as recruiting camps for prostitutes. In grasping for a new family structure, many kids of the era wound up with surrogate parents more cruel than the ones they left home.

Terms like "hippies," "love generation," and "flower children" belonged to the press. Magazines and TV codified the movement for the benefit of small-town America, but it would be absurd to say that the media invented the hippies, for an amorphous, let-me-alone attitude was spreading like an epidemic among youth.

They came to the Lower East Side and became part of the already existing cultural fruit salad: Ukrainian crones in babushkas waddling out of bakery shops, dashikied blacks with new Afros practicing Islamic chants on stoops spread with pieces of carpet, Puerto Rican kids boogeying to bongo drums, black-clothed Hasidic Jews clutching their breasts and scurrying along the sidewalk, mad artists dangling off fire escapes painting the sides of buildings, and vendors dealing grass from hot dog carts. Amidst this urban chaos came the hippies, skipping barefoot through the

Newark riots, 1967. Digger Abbie and friends.

Summer of Love, 1967, Central Park. Marty Carey, groom, Lynn House, bride, some of the 3,000 invited guests.

broken glass, shoving daffodils into your hand, murmuring,
"Help is on the way . . . loose change? . . . got a joint?" It was
an organizer's paradise, a real challenge because the reality and the
vision could be created from scratch.

At first I was cool to the hippie community. Dropping out I saw
as copping out—turning on as tuning out to social causes I believed
in. To me, hippies were just so many glassy-eyed zombies floating
through the neighborhood head shops. To them, I was too
"politico," "just another power freak." I expressed my criticism
in a *Village Voice* piece in which I mentioned the mind-blowing
contradiction of a peace-and-love rock group like the Jefferson
Airplane doing commercials for Levi's while southern blacks were
trying to unionize Levi Strauss and calling for a national boycott.
The Airplane, to their credit, quickly severed relations with the
company. In fact, of all the rock/protest groups I met only the
Airplane/Starship and the Grateful Dead came close to practicing
the community they sang about.

The League for Spiritual Discovery, a Timothy Leary and
Richard Alpert (later Baba Ram Dass) production, had opened just
around the corner from Liberty House in the West Village. I
drifted into meetings, playing the street politico. Leary and I had
many a run-in. I would argue that he was creating a group of
blissed-out pansies ripe for annihilation and Leary would just flash
a big grin and laugh a lot. Still, I studied his technique of karmic
salesmanship. In his famous *Playboy* interview, for example, he
reported women could have thousands of orgasms on LSD—what
a pitchman!

I went to see him in some hippy-dippy traveling carnival show at
the Fillmore—gongs, Tibetan bells, strobes, and in the center ring
Leary sat dressed all in white, barefoot, lotused-out on a pillow
and humming to a rapt audience. Turn on—tune in—drop out—
Eah! But Leary was tinkering with a form of communication that
deliberately broke with custom, carrying on in a way Stokely
Carmichael had suggested, and I thought more about how I should
say what I wanted.

Until that point, I had left my old hustler's sales rap back in
Worcester, with my suit and sample case. Social issues were
supposed to be debated Western style: rational arguments at
twenty paces. Tight organization, and a fast draw with historical

fact. Go for the head and their hearts will follow. In contrast, Leary and the other acidheads emphasized the inner trip: "Change your head and you'll change the world." He seemed to tunnel right inside, using acid to transmit directly to the mind-gut. Taking acid created a feeling of definite separation from those who had not. To this day, on some level, I still don't trust people who have not opened themselves up enough for the experience. On some anal-retentive level they are saying they fear looking inside, and grasp at any rationalization in reach to say "No!"

I saw the reverse of Leary's trip: change the world and you'll change your mind. Total absorption with the internal voyage made you easy to exploit and convert: change your shrink, change your diet, change your record collection . . . Columbia Records was actually running an ad campaign with the money-making slogan "The Man Can't Bust Our Music." In spite of our differences, Timothy later underlined his reassuring words by giving me a check to our newly formed community service group. Needless to say, it bounced. "It was the thought that counted," we reasoned. and never demanded that he make good on the money or anything else. Certainly not his word.

By the time I left Liberty House, Leary and company were closing down their LSD center and enough politicos and hippies were interscrewing their ideas for a community structure to emerge. I left Liberty House and headed East—to the East Side, that is. My job was on the streets now, which meant a shorter walk to work.

Love and Utopia
on the Lower East Side

If I had been born a woman I would have been Anita. Sometimes couples take fifty years of living together to get to look and act alike: we began right off. The first night we spent together we fell in love. She was a born rascal. A well-educated psych major like myself, she had been working in a mental clinic when we met at Liberty House. She had also suited up as a Gray Line tour guide, and as a Pinkerton guard at the World's Fair, where she once chased a pickpocket through the crowds only to release him when she realized she had more in common with him than with her fellow rent-a-cops.

Beneath a sophisticated New York exterior lay a heart-throbbing, romantic teenybopper. She was, as she often phrased it, "hopelessly in love." So was I. After a few weeks we rented a ground-floor hole-in-the-wall apartment right in the center of the Lower East Side street action, thirty-two steps from St. Marks Place and Second Avenue. Being broke but resourceful, we lived a life we called "primitive elegance," finding furniture on the street or making originals. I constructed a loft bed, there were big pillows on the floor for meetings and getting stoned—it was cheap but clean and cozy. We were never the stereotyped hippie slobs you read about as a media fantasy.

Anita made beads and sold them. Sometimes she worked as a psychologist, sometimes I got paid for making speeches: between her income and mine we supported ourselves. Subtracting the money I sent Sheila, it came to very little, but it didn't take much back then.

We had no way of knowing that we had just taken a $101-a-month front-row seat to the cultural revolution. The local counter-cultural institutions were all in a ten-block radius: Paul Krassner's *The Realist*, Ed Sanders and his Peace Eye Bookstore, resident poet Allen Ginsberg. . . . The *East Village Other* was a block away, the Psychedelicatessen, the country's first head shop, was around the corner at 10th Street and Avenue A, and Randy Wicker's Button Shop was right next door. Whatever cause people were pushing, they would go into Randy's and order a couple thousand buttons and get them for close to nothing. Buttons became a primary symbol of identity and expression.

The Group Image Band and Poster Commune, the second-hand hippie clothing stores, the community meeting center, Gem Spa, were all nearby. Bill Graham's Fillmore East was just around the corner. It seemed that every band that played at the Fillmore that year was discovered within three days and signed to a big record company: The Grateful Dead, Janis Joplin and Big Brother and the Holding Company, Jim Morrison and The Doors, The Band, Jimi Hendrix—they all went out the Fillmore's door straight to the big time. Sometimes Janis crashed on our living room floor. A sad cheeky poor little rich girl. She was the only person I ever saw use a needle. It gave me the shivers.

Across the street from my apartment Andy Warhol's Balloon Farm turned into The Electric Circus while I was sitting there, and Andy moved his factory north to Union Square, missing all the action.

At 31 I was older than the average runaway by some fifteen years, but those who took an interest in building a youth community on the Lower East Side were all over 30. Like myself, they had run away from mainstream life and were eager to pass their insights on to younger kids. An IBM executive moved down from Westchester County and founded "Food," a commune whose purpose was to pass out free food in Tompkins Square. Actors created street theater groups. Lawyers volunteered time for serious busts. Medical students set up a street clinic. Careers had come to be seen as strait jackets as the sound and smell of liberation filled the air. These were heady times.

The times also required a new operating style. Organizers are almost always outside agitators. Like anthropologists, they study the locals, learn their dialect, begin mimicking the style of speaking. This was what I had done in the civil rights and antiwar movements. But the rise of the hippie culture on the Lower East Side was different. Nothing like walking into some African tribe and organizing it, because the culture itself was just emerging, and it was us. Organizers were instigators of style and values. The way we spoke became known as hippie dialect. Our philosophy the hippie ethic. It was a two-way street: leaders learning the culture and helping to create it at the same time.

Something else made the scene on the Lower East Side different from other organizing experiences: long hair. It meant a lot at the time. First of all, it took six months or a year to grow a good, shaggy crop. Now that took real commitment, a lot different from being a weekend radical, going to rallies once a month, or sending in donations. In the civil rights movement many people would devote time and energy to what they believed in, but their beliefs were not something lived day-to-day.

Long hair wasn't that superficial. It caused hassles with family, school officials, the police. There was no way of hiding that your hair was getting long. You could hide in the closet if you were gay, a Communist, smoking dope, anti-war, or hated your boss. You could listen to the Beatles quietly in your room. But you just couldn't hide all that hair, and growing it was the coming out of the closet for the counterculture.

On the Lower East Side police would often grab kids by their long hair, throw them against the wall, and start searching them. Our organizing efforts really got off the ground over the issue of police harassment. One day we passed out leaflets urging people to come to a community meeting. We expected the usual ten or twenty concerned citizens. Instead, there were two hundred, almost all freaks. It was the first time I saw long-haired people at a community meeting.

We talked about a lot of problems—friction with the Puerto Ricans, with the Ukrainians, with landlords and the police. About bad dope, price gouging, street crime. Once the community had responded in force to a meeting, we planned more. At that time, of the half dozen or so who were emerging organizers I had the most experience, and of this group, two of us—Jim Fouratt and myself—were even put on the city payroll for a brief period. The *Daily News* blew this into a scandal and we were fired, but we retained our role as liaisons between city hall and Mayor Lindsay's representatives and the neighborhood.

We helped fill the gap between the community and the police, none of whom lived in the area. Soon, any cop who shoved a person around would find he had a crowd to deal with, for we organized community patrols to follow the police. In general, we were effective because we *were* the people we were organizing. Everybody would get together when the community's anarchistic, do-your-own-thing life-style was threatened.

The issues we organized around reflected what was going on in the neighborhood. When Gem Spa raised the price of an egg cream from ten to fifteen cents it became an issue, and we handed out leaflets calling for a boycott. It's amazing how a nickel raise for an egg cream can rouse a community, and if you're clever enough you can do a little educating about the nature of the profit motive in the process and build "people-power."

Most of the work took place right out on the street. The Lower East Side became our office, and we walked the streets, listened to tenants' problems, attended neighborhood ethnic group meetings, got people out of jail, established crash pads, attended to bad acid trips, struggled with speed freaks on rampages, and we did this twenty hours a day, for no money.

I loved it on the street. I panhandled there, ate there, sometimes even made love there. Just being on the street was thumbing your nose at a society that made "standing on the corner" a crime. As a kid I was taught that everything bad happened on the street. Disease lurked in the gutter. When you got fired you were "out on the street." Night and day we were warned about the dangers of the street. Just being there was liberating. I walked the soles off my boots three times that first year of the hippies.

By the fall of 1967 it was not unusual to see twenty cops patrolling a single block while hordes of undercover agents slouched against the buildings surveying the hairy swarm. I was busted six times on or near the Hippie Kingdom crossroads of St. Mark's Place and Second Avenue. For loitering, obstructing traffic, rioting—and each charge boiled down to "being on the street." Fortunately for me the local chief of police saw some value to my work. A patient, likable carrot-top named Captain Joe Fink, he quickly mastered the principles of symbolic warfare and adopted me as his wayward son, constantly worrying about me.

Despite the then popular rhetoric about "pigs" I always dealt one-to-one with those lined up behind the law. Fink, like a few police I've met, became one because of some deep social concern, and it showed. When I would come back to the neighborhood from the Tombs after a bust he would call Anita to make sure I was all right. When I kicked in his favorite trophy case window at the station house in protest over a police raid on a black family, he flew into a rage and personally busted me. The next day, after I was bailed out, I gave him twenty bucks for the window.

"I wanted blacks to see hippies stand up for them, Joe," I said. "It was nothing personal."

"I know. You get enough sleep downtown?"

Long retired, Captain Fink still keeps his worry-watch, advocating that the current charges against me be dropped.

Information became a crucial battleground. There was so much arrant nonsense in the media about LSD and marijuana. Banner headlines for a health official in Pennsylvania who claimed kids on acid had gone blind from staring at the sun (he later admitted he'd made it up) and stories about acid freaks walking right out of windows and jumping off roofs. Scientists on government grants would say they didn't know enough about the effects of grass, therefore it was harmful. Harmful? People had been smoking dope for thousands of years while most of the items in the supermarkets were known poisons, or junk, or both. I can't think of anything advertised on TV that's good for people. Kids heard of a new drug called STP and started mixing a little of Andy Granatelli's motor oil additive with crushed aspirin, not exactly the formula. Maybe it got them high anyway, like those who claimed that smoking bananas got you off. Marvin Garson perpetrated that original hoax. (Marvin wrote one of the better books on the era, *Inside Dope*.)

After all, suggestibility was a crucial factor in dope taking. Once, at a conference at the University of Buffalo, I ended my talk by scattering hundreds of joints to the audience. Everybody lit up and got high—even the Motherfuckers, ever ready to blow the whistle when they spotted me pulling what they considered a liberal phony, were taken in. The joints were rolled entirely from catnip. I expected to be busted and planned to flash the catnip boxes when the narcs appeared on the stage. Instead, I escaped in the midst of a communal catnip trip. Some people later said it was the best shit they ever smoked.

To fill the information gap, Jim Fouratt set up a communications center, located a mimeograph machine, and started printing. The main form of distribution was leafleting. I wrote reams of street literature; so did Ed Sanders, Allen Ginsberg, and a lot of others. A leaflet might give information about a venereal disease epidemic, warn about some bad news cat who had been ripping people off, rock concerts—all very low key, Yellow Submarine "peace-and-love" style with no confrontation politics, nothing heavy.

The words were often complemented by psychedelic artwork, and aesthetics became another way of contrasting what "we" were saying as opposed to what "they" said.

"Just look at this," I would say, holding up a copy of *The New York Times*. "Not only does it lie but it's ugly." We also evolved a form of poetic leafleting, not asking people to do anything but read it and enjoy. It was all hippie talk—cheery, very up, always optimistic, but generally related to something important in a silly sort of way:

> Pot get you high
> Whee
> Cop bring you down
> Oooh
> Pot love your chick
> Mmmm
> Cop scare your dick
> Owww
> Pot do no harm
> !
> Judge break your arm
> !
> Pot should be free
> Yeah
> Sun shine on me
> Yeah

That was the dream we lived. We saw ourselves as visionaries in the Mean Streets. A utopia would rise out of the garbage. BE REALISTS—DEMAND THE IMPOSSIBLE. We opened a Free Store on the Bowery. Like a Salvation Army depot minus the price tags. Less a store than a philosophical experience, the Free Store stood as the symbol of a new kind of economic exchange. GOODS FOR GOOD LOOKS, NO STEALING, YOU ARE THE FREE STORE, read the signs. Winos drifted in to pick up shoes some freak had discarded after high-school graduation. Kids emptied entire suitcases of worldly goods on the floor, saying, "I have enough, take what you need."

Two thousand people joined in a sweep-in, and one cross street in Manhattan was made to sparkle. Years later Reverend Moon appropriated the tactic, sending out smiling moonies in spotless white coveralls to clean up New York. The sight of them coming down the street with their brooms was chilling. The moonies are straight out of "Village of the Damned." Nothing but zombie assholes.

We held be-ins, sing-ins, tree plant-ins. Florists saw us as the best publicity stunt since Mother's Day and gave us flowers to hand out. Everyone went barefoot and painted their faces: a starry-eyed tribe of white Indians, we blitzed the streets of New York with our free medicine show.

When the Newark riots broke out we had a shuttle service from the Lower East Side to Newark, bringing in ten to fifteen truckloads of food, clothing, and blankets each day and giving them to local community organizers for distribution, helping their organizing as well.

The media were fascinated by the goings-on in the grimy enclaves of the counterculture. What do hippies do? Well, they lie around their crash pads, smoke a lot of dope, and when they get married they get all dressed up in crazy clothes and go to Central Park for a big celebration—like a wedding. That was Anita and me. We were *the* hippie wedding that June, the one featured in *Time*. (In color, you should know.) We sent out our wedding announcement in the form of a street leaflet, of course. Very flowery. The first multi-color one on the East Coast.

The ceremony was quite a contrast to the one Sheila and I had passed through seven years previous. Dope had replaced whiskey and soda. The chopped liver stayed but it received stiff competition from rice and veggies. Thirty-five hundred guests, our cultural relatives, attended. The minister was our buddy, Lynn House, a neo-American "boo-hoo" (a satirical religion). Lynn had just dropped the first STP tablet to hit the East Coast. Anita wore huge dark glasses hoping her parents wouldn't recognize her on TV. The groom was garlanded in daisies. The *I Ching* predicted a future locked in conflict for us as the Associated Press, our wedding photographer, snapped away. It was the event, however, and not the participants that was newsworthy.

Uncle Schmully and his wife came to visit us on the Lower East Side after we got married. It was the closest they had come to meeting actual hippies in a slum as all they knew was what they had seen on television. We had an American flag for a bed sheet and there was a semi-nude picture (decent—no genitalia showing) of Anita and me on the bedroom wall. My aunt took one look and said to Uncle Schmully, "Oh look, they're naked! Just like it said in *Time!*"

It was not all smiles and flowers in the slum. We had our Mansonesque moments. Murders, rapes, and sadistic beatings occurred and the papers magnified them as much as possible. They happened all right, but slum life is *always* violent. The practices of slum landlords and price gougers establish a jungle society at the onset, but the violence of neglect doesn't sell papers as fast as blood mixed with white suburban flesh and drugs.

Sexist attitudes also prevailed. Women beaded, cooked, and screwed their way through the era while their "old men" made the decisions. Racism Manson style was practiced by many harem lords like the legendary Galahad who forbade his "chicks" from balling "spades." But given all the seamier aspects of life on the Lower East Side, the hippie movement was still far more significant than any of the other youth fads encouraged by America's teen culture industry. Hoods, flappers, punks, disco mania come and go with the generational sign-offs, and rebellion has been neatly designated as something you do while young. To promote this belief the media traffic cops worked overtime to show that when our little dream was over, the hippies went home, grew up, and emulated their parents as if nothing had happened. *Woodstock Census*, an exhaustive survey by Deanne Stillman and Rex Weiner, reveals that the media vision of hippies-turned-Babbitts is far from reality. In time the hippie life-style that evolved in the mid-to-late Sixties will be seen as the force that broke the stranglehold of the Protestant Ethic, that spiritual underpinning of the profit greed-grab. It spread the morality of anti-war politics. Make Love Not War was our battle cry.

Personally, I always held my flower in a clenched fist. A semi-structure freak among the love children, I was determined to bring the hippie movement into a broader protest. Troop levels in Vietnam had risen to 500,000 men. The apocalypse was upon us. We activists had to harness our manic energies. Sure, I believed in the power of love, but the time had come to make outrage contagious on a grand scale.

There's a big difference between sitting around in a room bullshitting with your friends and making things happen. I sat and listened to people's fantasies, but then I was the "itch"—the one who ran to the phone or into the street to make it happen. Allen Ginsberg has spent a lot of time trying to teach me how to sit still. I always preferred the crapshooter's tension between fantasy and reality. *Come on, baby, light my fire. Freedom's just another word for nothing left to lose. I ain't got no satisfaction.* A good organizer should have "ants in his pants."

Typically American, we had no ideology. I developed my own methods of expressing indignation, using techniques that fit the time, the place, and my own personality. It was a theatrical period, filled with rebellion, naive optimism, moral purpose, giddy sex, and cheap dope. (Believe me, you can do a lot worse!) So we met, the times and me, down there on the Lower East Side. It was a nice fit; a great time to be alive. Each morning we would claim: Today is the first day of your life.

Museum of the Streets

The first time you may have seen me was in the gallery of the New York Stock Exchange, hurling money on the brokers below. Of course, you didn't actually *see* me because no photographs of the incident exist: newsmen are not allowed to enter the sacred temple of commerce.

It all began with a simple telephone call to the Stock Exchange. I arranged for a tour, giving one of my favorite pseudonyms, George Metesky, the notorious mad bomber of Manhattan. Then I scraped together three hundred dollars which I changed into crispy one-dollar bills, rounded up fifteen free spirits, which in those days just took a few phone calls, and off we went to Wall Street.

We didn't call the press; at that time we really had no notion of anything called a media event. (And to make one very important point, I *never* performed for the media. I tried to reach people. It was *not* acting. It was not some media muppet show. That is a cynical interpretation of history.) We just took our places in line with the tourists, although our manner of dress did make us a little conspicuous. The line moved its way past glassed-in exhibits depicting the rise of the industrial revolution and the glorification of the world of commerce. Then the line turned the corner. Suddenly, we saw hordes of reporters and cameras. Somebody must have realized a story was in the making and rung up one of the wire services. In New York the press can mobilize in a matter of minutes. Faster than police, sometimes.

We started clowning, kissing and hugging, and eating money. Next, some stock exchange bureaucrats appeared and we argued until they allowed us in the gallery, but the guards kept the press out. I passed out money to freaks and tourists alike, then all at once we ran to the railing and began tossing out the bills. Pandemonium. The sacred electronic ticker tape, the heartbeat of the Western world, stopped cold. Stock brokers scrambled over the floor like worried mice, scurrying after the money. Greed had burst through the business-as-usual façade.

It lasted five minutes at the most. The guards quickly ushered us out with a stern warning and the ticker tape started up again.

The reporters and cameramen were waiting for us outside:

"Who are you?"

"I'm Cardinal Spellman."

"Where did you get the money?"

"What are you saying? You don't ask Cardinal Spellman where he gets his money!"

"How much did you throw?"

"Thousands."

"How many are you?"

"Hundreds—three—two—we don't exist! We don't even exist!" As the cameras whirred away we danced, burned greenbacks and declared the end of money.

BYSTANDER: "This is a disgusting display."

ME: "You're right. These people are nothing but a bunch of filthy commies."

The story was on the air waves that night and our message went around the world, but because the press didn't actually witness the event they had to create their own fantasies of what had happened inside the money temple. One version was we threw Monopoly money, another network called it hundred-dollar bills, a third shredded money. A tourist from Missouri was interviewed who said he had joined in the money-throwing because he'd been throwing away his money all over New York for several days anyway and our way was quicker and more fun. From start to finish the event was a perfect myth. Even the newspeople had to elaborate on what had happened.

A spark had been ignited. The system cracked a little. Not a drop of blood had been spilled, not a bone broken, but on that day, with that gesture, an image war had begun. In the minds of millions of teenagers the stock market had just crashed.

Guerrilla theater is probably the oldest form of political commentary. The ideas just keep getting recycled. Showering money on the Wall Street brokers was the TV-age version of driving the money changers from the temple. The symbols, the spirit, and the lesson were identical. Was it a real threat to the Empire? Two weeks after our band of mind-terrorists raided the stock exchange, twenty thousand dollars was spent to enclose the gallery with bullet-proof glass. Someone out there had read the ticker tape.

In *The Theatre and Its Double*, Antonin Artaud called for a new "poetry of festivals and crowds, with people pouring into the streets." No need to build a stage, it was all around us. Props would be simple and obvious. We would hurl ourselves across the canvas of society like streaks of splattered paint. Highly visual images would become news, and rumor-mongers would rush to spread the excited word. Newscasters unconsciously began all reports of our actions with the compelling phrase "Did ya hear about ————.''

For us, protest as theater came natural. We were already in costume. If we went above Fourteenth Street we were suddenly semi-Indians in a semi-alien culture. Our whole experience was theater—playing the flute on the street corner, panhandling, walking, living protest signs. Our theatricality was not adopted from

Original caption: "A curly-headed young man burns a fiver." Burning
money in front of the Stock Exchange, April 1967. Helping Abbie are Stew
Albert and Jerry Rubin.

the outside world. We didn't buy or read about it. It was not a style like disco dressing that you could see in ads and imitate. Once we acknowledged the universe as theater and accepted the war of symbols, the rest was easy. All it took was a little elbow grease, a little hustle.

At meetings people would divide up in groups to work on one theatrical action or another. Some took only a few participants and others were more elaborate. Some had to be planned like bank robberies and others like free-for-all be-ins.

One night we decided to do something that would express the neighborhood's dismay over increased traffic and thought for the first time about using mobile tactics—people running around and creating a little chaos rather than just standing still. To get everyone assembled and disbursed we put out an anonymous leaflet telling people to gather at St. Mark's Place at 9 P.M., wait for a signal from God, then scatter through the streets. Two thousand people responded.

One of us (guess which one) had gone to a chemist's shop and bought two pounds of magnesium which we packed in coffee tins and put on the roofs around St. Mark's Place. Then we rigged the cans with delay fuses by shoving lighted cigarettes in match packs. Once done, we raced down to the streets where people were milling around, waiting for God. All of a sudden the whole sky lit up with a huge blast of exploding magnesium. People started running all over. Fire trucks poured into the area. Sometimes chaos makes a good point.

In incense-filled rooms we gathered cross-legged on the rugs, conspiring dastardly deeds. The Jokers would show Gotham City no mercy:

"We've just got to end this tourist gawking," complained provo agitator Dana Beal.

"Hey, how's this for the tourist problem?" said Radio Bob Fass. "Wavy Gravy gets dressed up real straight and buys a ticket to go on one of the tours. We all get dressed up as cowboys and hold up the bus when it turns the corner into Second Avenue. We board it, pull Wavy off and hang him from the lamp post."

"Hang him?"

"Well, not really. We rig up one of those harnesses under his jacket just like they do in the movies."

The major event that spring was the be-in in Central Park. That's when I really got hooked in to the whole idea. I was at Liberty House when Lynn House and Jim Fouratt came by and said, "We're going to put on this be-in."

I went on the air to promote the event and Bob Fass at radio station WBAI interviewed me. I started to fantasize about what the be-in was going to be about—no speakers, platform, leaders, no clearly defined format so people could define it for themselves. Folks would just come to the park on Easter Sunday dressed for the occasion and exchange things, balloons, acid, jelly beans, Easter eggs; do Druid dances, or whatever their hearts desired.

Thirty-five thousand people showed up. The traditional Fifth Avenue Easter Parade, our competition, drew less than half that. After the be-in, Anita and I walked out of the park and joined the Fifth Avenue Parade, singing "In Your Easter Bonnet." Our faces were painted silver and I was carrying a huge Easter bunny. In front of St. Patrick's Cathedral the loudspeakers blared, "Come in, come in and worship." Why not? But as soon as we mounted the steps we were stopped by a line of cops.

"You can't go in there looking like that."

"What do you mean, we can't come in? Don't you see who we're with? We're with the Easter bunny."

"The Cardinal says no hippies on Easter Sunday."

A crowd began to gather. We continued to "play the dozens" with the cops. The confrontation heated up so we staged a strategical withdrawal, already plotting a sequel: "We'll come back next Christmas. We'll rent a mule and get some dude with long hair, dress him up in a white robe and sandals, and have him ride right up to the door of St. Patrick's with people waving palm branches, and Cardinal Spellman will come out and say, 'You can't come in here . . .' "

It's so easy. All you need is a little nerve and a willingness to be considered an embarrassment. Then you just keep pushing it, repeating what they say: "You *mean* the Cardinal *says* . . ."

If observers of the drama are allowed to interpret the act, they will become participants themselves. Too much analysis kills direct theatrical experience. The put-on allows you to circumvent the trap. Smashing conventional mores becomes essential. The concept of mass spectacle, every-day language, and easily recognized symbols was important to get public involvement.

Artists, the vanguard of communication, had grown weary of decades of abstract shapes. Modern art was already institutionalized; ersatz Kandinskys hung in dentists' offices. Andy Warhol broke through the abstraction and let us see the raw stuff of art in supermarkets, on TV, in magazines, and at the garbage dump. Allan Kaprow and other artists were experimenting with a new form called "happenings"—half-scripted, half-chance public exhibitions—3-D art, with people as paint.

"Happenings" were an extension of abstract art and as such were designed for the ruling class. I thought we could improve on that. Perhaps the audience that appreciated *All in the Family* did not approve of our "message" but they *did* understand it. It was public and popular. If we were not accepted by the Archie Bunkers of America, then perhaps by the children of Archie themselves. That the Museum of Modern (sic) Art honored "happenings" and "pop art" while ignoring our brand of political theater just proves the connection between successful artists and the rich.

Lenin once wrote that art was counter-revolutionary because it showed beauty in the *present*, while revolution promised beauty in the future. It's true that art-for-art's sake leads to performing modern dance for Shahs and Sheiks or discussing sculpture at afternoon tea with the Rockefellers. Yet creativity is needed to reach people snowed under by ruling-class images, and only artists can manage the breakthrough. Artists are the collective eyes of the future. One of the worst mistakes any revolution can make is to become boring. It leads to rituals as opposed to games, cults as opposed to community and denial of human rights as opposed to freedom.

In organizing a movement around art we not only allowed people to participate without a sense of guilt but also with a sense of enjoyment. The use of fun in struggle was a new notion. Even in Mississippi where we were truly frightened most of the time with people shooting at us, living with the constant thought that we might lose our lives, it seemed like people enjoyed their "work." All I did was admit it felt good. There's no incongruity in conducting serious business and having fun. This pissed off the straight left no end.

One of the principles of good theater is not to overburden the audience with footnoted explanations of what they are seeing. In 1967 a picket sign saying END THE ————— was far more involving than one that said END THE WAR. People love filling in the blanks and you could always count on straight people to stick to the core message. A populist movement must allow people to define their own space, their own motives, to be their own critics. A good explanation is no explanation, keeping your mouth shut a correct response. There was, however, an even higher form of communication, since "no response" sounds the same as the bureaucracy's "no comment." Street players have nothing to hide. The solution lies in the zen axiom: say everything by saying nothing, remain silent by telling all. Any good Jewish comedian from Hillel to Don Rickles knows what I'm talking about. Partly truth, partly fiction, the "put-on" gets the job done.

GUARD: Sorry, hippies are not allowed in the Stock Exchange.
ACTOR: But we're not hippies, we're Jewish. Should we tell the press you kept Jews out of Wall Street?

Theater of protest, for me, was a marriage of circumstances and personality. After a while I couldn't keep it a secret who I was. At first, my identity was a bit of a mystery. I often wrote under weird aliases: George Metesky the bomber, Jim Metesky, which was a cross between him and Jim Piersall, a Red Sox ball player I liked, Frankie Abbott, a figure in the Amboy Dukes (dutifully reported in the *New York Times* as Mr. Frank Abbott), Free, The Digger, or just A. Hippie. (The period after A made it me.) After I became well known I couldn't continue the pretense, even if the attitude was right. It was all part of a reluctance (maybe an inability) to define. Definition always seemed to contain an element of control.

On April 15, 1967, the largest demonstration in the country's history, 700,000 people, marched to the United Nations to protest the escalation of the war in Vietnam. Our Lower East Side contingent assembled at Tompkins Square Park and marched north, gathering more people along the way. The artists all turned out, so naturally our form of presentation was pretty colorful: Ginsberg's bells and chants, The Bread and Puppet Theater group, gaily dressed and stoned, a Yellow Submarine, and a lot of people who looked like they had posed for the Sergeant Pepper album cover. (One of the first examples of a masterpiece entering the Supermarket.)

A month later the right-wingers responded with a Support Our Boys rally, and we organized a "flower brigade" to march in their parade. There were about twenty of us with flowers and banners that read "Support Our Boys—Bring Them Home," and we all carried little American flags. I wore a multi-colored cape with the word "Freedom" on it. Anita was all decked out in red, white, and blue. Joe Flaherty of the *Village Voice* came by and told us we were asking for trouble. Even the cops tried to talk us out of marching and wouldn't give us an escort for protection. But we saw the "Support Our Boys" stickers on their windshields and we knew we were better off without them.

For a while everything went fine. We marched behind some Boy Scouts from Queens ("Oh, look, they're kissing!" they'd squeal and break formation) and then walked straight into trouble. They came at us with fists, feet, beer, spit, red paint. They even ripped up our American flags. Then a flying wedge of cops appeared out of nowhere and escorted us, bleeding and limping, all the way back to St. Mark's Place.

Undaunted, we marched again, this time to Lincoln Center for a cultural exchange program. "March to Lincoln Center. Bring Your Own Garbage. Let's Trade It for Their Garbage—Even Steven," read the leaflets. About thirty of us walked from our neighborhood through the streets of Manhattan to newly-opened Lincoln Center with our bags of garbage and dumped them in the courtyard fountain, scattering in every direction when the cops chased us. The media got hold of it, turning the event into the potent image we had intended. "Oh, those hippies—they went up and threw garbage at Lincoln Center." That's enough, that was the message. The press didn't yet realize that these images were disruptive to society and they were quickly caught up in the excitement and fashion. Later, editors became more sophisticated.

Once you get the right image the details aren't that important. Over-analyzing reduced the myth. A big insight we learned during this period was that you didn't have to explain why. That's what advertising was all about. "Why" was for the critics.

Radical theater burst onto the streets with a passion. Our guerrilla band attacked Con Edison, New York's utility company. On cue, soot bombs exploded in offices, smudge pots billowed thick smoke into lobbies, black crepe paper encircled the building, and a huge banner hung across the front door: BREATHING IS BAD FOR YOUR HEALTH. Cops and firemen appeared on the scene. We ran in all directions, losing ourselves in the crowds. The six o'clock news opened with clouds of smoke, a pan shot of the banner, and strange-looking guttersnipes running amok. An official from the power company wearing a suit and tie explained Con Ed's position. As he spoke he nervously touched his face. Self-inflicted black spot marks appeared on his cheeks: the vaudeville show was completed by unwitting self-ridicule. The fatter they are, the harder they fall.

The Army recruiting center in Times Square was plastered with stickers: SEE CANADA NOW. Stop signs on street corners now read STOP WAR. Witches in black robes, bearing roses, exorcised the FBI building of its evil spirits. Hundreds crowded the lobby of the *Daily News* smoking grass and passing out leaflets to employees that began, "Dear Fellow Members of the Communist Conspiracy." A tree was planted in the center of St. Marx Place (we took the liberty of changing the spelling) while 5,000 celebrators danced to rock music. Midnight artists snuck into subway stations and painted huge murals on the walls. Naked people ran through churches. Panhandlers worked the streets for hours, took the change they collected to the nearest bank and scattered it on the floor. A giant Yellow Submarine mysteriously kept appearing in tow-away zones. Tourist buses, now detouring to watch the hippies cavort, were greeted by freaks holding up huge mirrors, screaming, "Dig thyself!" All this and more Anita and I got high doing.

Some events grew out of unexpected donations. A person called up, "I've got 10,000 flowers you can have." I had an idea: wouldn't it be great to have these flowers come showering down over the be-in in Central Park? We had to get hold of a head who knew how to fly a plane and was ready to risk arrest. I found one in New Jersey and told him to act fast. He raced to the airport on his motorcycle, smashed-up, left his bike on the street, called a cab and arrived just in time. All the connections were made perfectly except the last one—he dropped all 10,000 flowers blocks away on an empty side street.

If street theater is to avoid growing tedious, it benefits from an edge of menace—a touch of potential violence. When Secretary of State Dean Rusk came to town to speak to some war hawk assemblage at the Waldorf-Astoria, we rallied at 57th Street and Seventh Avenue, ready to "bring the war home." Plastic bags filled with cow's blood flew through the night air. Tape recordings of battle sounds screamed above the crowds. Urban monkeys (not yet guerrillas) with painted faces and water pistols attacked tuxedoed enemy collaborators. Fire alarms were pulled and swarms of angry demonstrators shouting, "Hey, hey, LBJ, how many kids did you kill today?" surged through midtown.

A couple observing the melee said, "What's going on?" "There's a war on, can't you see?" I answered as the police on horseback began to attack. We scattered the sidewalk with marbles and the horses slipped and stumbled. Innocent bystanders (no bystander is innocent) were caught between the clashing armies. The cops waded right into the crowds of people, clubbing away. Crunch! I got carted off to jail.

The head of a pig was delivered to Hubert Humphrey on a silver platter before a shocked throng of liberals. Shelley Winters, that pompous phony, denounced us. Mice were released at a Dow Chemical stockholders' meeting. Cardinal (Pass-the-Lord-and-Praise-the-Ammunition) Spellman, who went to Vietnam and posed behind a machine gun, was confronted by angry Catholics during a church service.

When all else failed, we simply declared the war over. Five thousand of us romped through the streets, hugging people in stores and buses. "The war is over! Hip-hip-hurray!! It's over!!" Balloons, confetti, singing, dancing. If you don't like the news, we reasoned, make up your own.

America Has More Television Sets Than Toilets

Valentine's Day had special significance. For its celebration I concocted a gift of love, compliments of the counterculture. Three thousand persons selected at random from the phone book were sent a well-rolled marijuana cigarette with a card saying: "'Happy Valentine's Day. This cigarette contains no harmful cancer-causing ingredients. It is made from 100 percent pure marijuana." Directions followed on how to smoke it, so the recipients could cut through all the baloney and make up their own minds. A postscript warned: "Oh, by the way, possession of the item you now hold in your hand can bring up to five years in prison. It matters not how or from whom you got it."

The press reacted as if a plague of killer-weeds had descended on the defenseless Big Apple. Special squads of narcotics agents, they reported, had been dispatched from Washington to ferret out the perpetrators. Newscaster Bill Jorgensen, then of Channel Five, played the perfect straight guy. Midshot: "Good evening, this is Bill Jorgensen with the evening news. This (*dramatic pause*) is a reefer. It is made from an illegal substance, marijuana. Thousands of unsuspecting citizens of New York received them today with the following Valentine message," he said, straight-faced. "The police has set up a special number to process complaints" (the number flashed across the screen). "We are now going to call that number." News and commercials filled the next twenty minutes while much of New York waited with bated breath. Near the end of the show, the announcer invited two trench-coated men, playing "Dragnet" clones, to come onto the set:

ANNOUNCER: You're the police?
POLICE: That's right.
ANNOUNCER: I received this in the mail.
POLICE: Approximately what time of day was that?

ANNOUNCER: It came in the morning mail.
POLICE: What's your name and address?
ANNOUNCER: Bill Jorgensen.
POLICE: Do you have any identification?
ANNOUNCER: (*puzzled*) Why, I'm Bill Jorgensen. See the sign? This is the Bill Jorgensen news show.
POLICE: We'll still have to see some I.D.
ANNOUNCER: What about what it says here (*pointing*) about me—holding this reefer could earn me a prison sentence? Is that true?
POLICE: That's not our department. You'll have to ask the D.A.'s office.
ANNOUNCER (*even more puzzled, faces the camera*): Well, that's all we have time for on the news tonight.

All this actually took place on New York television. A New Jersey radio station went so far as to report Bill Jorgensen had been arrested for possession of marijuana while delivering the evening news. Of course no one, including sourpuss Bill, took a fall on the prank, but for days the most amazing stories circulated. Trying to separate news from gossip has been a lifetime endeavor and I'm unconvinced there's any difference. All is subjective, all is information molded by distortion, selection, exaggeration, emphasis, omission, and every other variable of communication. Walter Cronkite just leans over the country's back fence and tells his stories. There's a lot of bias.

Broadcasters report "news," the enemy engages in "propaganda." Our "soldiers" and allies must kill to defend freedom, their "terrorists" kill for criminal reasons. (Remember, no terrorist bombs from a jet plane, therefore only enemies of imperialism can earn that label.) Unions are to blame for strikes, never management. Murders are newsworthy, corporate price-fixing too "abstract." Even the newscaster I most respect, Cronkite, is prone to using cold-war imagery. In covering the Vietnam War, for years he described it as "our American way of life" or "the Free World battling Communism." Home-grown culture versus foreign ideology. No U.S. broadcaster or reporter can ever speak of "capitalism" or "imperialism" being "our way of life," with "cooperation" being the social dynamic of communist countries. It's our "leaders" against their "rulers." Our "free press" compared with their "party-line." Our government, their regime.

On domestic news, I heard of many cases where an editor would tell a reporter, "Ten thousand at that rally? That's too many. Make it 3,000." The reporter would say, "Sure," then go out and get drunk. When you turn on the telly or pick up a newspaper you are tuning in on the boss's gossip and propaganda. If you believe America has a free press it just means you haven't thought about it enough. Everyone who makes and reports the news knows what I'm talking about.

(In case you're curious, Jimi Hendrix financed the entire marijuana mailing.)

Theater of protest expanded from the streets to the television studio and into the home. Keep in mind, there was a television rule that they only invited a person with any kind of radical ideas on a show for ridicule. Knowing that, I approached talk shows as you would enter a war zone. I brought every conceivable kind of verbal ammunition, prepared for any situation, and before every appearance I spent hours studying the show's format.

It was very tricky business. What I lost by going on these shows was a reinforcement of the idea that America is a free and open society. One of the first questions I'd be asked would be, "If you're so censored how come you're sitting here with me on nation-wide TV?" I was also allowing myself to be edited, to fulfill a personality role in a play designed by the producers of American society. "He's just another pretty face." Keeping all these pitfalls in mind, television was nevertheless an enormously successful vehicle for making statements to a mass audience, and I used it as a form of theatrical warfare. Readers should understand television interviews are edited to make the interviewer, not the interviewee, look good. They are "based" on reality, just as all other fiction in the media.

Invited on the David Susskind Show, we were ready for America's star performing intellectual's attempt to neutralize us by forcing explanations. "How do you eat?" queried the Skeptic, and we passed out sandwiches to the audience. "But what *is* a hippie?" pressed the emissary of New York's literati. A box opened as if by magic. "Why don't you ask him, David, he's a hippie?" I

said and a duck flew out of the box. Around its neck was a sign
saying I AM A HIPPIE. Susskind exploded, "Catch that damn duck!"
The duck, scared out of its wits, kept flying into the klieg lights.
Chaos, the intellectual's nightmare, broke loose. Staff hands tried
to grab the elusive duck. Each time the duck took off he crapped in
midflight. Hippie-duck shit-bombs fell on the audience.

"That duck goes," screamed Susskind. "Hold the cameras!"

"David, you're television's worst C-E-N-S-O-R" (a particularly low blow). "No duck, no hippies," we shot back. Negotiations. The duck will stay, the duck shit goes. Later, when the show
was aired, Susskind reneged and cut the entire scene. For a week
he got late night calls: "Quack, quack, quack!"

The goal of this nameless art form—part vaudeville, part insurrection, part communal recreation—was to shatter the pretense of
objectivity. The calm, patriarchal voice of reason, embodied in an
Eric Sevareid or a David Susskind, could be a greater danger than
shrill Red-baiting. We learned to sneak onto the airwaves with
Conceptual Art pieces that roused viewers from their video stupor.

To do that, we had to study the medium of television. At first we
aimed at the human-interest slot near the end of each news program
called the "Happy Talk" segment, offering some freaky tableau to
contrast with the nightly news blur. We infiltrated news by entering through the back door and slowly worked our way up to the
lead items. To find us in *Time* and *Newsweek* you had to turn to the
back pages. Of course, any clever student of mass communication
knew most people read those two magazines backwards anyway.
Everyone paid attention to Happy Talk because in being personal it
deviated from the prepared script.

The things about television you weren't supposed to take seriously I took very seriously, and vice versa. Everybody knows that
studio audiences are primed to laugh, applaud like crazy, and look
generally ecstatic, but it's easy to forget how contrived and manipulated the situation is. I used this distortion of reality to my own
advantage on the David Frost Show, pumping reverse responses
out of the studio audience.

During the commercial break I got out of my seat, already
creating a little chaos because guests aren't supposed to get out of
their seats on talk shows unless the host tells them to get up ("How

'bout a song?'' "Yes, sir"). I walked right up to the audience and started conducting them:

"Come on, you're not angry enough! I'm a gook. I'm a nigger, I'm a kike—come on, get it off your chest!" They started yelling and getting up out of their seats, enraged and shaking their fists at me. It was a symphony of hate. By the time the commercial break was over I was back in my seat, smiling like an innocent lamb, while Frost worked me over and the audience roared and snarled. Then I jumped up and played hate conductor again. It came off very effectively.

On the same Frost Show I waited until the camera was on me while I was talking, and near the end of my rap I mouthed some words soundlessly, putting in the word "fuck" for those who were up to a little lip reading. People watching said, "Oh my God. They've censored him. They blipped him right there! I saw it!"

To practice this reverse manipulation you had to be very much in control. People weren't supposed to do these things in the television studio. The point was to give the home audience a different message, one closer to reality. I mean, who really gives a fuck about how hard it is for actors to get up at 5 A.M. to powder their noses?

Radio needed another frame of mind. I studied how it was different, always preferred it to TV, and felt I was better on the radio because the listener couldn't see what was going on and respond to certain visual images I had to create. One night I was being interviewed by a hostile host live on New York radio station WNEW. I picked up my host's pack of cancerettes and said, "Can I have a cigarette?"

"Sure, help yourself," he said, and I took one and dragged on it slurpily. "Hey, this is really good stuff here, man," I said, imitating the stereotyped stoned musician. The host got all flustered and announced, "Ladies and gentlemen, he's just smoking a plain Marlboro cigarette." "Tell them that—tell them it's just a cigarette, man," I agreed, then apologized profusely. "Oh my God, ah shoudna done it. . . . I'm sorry, I don't wanna blow your gig. So cool, though, man, disguisin it as a cigarette." There was no way the host could get out of the little trap with just words. He completely lost his composure, but he had me back.

On another talk show, I got a call-in death threat. I said over the air that I'd be leaving the studio at 5 o'clock and went on to describe myself, only using the appearance of the host. "I got horn-rimmed glasses and a brown and white-checkered sports jacket." Most of the time I'd talk about the war or other social issues, using humor as a hook. I would use the opportunities to advertise upcoming demonstrations. It was free space and effective. Before Disco, people actually talked on radio. Now it seems like everyone, disc jockeys, broadcasters, newsmen, are all hopping to the same monotonous beat. One-two-three. One-two-three.

I practiced talk shows and press conferences just as singers and comedians practice their routines. You train to improvise. Most TV dialogue is canned, but I never read prepared lines. Talk show questions are sometimes given, often requested, from guests. Press conferences by politicians are carefully orchestrated. What viewers are led to believe is that all is "totally unrehearsed." Yet most, if not "rehearsed," is certainly "arranged." For example, take a presidential press conference. Only mainstream (controllable) reporters are allowed in the White House press corps. The safest, most controllable (TV commentators) are recognized for the first questions. Jumping from reporter to reporter, from question to question, lends the appearance that a free and open exchange is taking place. As one who has played both sides of the Q and A, I know that no format lends itself more to burying the truth beneath public relations gloss. Everyone on TV works on a media "presence." From the White House briefings to The Gong Show, entertainment rules the tube. The similarities between Rona Barrett and Walter Cronkite are far more interesting than the differences. And, if we are talking of accuracy, Ms. Rona is far ahead of most so-called news reporters. Obviously there is *some* freedom in the U.S. media, but rather than pay it unbending homage is it not better to educate the public in the ways it is *not* free? Like not being free to suggest an alternative to our economic system.

My television act was close to my everyday life. Close, in fact, to my unconscious world. I personalized the audience. I think aloud. Recognizing the limited time span of someone staring at a lighted square in their living room, I trained for the one-liner, the retort jab, or sudden knock-out put-ons. I practiced with friends, waiters, people on the street, cab drivers, mayors, movie stars, cops, reporters, and relatives. When no one was around to practice with, I turned on the TV set and played each character, internalizing their questions and answers. What I'm trying to say was I didn't practice at *all*, that all communication is the same—face-to-face or face-to-camera.

I read *Variety, Show Business, Billboard*, and other trade papers far more probably than any radical organizer in history. It would be little problem for me to recite the ten top-rated TV shows or movies of the week. I tried to study things such as the effect of looking at the camera as opposed to the host (it depends) or whether or not to wear makeup. No makeup, although visually handicapping, gave me a bottom-line edge; if I was accused of being a phony I could respond: "It's funny, Dick, people who say that to me are always wearing makeup." Immediately the audience at home could "see" the difference between us and have their consciousness raised about television information. There is nothing more radical you can talk about on TV than TV itself.

In analyzing word communication, I've arranged a list of the ten most acceptable words. The most popular word in the American language is "free," "new" is second. The word "less" is more acceptable than "more." The potential customer is suspicious of "more"; he knows the maxim—you pay more, get less. Television advertising is the height of fantasy manipulation. I tried writing commercials for revolution to learn the rhythm of the medium.

My work in TV was a long way from accepting its format. I entered the world of television to expose its wasteland. The top one hundred corporations control eighty percent of all network air time. Robert Hutchins once said: "We can put television in its proper light by supposing that Gutenberg's great invention had been directed at printing only comic books."

Later a group of us performed a guerrilla theater piece which adequately summed up our attitude toward television. While Nixon addressed the nation on the need for invading Cambodia, we set a twenty-four-inch receiver on a pedestal and before twenty thousand angry protesters pick-axed the flickering image. Electronic voodoo. Sometimes the proper intellectual argument is "FUCK YOU!"

Cast of Characters

Ideas are free. There is a big difference between having an idea and
making it happen. Being an activist is not a designated job in our
society. An intellectual/artist working to change the power structure has no legitimate occupation. "What's with all the fancy
language?" my father would have said. "What you're describing
is a bum." Some of the other "bums" who worked the streets
deserve mention because they were the conspirators who brought it
all together.

The first time I met Phil Ochs, in 1962, he was touring the
country for SDS, trying to build a socialist movement through
protest songs. If he had cut himself off from the movement to
concentrate on his singing career, he would have become a star and
pulled in millions. He chose, instead, to shuttle back and forth
between the streets and the recording studio. A tough gig. He sang
satirically of "liberals" when he, like us all, had some liberal
blood in his veins. He loved Ho Chi Minh and the Kennedys.
Socialized medicine and TV game shows. Eventually Brother Phil
could no longer keep it all together. He ended his life, hanging by a
rope in his sister's bathtub. Poor Phil's now dead and gone, left us
here to sing his song.

Ed Sanders inspired a good chunk of the Lower East Side street
theater. A great original, Ed never entertained a thought not
uniquely his own. I first tuned in to him circa '65, when he and
fellow peace creeps swam aboard a nuclear submarine off the coast
of Connecticut. Student of Egyptian hieroglyphics, detective,
storekeeper, rock singer, and preacher man, he fashioned a poetry
that raced through the streets stopping only to worship at the feet of
a mythical slum goddess. His raunchy rock-group creation, The
Fugs (book censors had for years forced writers to use *fug* for
fuck), were steady repeaters at rallies and benefits. Ed was the
Yippies' Homer, his "Shads of God" our Iliad. Tuli Kupferberg,

another Fug, spewed forth the uninhibited semen thinking of a sexual anarchist. Years before, Tuli had jumped off the Manhattan Bridge, somehow managing to survive the fall. He went on to invent 1,001 new ways of making love. Late at night you could see him scrawling his poems on the walls of angry tenement houses. Tuli was the madman possessed by compassion.

Jim Fouratt, gay blond-on-blond cherub, off-Broadway actor, put every muscle into trying to make the street sing. The original flower child, Jim played the perfect innocent, constantly popping up in the middle of violent chaos with a surprised "what me?" look on his face. When we caused problems for the Newark police by smuggling truckloads of food and equipment into the black ghetto riots, Jim managed to upset the cops so much they pistol-whipped him and locked him in the can. Once late for a meeting, Jim ran through the streets, bumped into a policeman hard enough so the ice cream in his cone swan dived onto the cop's jacket. He got busted for assaulting an officer with an ice cream cone. Pure Fouratt. I had many a vision of Jim's alabaster body, topped by Peter Frampton–like ringlets, hanging blood-spattered from a corner streetlight. Indeed, I had come to think of a "Fouratt" as a special act of courage. Last I saw Jim was '71-ish at some close-out antiwar rally. He was giving a speech dressed as a woman. "You don't know freedom," he proclaimed to the crowd, "unless you've put on the dress."

Paul Krassner was the legitimate father of the underground press. His *Realist* magazine best combined the politics and humor that led to the thousands of offset street papers that appeared during the period. Satirist extraordinaire, the Krass had zeroed in on governments for years. "Grab their balls and their hearts and minds will follow," was original Krassner. LBJ ripped off the phrase, failing to give due credit. Krassner was a lonely person who always insisted everything be reduced to the absurd. A funny guy, Paul was a comedian who drifted into the counterculture. We may have looked the same, but there was always some friction between us. Called as a witness during our Chicago trial, he dropped acid the morning he was to testify and broke down on the witness stand. None of us knew what was going on at the time. Kunstler had to get rid of him prematurely. He was our worst witness, and the only one more concerned with making his own hit than helping us beat the charges. That was Paul's kind of anarchy. Together we could have planned the LSD venture and expanded it into a nice trial vignette. If he told us we could have had Kunstler ask him the question, "Are you now on LSD?" That would have stunned the midwest jurors—actually seeing a person in the flesh taking a trip. There were scores of incidents like this constantly getting in the way of our friendship. Paul just regards everything that passes through his life for the public record, and maintaining deep friendships with people who do that is near-impossible. It's best to aim for a formal friendship.

Bob Fass, communication pioneer, invented the free-form radio style which became the verbal trenches from which we made war on plastic culture. New York City is media central. The place you plug it all in. Bob Fass was the secret weapon. Today FM equals AM equals canned, pressure-treated nonart for money. Big Bob favored principles over fashion. Now he's out of work.

In Europe there were several anarcho groups working on similar tracks. From Berlin came word of Fritz Teufel, Karl Pawla, and Kommune #1. The story that crossed the Atlantic was that Pawla had, during one of his many trials, pulled down his pants and defecated on the courtroom floor, wiping his ass with the subpoena. In Paris, Jean-Jacques Lebel, a disciple of Artaud, had been strangling chickens and smearing the blood on U.S. embassies. When Lebel made it over to the States, we met our European connection. He had the ability to space-travel instantaneously from one culture to the other. Like Alec Guinness in *The Captain's Paradise*, Lebel pressed a button and could be at home on both shores. Lebel linked the anarchism of the Left Bank to the street culture of Haight-Ashbury and the Lower East Side.

Emissaries from Rome, Tokyo, Mexico City, began plugging into what we were doing. Ideas. Energy. Commitment. Trust. Unsigned treaties of global consciousness happened with a speed befitting the electronic age. In Amsterdam, a particularly advanced corner of the planet, street players dubbed themselves the "Provos" (short for provocateurs). Practicing the politics of "free," they opened the parks to free concerts, established crash pads, and ladled out soup to moneyless hungry customers. Their symbol became the white bicycle. Second-hand wheelies were painted white and left around the city. Whoever needed one could take one, pedal away, and leave it at another location for the next. The Provos became so large they even managed to get several members on the city council. Eventually factional neurosis destroyed the Provos. Not, however, before they had established a community ambience that would be held up as a model by all of us.

Dana Beal picked up on the Provos and founded a chapter on the Lower East Side. Dana was a strange duck. A short, extra-longhaired WASP who works twenty-five hours a day trying to structure anarchist revolt on turf heavily populated with kikes. In a burst of ecumenical genius, Dana once showed up at a tribal council meeting with a bag full of free corned-beef sandwiches. Slight snafu, they were all on Wonder Bread. How was he to know Jews think white bread causes brain damage? Thirteen years later Dana is still down on the Lower East Side trying to hold his act together, still getting busted, the perennial Peter Pan. But a fanatic attracted by the ritual of Yippie rather than the game.

Aside from the Provos, one other model was naturally California's Haight-Ashbury community (see *Slouching Towards Bethlehem:* Joan Didion). Berkeley gave birth to protest politics, and by '67, the people, through a massive street march on the Oakland Induction Center and a huge rally at Kezar Stadium, had mobilized thousands of antiwar demonstrators. Cultural-political friction was symbolized dramatically when a Trotskyite mini-faction pulled the plug while rock singers Country Joe and the Fish were performing at Kezar.

Culture freaks headed across the bay and set up camp along the Haight. There was strength in numbers, and quickly the beads and feathers appeared. Free clinics, head shops, and communes multiplied. The world's first be-in took place in Golden Gate Park. Berkeley and Haight forgot their differences and on one glorious day brought it all home. Thirty thousand people blissed out. The hope. The creative. The good. The potential. All erupted in magnificent splendor.

Two creative forces worked the Haight. The *San Francisco Oracle,* a psychedelic, multicolored tabloid, was the most beautiful newspaper ever seen on the streets of the planet. Our version of the illuminated manuscripts of the Middle Ages, it was, to use an expression of the times, a "mind-blower." The *Oracle,* though the least political of all the underground papers, embodied the

passion for beauty in a new and exciting way little understood by
political people. Old copies of the *Oracle* should be dug up and
studied. They were the Real McCoy.

The other force guiding the swarming mass of Haight culture
was the Diggers. Outgrowths (some say outcasts) of the San
Francisco Mime Troupe. Arthur and Paula Lish, Peter Berg, Peter
Coyote, Batman, Motorcycle Ritchie (rest his soul), the Buffalo
Man, Nicki Wells, and the others I've been careless to forget
combined Dada street theater with the revolutionary politics of
free. Slum-alley saints, they lit up the period by spreading the
poetry of love and anarchy with broad strokes of artistic genius.
Their free store, communications network of instant offset survival poetry, along with an Indian-inspired consciousness, was the
original white light of the era. It lit up many an East Coast mind.

And then there was Emmett. Emmett Grogan was the hippie
warrior par excellence. He was also a junkie, a maniac, a gifted
actor, a rebel hero, a rock singer groupie, and above all a pain in
the ass to all his friends. Emmett hurt me. Not in the way he or
others thought, of course. A stab in the back by someone you
respect is not easy to absorb. *Ringelevio,* his half-brilliant book on
this era, is marred by Emmett's paranoia and immaturity. Forever
the punk kid, Emmett strove to be the darling of the rock promoters, and the street-chic rebel of New York liberals. Anyone who
loved the guy knew he lied like crazy—not fibbed but lied. Nothing he said should ever be considered history. *Ringolevio* was
penned as an act of revenge, not love. It was Emmett's Altamont
(an event he was partly responsible for) set to words. A sad book
reflecting a sad clown not unlike Emmett Kelly at the center of it
all. Bad blood existed between us. On my last night in the Chelsea
Hotel, two weeks before going underground, I saw him pass,
locked in his lonely shiver. Gregory Corso delivered my message.
I wanted to fight him that night down in the lobby. It would have
been an interesting match-up of macho miscues, but fortunately or
unfortunately, depending on which type of theater you relate to,
Emmett didn't show. For the following year I felt he chickened
out. The next year I grew less bitter and figured he or Corso
dropped the message in the snow and nodded out to sleep instead.
Then, by chance, he and I talked on the phone. He was at the office
of *Oui* magazine, I at a roadside telephone outside of Santa Fe. We

made our peace. It was the last time we would ever speak. Next came word that Emmett's body had been found riding the midnight subway to Coney Island. He lived and died a legend, fulfilling Thomas Wolfe's dictum about only the dead knowing Brooklyn.

In the early sixties I gained inspiration from two red see-through discs pressed by Fantasy Records. The first, Lenny Bruce's "Picnic in a Graveyard," will make me laugh for a hundred more years. For a long time I found myself imitating his nasal whine and sharp barbs. There's not enough space here to talk about Lenny Bruce. In '61 I hitched to New York to see him at the Village Vanguard. Chuck Isreals, a Brandeis classmate and bass player sharing the program with Lenny, introduced us. Even knowing Bruce's routines by heart, his spontaneity amazed me. Once, during one of his monologues, there was a loud thud on the floor above; he jumped on a chair, pounded on the ceiling, and screamed out, "Hey, Frankenstein, quit jerkin' off!" He completely cracked me up. Of all today's comedians, only Richard Pryor can top the Bruce on quick-draw humor. 'Tis a pity Lenny's gone. I dedicated *Woodstock Nation* to him. We all know Lenny's story. Mother fuckin'. Shit. Piss. An Anglo-Saxon hero.

The creator of the other red Fantasy disc, Allen Ginsberg, still grows on the planet. Excluding some of T. S. Eliot, "Howl" is the greatest twentieth-century poem in the English language, bar none. Ginsberg wrote the whole thing in about an hour and a half, sitting on a hill overlooking North Beach, San Francisco. It was inspired by the gods. Just as they had spoken to Isaiah and Jeremiah, they talked to Ginsberg and Ginsberg took his poetry into the streets. Jews don't have saints, they just have Ginsbergs every once in a while.

Ben Morea's Up-Against-The-Wall-Motherfuckers gang was probably the most anarchistic local group of all. The Motherfuckers lived like gutter rats and supported themselves any way they could. They dressed in black and brown and snarled a lot. They presented themselves as the middle-class nightmare. An antimedia media phenomenon simply because their name couldn't be printed. When they were mentioned in the press as "a group with a certain unprintable name," every reader was immediately interested.

There were many others. Anne Waldman, fast-talking founder

of the St. Mark's Poetry Workshop. Marty Carey, my high-school friend from Worcester, plastered his utopian reveries onto free posters and leaflets circulated on the streets. Trina Robbins developed into our best cartoonist-pamphleteer. Alan Katzman and Walter Bowart managed to get out the weekly editions of the *East Village Other* (*EVO*), our counterpart to the ritzier, more liberal *Village Voice*. Keith Lampe, a zany peace creep who liked dressing up as a Keystone Kop, shuttled between the organized antiwar groups and the street people. Judy Lampe, meanwhile, designed most of our agit props, including all our protest buttons. Anita also wrote for *EVO*, and her later novel, *Trashing*, although overglorifying the times, still had the flavor that can only come from someone who was there when the fire was hot. Robin Morgan was another activist poet who would later go on to play a leading role in the women's movement. Her chop jobs on all her former friends were legendary. Her accusation, which was printed in *Sisterhood Is Powerful*, of a famous sexist quote I made was pure fabrication. I challenge her to document the quote or be accused of being a liar.

The ease with which the larger society absorbed and diluted hippie culture I still regard as a defeat. Long hair, dope smoking, and freaky clothes have long since lost their social bite. The spontaneity of the counterculture press was absorbed by *Rolling Stone* and hip capitalism became the sponge used to mop up hippie originality. Jann Wenner sold the record companies on the idea of a national "underground" newspaper which would play it cozy with the industry in exchange for their centralizing their advertising under the *Rolling Stone* banner. It was not long before the counterculture fashion and fad were to be manipulated by the Kinney Parking Lot System. In all the analyses of why hippie culture seemed to wilt on the vine, I've yet to see much mention of the crucial factor of *Rolling Stone*'s cooptation of the underground press. Without record company advertising, the papers lost their financial underpinnings, and with a slick journal clinging closely to mainstream mores, the dominant culture could more easily direct the course of events. Jann Wenner was the Benedict Arnold of the sixties.

In October of '67, the Haight community, sensing that *Rolling Stone*, the musical *Hair*, and other watered-down versions of counterculture media were about to do a Dracula, chose instead to bury their own culture first. In a somber, shrouded wake, a coffin marked DEATH OF HIPPIE was paraded through the streets of San Francisco. The bells of closing rang across the land. Within a few years Altamont and Charlie Manson banged the final nails in the coffin.

Even guerrilla theater grew tedious by repetition. I remember getting arrested in Chicago for scrawling a four-letter word across my forehead; a year later, flying to Seattle, I was greeted at the airport by thirty kids with FUCK painted on their faces. Indeed, as Marcuse pointed out correctly, by 1971 swearing itself had lost its shock value and was no longer a necessary form of communication.

(Most people thought the "*fuck*-on-my-forehead" was inspired by Lenny Bruce, but I had another incident in mind. Jack Kerouac, after once meditating on a mountaintop, descended to the press with a cross around his neck. The press took photos, but the cross got airbrushed in all the morning editions. I wanted to see if they'd airbrush my face.)

By going underground—forced to become a new person—I probably overcame much of the tendency to look back at those years with teary fondness, like an American Legionnaire getting drunk and blabbering, "Wanna know what it was like in Guam?" I don't just define myself as an antiwar veteran. Nostalgia is a mild form of depression. Unhappy with the present, fearful of the future, we cling to the past. There were the Beatles, and there is *Beatlemania*.

The sixties were so earth-shaking that the seventies can only be defined in contrast. The seventies were *not* the sixties—that's how they'll lead off the "CBS Decade Round-Up." Then we can turn the corner, leave nostalgia behind, and begin studying the period with the necessary historical overview. There are signs. . . . One time recently I was in New York and I saw actual, authentic-looking flower children. "Where are you from?" I asked. "Oh, we're not hippies, we're extras from *Hair*. We're shooting a be-in in Central Park." Fancy that, I thought: period dress in less than a decade.

Rubin and the Rising
of the Pentagon

Never for a moment did I believe guerrilla theater or "monkey warfare," as I had come to call it, could alone stop the war in Vietnam. But it did extend the possibilities of involving the senses and penetrating the symbolic world of fantasy (television's primary aim). Had there not been another equally strong appeal to reason—a more conventional mode of communication—our efforts would have been in vain. That responsibility rested with a group called the National Mobilization to End the War in Vietnam. Not exactly the easiest thing to stamp on a button, but a relatively well-organized method for mobilizing pacifist resistance. Not needing *or* desiring to split U.S. culture into two distinct camps, the Mobe could reach into age, class, educational, and union groups which might have been turned off to our particular style. Never the hippie nationalist, I had always considered myself a secret member of the Mobe steering committee. For good organizers such as Cora Weiss, Sidney Lens, Sid Peck, Norma Becker, and Dave Dellinger to have dropped acid, donned hippie garb, and run through the streets with spray cans would have been absurd. When the movement began to grow beyond anything we had come to know as "our limits," when we went truly "national," most of the major demonstrations were carefully coordinated to allow space for the two styles.

In the spring of '67, just before the great summer of love, the Mobe successfully put together the largest single street demonstration in the history of the United States. A march on the United Nations drew something like seven hundred thousand people. Three times as many as had gone to Washington in '63 to boost the civil-rights movement. With the legacy of repression and intimidation of the fifties far behind us, knowing our movement was reaching deep into the heartland of America, and seeing the swarms of countercultural communities forming, we expected a large crowd—but this outpouring exceeded all expectations. For every person honest and daring enough to venture off the curb-stone, leave his or her living room, and join in a protest march, there are perhaps a hundred people similarly inclined who stay away. To be there was to know we could force the U.S. out of Vietnam. Mark you, this was no easy task. Never had a people risen up and defeated its own government's imperialist war. André Glucksmann, France's best "new philosopher," told me that the antiwar movement in the U.S. will be a symbol of freedom for a hundred years to come. "It showed," he said, "the strength of people even when confronted by highly sophisticated repression." In the spring of '67, we realized our determination to make our stand against the war. What the march on the U.N. showed us was that we had the numbers to win. National demonstrations were the top of the iceberg. Our way of polling the population. They were what held local grass-roots organizations together, making iso-lated groups and individuals feel part of something bigger. No wonder that, within a year, Congress signed into law the Interstate Riot Act. (Still in force, and as yet untested in the courts, it just about made *all* national demonstrations illegal, if the government chose to prosecute.)

It was just along here that I met Jerry Rubin face-to-face. For just as Che needed Fidel and Costello needed Abbott, Jerry Rubin and I were destined to join forces. Conceived not in heaven but in the streets, in war not peace, it was nonetheless a partnership of surprising endurance. In a community of individual egos, we at least managed to expand to an ego of two. (We are, by the way, still close friends.)

Jerry was from Cincinnati, Ohio, a middle-sized, anti-union town very similar to Worcester. He was an action freak and an anti-intellectual like myself. It was to be the similarities, not the differences, in our personalities that would make the combination work. We both had a willingness to go beyond reason. Like me, Jerry was a populist who watched TV, went to mass movies, and understood how to turn ideas into action.

We became friends. I told him I would support what he was doing in the national antiwar movement and give him access to the counterculture. I took him up to WBAI and interviewed him on

Bob Fass's show—translating what he was saying for the hip audience, as he was still unfamiliar with making language and imagery fit the style of the times.

Although Jerry was familiar with the be-in style, having been a participant of the first one in San Francisco, his presentation was still too forceful and rhetorical. It didn't have a silly element and the appeal to the spirit. This was how I complemented Jerry. In turn, he was more versed than I in getting the cultural revolution incorporated into a broader structure. We were two people who sensed the opportunity of blending the political and the cultural revolutions. Jerry's forte was the political timing, mine dramatic. I trusted his political judgment more than anyone's in the country. We were anarchists, but even among anarchists there are not that many who can map out a strategy and lead. Some anarchists are just more equal than others in that ability. Stubborn, attentive to the ways of power and the universe, Jerry had the drive and the political instincts to ride the movement waves.

I knew Rubin before he knew me. A few years earlier, aided by the movement's best legal strategist, Arthur Kinoy, he had defied the archvillain HUAC in a unique way. Dressed up as an American revolutionary (from the first revolution) Jerry successfully engaged the enemy in symbolic warfare. A delicate form of protest art, symbolic warfare insists one must love one's country in order to overthrow its government. The way in which a revolutionary uses past national heroes, myths, the flag, popular legends, and the like has to be exceptionally cunning. Jerry was a lovable, cunning bastard all right. I had begun to track his efforts when he returned to Berkeley. When he organized political rallies emphasizing the cultural ingredient. When he led attempts to stop troop trains headed for ports with Vietnam beyond. And when he ran as a candidate for mayor. I knew it was as if I had never left Berkeley. Dave Dellinger also had eyes on the energy ball called Rubin and after the U.N. march invited him to come East as a project director of Mobe. The East was the center of power. Rubin made the correct tactical move and I could not have asked for a better comrade in arms.

My take on first meeting Jerry was not without criticism. In spite of all his revolutionary highjinks, he played it deadpan and took himself as seriously as any other left-wing preacher. As soon as he and his friends hit shore, I took them down to Wall Street to burn up some money—the best teacher is the best student. Rubin got the message as quickly as I had internalized his HUAC costume show. I lured him to the Lower East Side. He lured me to the Mobe headquarters and into the conspiracy to attack Washington that fall. "Abbie, why don't you get all those freaks off their asses and join us in Washington," he suggested. "Don't worry, I'll cover all the flack from the straights," he promised. Noticing his hair was growing faster than marijuana under a Gro-lite, I began to respect his judgment.

In one glorious night of religious group-grog rivaling any Druid ritual, Ed Sanders, his eyes redder than a baboon's ass from smoking pipefuls of weed, implored the gods to guide our decision. "A pentagon is a five-sided symbol of evil," he assured us. "Lordy, Lord," he yodeled, "suck my pork-pine of inspiration." The heavens parted. The gods spoke: "Make it rise, you motherfuckers. If you're so goddam good, make it rise in the air."

Magic Foils the War Machine

All Indians, even the electronic variety, must employ a certain element of magic if their battles are to be successful. Spiritual purification is sought as an antidote to the demons present in all imperialist war machines. On October 21, in the year 19 and 67, we would launch our holy crusade to cast forth the evil spirits dwelling in the Pentagon. It was written in the books of several religions that five-sided figures were devil-created. No one who read the fine print of *The New York Times* doubted that Vietnam War policy was the creation of Lucifer. What should one make of cluster bombs—that open a hundred meters above the ground, releasing bomblets which in turn release a spray of deadly needles killing all that is human in their wake? Silent penetration of body flesh. Can one talk in civil terms about saturation bombings, strategic hamlets, and free-fire zones? Could you describe napalm

to a ten-year-old? Dropped in large barrels, a jelly-gas that spread
rapidly through villages and stuck to the skin with a fiery grip. Or
herbicidal defoliants designed to poison miles upon miles of plants
and trees. Not since the Romans, in revenge, salted the earth of
Carthage, has the world seen such a calculated wasteland. And the
enemy? The "gooks" our young boys were commanded to kill in
order to preserve the American Way of Life? Is there anyone now
who believes God and napalm could ever end up on the same side?
I knew the U.S. was not to triumph in the war on the day a wise
Vietnamese colonel named Xuan Oanh (pronounced "wine-
own") told me the following:

> You must come to realize how we Vietnamese relate to the
> war. Many of us had never seen an airplane before. In the
> mountains and jungles the people believed they were flying
> dragons, dropping fire-eggs on their villages. The fear is
> beyond comprehension to Westerners. We trained villagers
> not to be afraid. Farmers learned to stand in their fields and
> shoot rifles at jet planes. Several times they would be success-
> ful. It would be foolhardy to dismiss supernatural forces as
> allies.

Xuan Oanh was an extraordinary warrior. A superior jungle
fighter, he could also don the diplomat's garb when it became
necessary to negotiate with Kissinger in Paris. In his mid-fifties,
though he looked twenty-eight, Xuan, a soldier for some forty
years, remained a man of peace. He was the counterculture's man
in Hanoi, in Paris, and in the tunnels and trenches of South
Vietnam. Lacking formal education, he nonetheless managed to
speak five languages fluently. Though he never mentioned it,
many in his family had been tortured by Saigon intelligence
officers trying to track him. His evasive tactics were legendary.
Once when I saw him in Paris, he mentioned he was going home.
"How do you go back, Xuan?" I queried. "I fly by commercial
airline to Moscow, then transfer to a fighter jet headed to Hanoi.
That takes about sixteen hours, then I walk home. That part takes
six months." Knowing the magic of time travel, he could adapt to
all the world's jungles. He also had an uncanny ability to begin

conversation on exactly the right note. Once during a visit, after Woodstock, he asked Anita if she could send him a Janis Joplin record. Later, in exchange, he presented her with a hash pipe fashioned from the metal wing of a felled jet plane. "Amazing," she exclaimed on the taxi ride from the embassy, "I swear he read my mind. He knew I had run out of rolling papers."

Needless to say, we had a different view of the Vietnamese than did the Pentagon. Coming out of Buddhist culture, they understood the significance of American martyrs dousing themselves in gasoline and torching their bodies in protest. They would not dismiss as frivolous attempts to exorcise the Pentagon. To the contrary, this was one conspiracy that actually could have hatched in Hanoi. Without saying a word, Xuan Oanh could easily let us entertain the illusion the idea was our own. Being young and hungry, we acted on that illusion. What the heck!

Marty Carey and I began the ritual by standing in no-trespassing territory on the lawn surrounding one flank of the granite beast. (Just in case you have trouble distinguishing guerrilla leadership from an imperialist high command, consider the headquarters of the National Liberation Front—a floating collective moving by night from hand-dug jungle tunnels to secret back rooms inside Saigon. The U.S. forces, on the other hand, were directed from the world's largest office building.) Marty brought some incense and Tibetan bells, we improvised an Apache war dance and proceeded to measure at arm's length the distance from one corner to the next. "What the hell is going on here?" screamed the M.P. sergeant, racing up to us with bayonet poised. Paying no attention, we continued.

"One hundred and one, one hundred and two, one hundred and three . . . ," we counted, exchanging positions with each number. Soon there was a circle of concerned officials. Braided uniforms signifying Army brass. Suit-and-tie costumes of public-relations men. "Just what's going on here?" asked a uniform.

"Well, *corporal*, as you know, five-sided objects are evil. We're here to begin the exorcism of the Pentagon," said Abbie.

"Now wait a minute. This is government property, and it's *captain*."

"We'll be done soon," explained Marty. "We just have to measure one side and multiply by five. We have to see how many witches we need to circle the Pentagon."

"Circle the Pentagon? Sergeant, what in God's name is going on here?" shouted the captain.

"Exactly," responded Marty. "See, as part of the levitation ceremony . . ."

"Levitation!" he exploded.

"Don't worry, general, we're applying for a permit. We want permission to raise the Pentagon one hundred feet," continued Marty.

"It'll all be legal," I added in a responsible tone.

"Goddamn it, sergeant, arrest these lunatics!"

The arrest created national interest. "We'll be back with fifty thousand more next month," we announced.

"Did you get the permit?" inquired the press.

"We are negotiating permission to raise this hunk of granite one hundred feet, the generals so far agree to only ten. We're reasonable, ten feet will have to do. See you next month, boys and girls."

Witches were recruited from central casting (St. Marx Place), costumed appropriately, and sent on TV talk shows to entertain and inform the people of our plans. Hildi Hoffman, chief witch of the Group Image, baffled one host when she poured red sand on his studio floor, drew a pentagon figure with a stick, and starting weirding out on incantations. We constructed a huge plywood replica of the Potomac monster, and at a dress rehearsal on the stage of the Fillmore East managed to get the bugger to rise. It took Fugs, music, smoke bombs, and a network of thin piano wires slung over the rafters.

When the Washington police announced they were prepared to use the dreaded mace spray to blind demonstrators, we announced that our scientists had invented a new drug called—"Lace." "Lace is LSD combined with DMSO, a skin-penetrating agent. When squirted on the skin or clothes, it penetrates quickly to the bloodstream, causing the subject to disrobe and get sexually aroused," I announced to a bewildered but horny press. For the few cynical holdouts we staged an orgy. Water pistols were loaded with the secret Lace which had been smuggled into the U.S. from Taiwan in plastic containers labeled "Schwartz Disappear-O!" Marketed as a novelty item, it appeared to cause a purple stain, then vanished before your eyes. Magic!

I called some reporters and told them we had a new drug that made people want to fuck. "How do we know it's true?" they said. I told them to come over to the house for a demonstration.

They all showed up, and we ushered them into a room we had set up with pillows on the floor, assembling the reporters against the wall and introducing them to the two couples who were to demonstrate the effects of Lace. I gave a little speech full of mumbojumbo about the new drug, cautioning them not to touch the containers as the stuff hadn't been tested yet.

After my speech, I had to slip out to speak at a church. Having no idea the couples were going to go all the way, so to speak, for the revolution, I'm annoyed to this day that I missed the orgy. The subjects shot themselves with water pistols full of purple Lace, took off their clothes, and fucked. Then they put their clothes back on, and the reporters interviewed them. "What did it feel like?" they asked.

"Well, after about five minutes I began to see all sorts of colors . . ." Their answers were merely recollections of past acid experiences.

Within no time at all Johnny Carson was talking about the new and potent sex drug, Lace. At the time there was a lot of scare talk about drugs—LSD, mushrooms, STP, and Morning Glory seeds—there were many new names floating around and a lot of stories that usually involved dopers doing bizarre things. People suspected the Lace demonstration was a put-on, but then again. . . . Hippies, drugs, orgies: it was all perfectly believable. A good joke and a good ad for the march on the Pentagon. Whatever terror ploy the Washington cops could dream up, we could top.

So two truckloads of Disappear-O!, water pistols, smoke bombs, Halloween masks, and noisemakers went south and were distributed just before dawn on the banks of the Potomac. One hour later, word came that one of our secret battalions, led by Walter Bowart, had been arrested at the airport. Busted with them were ten thousand flowers. They were nabbed boarding a small Piper Cub which was to penetrate the artillery defenses and flower-bomb the Pentagon with lilies. Some rat-fink had snitched the plot before the plane had a chance to challenge the radar.

Caravans of demonstrators began arriving from all over the country. At noon we assembled in front of the statue of Honest Abe Lincoln. It was warm for an October day, and young people stripped and swam nude in the reflecting pool. Radio Bob got into an early altercation with some Nazi hecklers and was hauled off to prison in a makeshift jail somewhere below the Washington Monument (about where the left testicle would be if the phallus had balls). Thousands, more than a hundred thousand in all, turned out. The air rang with anticipation as the crowd heated up to the speeches and singing.

Then Dave Dellinger announced the ground rules: "No pushing, no shoving, no *violencia*; but those who so desire should now proceed to the walls of the Pentagon for civil disobedience." "Hup-Two-Three-Four, what the fuck are we fightin' for!" The war was about to come home. Welcome sisters and brothers to the Second American Revolution!

"Out demons out! Out demons out!" The chanting grew louder. Fugs and medicine men on flatbed trucks filled the air with the sounds of tambourines, drums, and screaming incantations. Anita, dressed as Sergeant Pepper, and myself, as an Indian with an Uncle Sam hat, held hands. We split our last tab of acid, hurtled the highway barrier wall, raced across the traffic, and scampered up the embankment. From there we could see the five-sided hulk stretched against the Virginia horizon. To the left and right were flanks of demonstrators crawling up the slope. Several carried Viet Cong flags. College pennants fluttered alongside banners proclaiming antiwar slogans. M.P.s in white helmets chased stragglers who raced through the highway traffic and disappeared into the bushes. Once on the top of the plateau, the plain ahead was flat, and the Pentagon was clearly visible. Helicopters whirled overhead. Thousands spread out in formation. "CHARGE!" I screamed at the top of my lungs, lunging forward. "To the walls! To the walls!" Adrenaline shot through the crowd's bloodstream. A swarm, fifty thousand strong, raced across the grass and hurled itself as one mighty mudball against the Pentagon. Dancing and cursing, we tried to encircle the joint. Between the building and us were platoons of soldiers, rifles and bayonets outstretched in menacing formation. A hush came over the crowd, instant leaders urged the people to sit down and be calm. The singing began:

I lay down my sword and shield, down by the riverside,
Down by the riverside, down by the riverside.
I lay down my sword and shield, down by the riverside,
Ain't gonna study war no more. . . .

Super Joel, one of Berkeley's best street people, walked up to the bayonets and, in a gesture of courage and love, inserted a flower into a soldier's rifle barrel. It has remained one of the classic photos of the sixties.

Hours passed. Graffiti covered the outer barrier walls. HO CHI MINH LOVES LBJ, END WAR! THE NLF IS GONNA WIN, GUMBO WAS HERE. "Beat Army! Beat Army!"

Night came. Fires were lit to keep warm. People huddled under blankets. It was Valley Forge revisited. When the TV camera-eye could no longer see, the order went out and heads were busted. Some people fought back. Rumors flew. "Soldiers are deserting!" "Someone got shot!" Helicopters with spotlights hovered in the darkness, eerie reminders of Vietnam. The breath froze in the chilly autumn air as we scrambled on the ground to keep our hard-won turf. Paddy wagons and ambulances moved into position as the long tedious ritual of dragging people off to jail began.

Just before dawn, eleven of us assembled at the west wall. Our bellies ached from hunger, our fingers were stiff from the frost, paint and mascara streaked down our faces. The acid had long since worn off, leaving parched throats and lips begging for Chapstick. A Shoshone medicine man asked Anita to sit cross-legged facing the sun and lead us in prayer. Spontaneously an undulating sound arose from our circle of comrades. It was not unlike the battle cry of Algerian women. Words that shall remain secret were spoken by the shaman. Then Anita rose tall and proud, and in a voice possessed roared: OM AH HUM. OM AH HUM. OM AH HUM. The ground beneath us vibrated. The granite walls began to glow, matching the orange of the new sun, and then, before our very eyes, without a sound, the entire Pentagon rose like a flying saucer in the air.

What impressed me the most was the ease with which it happened. Child's play really. Of course, to "see" the levitation you had to be there that moment. Even being there in the physical sense was not enough, one had to master Don Juan's technique of *not-doing*—one had to learn how to stop the world. Xuan Oanh told me he had felt the Pentagon move while walking along the Ho Chi Minh Trail on his way home.

Quite apart from the metaphysics, the sight of the most famous war-making symbol on the planet under siege by thousands of its citizens was instantaneously transmitted around the globe. That needed no interpreter, no hocus-pocus.

Released from the D.C. jails, we headed back to our local communities: Madison, Atlanta, Ann Arbor, Berkeley, New Orleans, the Lower East Side. We already knew our next national rendezvous. In eight months we would reconvene outside the gates of the Democratic Convention. The location had no sooner been announced than we made our intentions clear. We would bring the war home to Chicago. Confidence high. Experience and courage already tested. We would stalk Lyndon Johnson as he campaigned throughout the land, building armies of protesters who would then flock to the Midwest and confront the policy makers with their own madness.

Little did we realize that old warhorse LBJ would soon quit. Just one of the many surprises the next year would present. Seeing the Pentagon rise was one thing; seeing 1968 before it happened would have required clairvoyant powers beyond our capabilities. Brace yourself, sports fans, for we are about to enter the Apocalypse. Happy New Year 1968! You were the greatest of them all.

1968: The Year That Was

A word was born on New Year's Day.

Five conspirators lay scattered on the pillows adorning the postage-stamp living room of our Lower East Side flat. Paul Krassner, suffering from an acid hangover, staggered around asking, "Why? Why? Why?"

"Look," he said, flash bulbs exploding in his chromosome-damaged mind, "when you make the peace sign of the V the extension of your arm makes it a Y."

"I, EYE! EYE! EYE! I love you very much," chimed in Anita. "PEE-PEE," piped Jerry Rubin, his Rolodex brain already connecting the concept to structure. "You need a little pee-pee in every movement."

"I again. I am the Walrus, I am the Eggman," said Abbie. "E is for everybody, energy," exclaimed Jerry's girlfriend, Nancy Kurshan. "Yippie!" shouted the chorus. The exclamation point would carry us to victory. Its good vibes would conquer all question marks and get us to Chicago. If the press had created the "hippie," could not we five hatch the "yippie"? A political hippie. A flower child who's been busted. A stoned-out warrior of the Aquarian Age. "What's a yippie?" they would ask. "A yippie is someone going to Chicago." The tie-dye had been cast. Our hair was in the ring.

Outside it was probably snowing, the TV was crowded with the usual football games. Five years before, I would have been frantically trying to get down one last bet before the Cotton Bowl drifted into the Rose Bowl. Pasadena was now a long way from the Lower

East Side. Fondness for games had been transferred into devising guerrilla theater stunts to change the world. In athletics, with the exception of Joe Namath's knees and Muhammad Ali's left jab (in those years stilled by racist warmongers) there was nothing worth noting. All my enthusiasm for sports had been channeled into the Big Game—the battle with the government.

The year began with a scattering of early warning shots. The good Dr. Spock and four others were indicted in a Boston federal court for aiding and abetting draft resisters. It was the second of the great conspiracy trials, Oakland 7 having been the first.

In Congress, a debate was raging over the controversial civil rights bill. In the land of equality, 190 years after the fact, politicians still argued about skin color as a factor in determining where a person could live and work. After the usual watering-down process, the conservatives would agree to go along with the bill if a series of restricting riders were attached. One rider to bill HR-17893 made it unlawful to cross state lines with the intention of inciting a riot. Familiarly called the "Rap Brown Law," it was—and still is—the most antidemocratic law on the books. Once Congress passed the civil-rights package in April, all national demonstrations were by definition "riots." Leaders, those nefarious villains that government bureaucrats, denying popular protest, saw in their fantasy world, became subject to ten-year prison terms. The stakes, like the tempers, were rising.

That spring the Tet offensive had begun in earnest. Nixon announced he was going to run for president. In Orangeburg, North Carolina, militant blacks took on the police in pitched gun battle. Lyndon Johnson announced he would not seek a second term. A week later Martin Luther King, Jr. was assassinated.

During the final week of that chaotic April that had begun with King's assassination, radical students, attempting to build a coalition with the neighborhood black community and to purge their university of its connections to the Vietnam War, turned Columbia University into a raging battlefield. A decade before, this Ivy League bastion had given the world Pat Boone. Times change. White bucks and crew cuts had long since passed from campus life, and Columbia's new rock and roll singer was a baby-faced lad with a shock of sandy hair and an equally good voice. He used the stage name Mark Rudd because, like me, his Russian roots had been sanitized by some border guard at Ellis Island. Make no mistake, Mr. Rudd was a member in good standing of the International Jewish Conspiracy.

You cannot conduct a war like Vietnam without the complicity of the universities. They are important research centers for sophisticated weapons and communications tools. They train those needed to carry on the false public relations necessary to convince young people to go die in old people's wars. Politicians, generals, movie producers, even revolutionaries come from the universities. Columbia University, like Dow Chemical, had a financial investment riding on the Vietnam War.

Events on Morningside Heights snowballed. First the occupation of the dean's office and the storming of the chain-link fence around the gymnasium construction site, a symbol of the destruction of the Harlem community for the recreational benefit of the university. Then the occupation of seven major campus buildings. The university ground to a standstill. Avery Hall was the site of a counterculture wedding. At the Low Library radicals repelled the attack of soused-up football players and fraternity jocks. In the Administration Building, compromising files were uncovered. In Mathematics Hall we, the denizens of the Lower East Side, held the fort.

The Motherfuckers, Jim Fouratt, Anita—the whole gang was there, all battle-wise veterans by the spring of '68. Our colors were anarchist black or yippie pink and purple. Not exactly the hippie-flower motif of Avery Hall, not as severe as the SDS students in Administration nor practicing the military discipline of the blacks who held the fort in Hamilton Hall. Like the Paris uprising of the same year, there was little centralized leadership. We had walkie-talkie communication between buildings, but everything that went on was more or less spontaneous.

I shuttled between the barricaded hall and the outside world. I came and went through secret passageways we had discovered, avoiding the right-wing students who locked arms and encircled the occupied buildings in an attempt to starve us out. By that time our communications network was well developed. Using radio station WBAI, and a lot of street leafleting, we urged the faculty and the community at large to come to Columbia, join us, and prevent a police occupation. What was about to happen, we knew, wouldn't be in the usual dark alley, Lower East Side style. "Here's a chance to show what's coming down on the street," we urged.

Behind the barricades we acted like everyone who has ever experienced being under siege—we spent most of our time discussing what we would do when the police came. For those participants facing their first police confrontation the yippies were a walking encouragement: we'd been through it and were still alive and kicking. We also discussed defensive tactics. Someone brought up spraying foam from the fire extinguishers on the stairs to slow down the police. It was voted down. We taped the windows to keep them from shattering, and along with the food that was smuggled in came Vaseline and plastic bags—protection against mace.

Outside the buildings students and faculty took sides. A right-wing group called the "Majority Coalition" opposed the demonstrators. Faculty members hoped to keep tempers cool and prevent violence.

Inside, we posted guard around the clock and waited hour-by-hour those five days for the police to come. Bodies sprawled all over; rock music blared. We talked endlessly of issues and strategies, fought boredom, fought fear, got hung up on how decisions were to be made, worked out evacuation routes, laughed, made love, smoked dope, sang, argued, and waited.

People learned this way. They gained experience in how to push confrontation, for that was what the occupation was—a piss-or-get-off the pot situation for the establishment. Not for a minute did we think we were taking over Columbia or closing it down for more than a brief time. The point was to show that those who called in the police didn't have the students' interests at heart and never did; that what was happening at Columbia—weapons research, think tanks, financial investments—had nothing to do with students, teachers, and learning; that learning was academic window dressing to a profitable business.

Around 3 A.M. on April 22 I left WBAI and returned to the campus with boxes of donuts for everybody inside Mathematics

Hall. I arrived together with the police. What I saw was unbelievable, an original nightmare drama staged for television. Spotlights lit up the entire center compound, the hundred-and-sixteen-year-old statue, and the pseudo-Greek buildings with their ivy beards.

A caravan of police vehicles moved onto center stage. The back doors of the vans sprang open and the cops came rolling out. Thousands of students booed and threw paper cups at them. The cops looked very formidable: beefy, visors down, dressed in leather, flapping their black jacks, mace at the ready, and swinging their clubs ("the police were not allowed to bring their clubs on campus," we were later told). They were nervous, too, but they were going to deal with their nerves in a macho way. Battered to the ground by the swarming blue, I was picked up and bodily thrown into a waiting paddy wagon. Meanwhile, the police were entering Mathematics Hall, yelling, "If you don't come out you're going to be sorry." Everyone inside refused to walk out and the cops used the opportunity to club them all the way to the paddy wagon.

At the precinct I was booked with illegal trespassing in Avery Hall. Although I had never set foot in that building, I eventually pleaded guilty to the charge and accepted a year's probation. Of the more than five hundred demonstrators arrested, less than a dozen of us paid any penalty. Marty Kenner, my old friend from Berkeley, Gus Reichbach, Jonah Raskin, and the others the police infiltrators targeted as "leaders." Mark Rudd, expelled from school and facing several charges, paid the stiffest penalty.

I related to Mark like to a younger brother. He had zero experience but a natural instinct for making good trouble. He built the issues of the gym and the research institute into a battle that went beyond the campus. The institute was little more than three professors in their seventies, and Mark later admitted he'd never even been to the gym site. He saw that the principle of organizing was biting the tail of the tiger and holding on tight, forcing a confrontation and making the fencesitters take sides. While the West Side liberals rushed home to their brownstones and debated the nature of the university, Mark saw that the issues were to a large extent fabricated, a way of making concrete an abstract concept.

Although we were close, Mark considered freaks an interesting sideshow to the main event, your standard commie interpretation of anarchist history. He was ashamed of his drug bust and would never tell anyone about it. He didn't see the link. On the other hand, the old leftists hardly appreciated him. They would never forgive him for his rudeness in challenging their domain, and he remained their *bête noire*. It mattered little to Mark; in eighteen months he would be waging war from the Weather underground.

Violence on the part of New York's Finest was nothing new to us. Once, after the Dean Rusk demonstration, I was in a group of arrestees being processed at a midtown precinct house. Two right-wing cops pistolwhipped a demonstrator whose hands were handcuffed behind his back. They beat him for a full agonizing ten minutes. All of us tried in small ways to interfere with the beating. When we were herded into the van to be taken to the Tombs he was left behind, for the cops had to wait until he stopped bleeding before they could clean him up a little and send him downtown to court. We all filed complaints with the review board. Nothing happened, of course, but I always wondered what happened to that heavyset, dark fellow with the moustache who held his dignity so well while his flesh and blood splattered in the air.

A month before Columbia, in an action foretelling the confrontation in Chicago, we held a Yip-in celebration at midnight in Grand Central Station. Our leaflets called for a joyous equinox mating, a pre-Chicago festival of life with balloons, roller skates, and dancing. Six thousand people showed up and frolicked under the vaulted ceiling. Everybody was enjoying themselves when one eager beaver scampered up on the information center and yanked off the clock's hands. Could this gesture prevent the trains from running on time? Was this equal to tearing down the flag? Obviously it was of major importance, for the act resulted in cops going berserk. They began bashing heads without warning. Police officials repeatedly refused to allow me and other community leaders to address the crowds not to panic. Barry Gottehrer and other well-meaning Lindsay aides were also kept from cooling things down. Cultural civil war erupted in the vast chamber, but it was unevenly matched: only one side was armed. There was no escape route except through a gauntlet of clubs. The place had become an enclosed tomb in which the cries of the people were magnified, increasing the horror. The scene was more frightening than anything that was to happen in Chicago.

An elite force bee-lined for me. Yippie Ron Shea was bodily thrown through a plate-glass window trying to protect me. His hands were broken and vital nerves in his arms severed. Then Nancy, Anita, and another friend, Brad Fox, covered me with their bodies. The cops had other plans. Peeling them off, I was clubbed on the back until unconscious. The beating resulted in a damaged vertebra that still acts up. Somehow we made it outside. Barricaded off by police, 42nd Street was a maze of ambulances and white clad orderlies bearing stretchers. The Grand Central Massacre had occurred. It did not keep us from Chicago; it merely sharpened our determination.

In Chicago, too, there had been signs of the clash to come. During the uprisings following the killing of Martin Luther King, Jr., the South Side of Chicago exploded with a fury. If someone spit on the sidewalk of his city, Mayor Daley was personally insulted. To set it ablaze drove the Irish warlord bananas. He issued the following proclamation:

> Shoot to kill any arsonist or anyone with a Molotov cocktail in his hand and shoot to maim or cripple anyone looting a store in our city.

Never a namby-pamby, Daley established a rigid stance he was to maintain throughout the coming months. He was determined to play the kingmaker/host at the August convention. Within the Democratic party he was maneuvering between the Humphrey and Kennedy forces. No one would gain the nomination without the blessings of America's most celebrated ward politician. No niggers, commies, or hippies were going to sabotage his plan.

In the spring, when Rennie Davis and other organizers staged a peaceful antiwar march, Daley's police along with thugs waded into the marchers with a fury that matched that of the police at Grand Central Station. To a lesser degree, similar scenes were occurring across the country. In Madison, Wisconsin, in San Francisco, wherever the building campaign brought Nixon or

Humphrey. Meanwhile, Gene McCarthy's campaign was turning
into a crusade of virtuous irrelevance. On the other hand, Bobby
Kennedy was rising faster than the new Rolling Stones album.
When yippie scouts reported rumors in the counterculture that
JFK's kid brother smoked grass, we realized he was the candidate
to beat in Chicago. Kennedy would have been our real challenge,
maybe even our own candidate, if events had not, during the past
five years, removed us so far from mainstream politics. Perhaps if
he had not gone after Jimmy Hoffa. Perhaps. . . . perhaps. . . .
the history of politics is swaddled in layers of "perhaps."

On June 5 in a Los Angeles hotel kitchen, speculation was to
cease. Sirhan Sirhan, an intense Palestinian with a small hand gun,
was to cast his primary vote. The image that sticks in my mind is
the back page of the *New York Post*, the full page occupied by the
sprawling bloody body of Robert Kennedy. On the top was the
familiar heading: *New York Post: Sports Section*. One could
reasonably make the case that Sirhan was an agent operating under
the influence of the National Football League. That everybody's
favorite lineman, Rosy Grier, grabbed the gun further proves the
point. But again a Kennedy lay dead and the country (all of us)
shuddered at the recognition of our collective frailty.

Despite all these national jolts, the yippies (at times now called
the Youth International Party) moved steadily forward toward our
climax with destiny in the windy city. Crack YIP organizers
throughout the counterculture held meetings for our planned Festival of Life. Events all around us were giving credence to our
capsule scenario: the Democrats would gather in Chicago for a
convention of death; in juxtaposition, we would gather to celebrate
life. We would run a pig for president and our campaign pledge
would be, "They nominate a president and he eats the people. We
nominate a president and the people eat him."

We would secure a large park, sponsor workshops, exhibits,
demonstrations and rock concerts in contrast to the deadly dol-
drums that would go on inside Convention Hall. True, there would
be monkey-warfare highjinks, but our strategy did not include
plans for organized violence or riot although our fanciful literature
carried our dope-induced hallucinations. We revealed that the
Potheads' Benevolent Association had been busy all spring strew-

ing seeds in the vacant lots of Chicago, anticipating the ideal growing weather of the predicted Long Hot Summer. We spread the rumor that battalions of super-potent yippie males were getting in shape to seduce female convention-goers and that yippie agents were posing as hookers. There was no end to our nefarious plans. We would dress up people like Viet Cong and send them into the streets to shake hands like ordinary American politicians. We would paint cars taxi-yellow, pick up delegates and drop them in Wisconsin. Planning to hijack the Chicago office of the National Biscuit Company and distributing bread and cookies to the masses might have sounded a little incendiary, had there been a Chicago office of Nabisco. There wasn't. Later HUAC took all this dead seriously, even suggesting we had planned to blow up a baseball diamond in Lincoln Park.

We encouraged everybody to run for president. "Vote for Me" signs would sway in the breeze, thick as Illinois corn. One presidential hopeful, Louis Abolofia, sent out flyers of himself nude with the slogan, "What have I got to hide?" We promised the Vikings would land once more on the shores of Lake Michigan, only this time in yellow submarines. America would be rediscovered!

Night and day we organized. Our office in New York, under Nancy Kurshan's direction, printed tens of thousands of the famed yippie buttons, posters, and leaflets designed to bring people to Chicago. Freewheeling meetings, open to street rumblers and government agents alike, were held weekly at the Free University. The Liberation News Service, then under the leadership of Marshall Bloom and Ray Mungo, wired daily messages to the hundreds of underground newspapers, now local hotbeds for organizing yippie chapters. Rock and folk singers were solicited. Many agreed, although all but Phil Ochs and the MC-5 out of Detroit would eventually chicken out. Many succumbed to threats laid down by Daley and his police department, but most gave in to their managers' desires to avoid politics with a passion.

Faced with the task of getting huge numbers of people to come to Chicago along with hundreds of performers, artists, and theater groups, operating with a ridiculously small budget (we probably spent a total of $10,000 on Chicago) we created a myth. What is a yippie? A hippie who is going to Chicago. Who is a yippie?

Anyone who wants to be. Yippie was the name of the myth that created free advertising for our Chicago confrontation. We never had to pay for ads. The papers and the electronic media provided us with free coverage. We stole thousands upon thousands of dollars' worth of free publicity using gimmickry. I don't think it would surprise anyone to learn that after Chicago, three ad agencies tried to hire me and Jerry.

Behind the myth, of course, was an enormous amount of traditional organizing. When you're busy creating an aura of spontaneity you don't have cameras come in and focus on the people at their desks answering telephones nine to five. This reluctance to explain away the mystery contributed to our image of not being serious. We didn't want to show the back stage *deus ex machina* that created the magic. People, even comrades in the antiwar movement, would say, "You're a non-group. You don't exist." When reporters accused us of the same we would say, "You're right. This is magic. It just happens. We just rise up out of the sewers."

"Where will all these people go to the bathroom?" they would inquire.

"Yippies don't go to the bathroom. Did you ever see a yippie go to the bathroom? See—that's not a problem." Newspapers just want "good copy" anyway. Funny term for journalism—good copy.

Meanwhile, we had worked out all those logistical problems long ago and lined up churches and homes near the park site. In time our announcements would contain factual detail.

Forty thousand people attended our Yip-out that Easter in Central Park to hear speeches and get themselves primed to go to Chicago. Campus organizers turned out large audiences for Jerry or myself as we brought word of upcoming events and raised funds. Throughout July and early August we carried on negotiations with Chicago city officials. Chief negotiator for the city, one David Stahl, gave credence to his name—he stalled. Negotiations are a complicated affair. It's cat and mouse, not a game where saints wait for the opportunity to become martyrs. If the city granted us permission to camp in Lincoln Park then perhaps 100,000 people would come, resulting in large-scale yet peaceful demonstrations. On the other hand, if no permits were forthcom-

ing, we would all essentially be "criminals guilty of illegal trespassing and parading without a permit." The numbers would be
fewer, but they would be angrier. The Constitution of the United
States guaranteed us the right of assembly and protest, but Mayor
Daley saw fit to overrule the founding fathers. In one of Daley's
more prophetic slips of the tongue, he said at a press conference,
"The police are not here to create disorder, the police are here to
preserve disorder."

The negotiations went on as yippies all over the country made
their preparations for the festival:

> This will be the first coming together of all people involved in
> the youth revolution. It should be a beautiful week. This is the
> first day in the rest of your life. See you in Chicago.
> YIPPIE!!!!!!!!!!!!!

In early August, I flew alone to Chicago, prepared not to leave
until we had made our point. I had about thirty-seven bucks in
cash, a change of clothes, and a bundle of determination. The lone
gun on his way to clean up Dodge City. Just like Henry Kissinger!
Before boarding the plane, I filled out a life insurance policy
making the National Liberation Front of Vietnam the beneficiary
should the plane crash. It didn't, but in a way Chicago did. For a
good number of years it would be less a place on the map and more
an event symbolizing a civil war.

Chicago: The Whole World Is Watching

Chicago, as the song and I agree, is a wonderful town. A place to
lose your blues. No city in the land is more typically American.
The heart of the heartland. Railroad trains, pulsing along its vital
arteries, rush raw materials from the mouth of the Midwest to the
body of the nation. Nowhere in Chicago will you find the snobbish
sophistication of New York or the cosmopolitan airs of San Fran-

cisco. New Orleans has its charm. Los Angeles has Hollywood. Houston and Dallas the mad money of oil and cattle. Chicago has none of this.

Its urban character has been determined by its geographical location. The Windy City is smack dab in the middle of the world's most productive breadbasket. Its great natural resource is its workers. Immigrants broke their backs building Chicago. Communists. Anarchists. Idealists. All drifted to Chicago in an effort to organize the swarm of cheap labor crowding into the city. Here the Haymarket police riots resulted in the country's most violent labor battle. (It is to the city's disgrace that it memorializes only the cops who died.)

In the twenties and thirties robber barons like Al Capone and Dion O'Bannion built underworld empires by combining good business management with mayhem. Without the productivity of Chicago, one could make a good argument that the allies would have lost World War II. Beef. Wheat. Hogs. Cotton. Coal. Commodity brokers for an exploding economy. Chicago serves the country well.

A good part of popular American culture sprang from Chicago. Jazz drifted up the Mississippi and broadcast its bebop and blues to the world from the South Side. It was from here Louie Armstrong made famous the tunes of W. C. Handy. America's greatest populist lawyer, Clarence Darrow, hung his hat here, as did everyone's poet, Carl Sandburg. Chicago's tradition of proletarian writers remains unmatched: Upton Sinclair. James Farrell. Nelson Algren. Studs Terkel. One story even insists B. Traven, my favorite worker-scribe, hailed from the immigrant quarters behind the stockyards. A brawling turbulent town, Chicago's legacy has been painted in blood. The Haymarket riots put it in the newspapers. The gangland wars got it in the movies. It would be the destiny of the yippies to shed their blood putting Chicago on the television screens of a watching world.

Knowing and causing, however, are not quite the same. That we indeed sensed a violent climax might lead the Monday-morning quarterbacks to conclude we encouraged it. I declare, ten years after, that that most certainly was not the case. We were aware, however, that Chicago was, in some topsy-turvy way, the largest "southern" town in America. Shoot-to-kill Daley made it known

Fred McDarrah.

Grand Central Station Yip-In, Spring 1968. Anita reaches for Abbie. Ten seconds later he was beaten to the floor. Dislocated vertebra.

Abbie, Allen Ginsberg, Bob Fass, Lincoln Park, Chicago, 1968. Ginsberg is holding secret Yippie plans in the box. Lee Balterman. Time-Life.

Honorary member of Chicago's finest. Nacio Jan Brown. Black Star.

at every turn that he played a rough-and-tumble game. The redneck sheriff of Cook County, one Joe Woods, had announced to the press his intention to "stick the yippies in underground mud tunnels and organize white vigilante groups." One could not naively venture to Chicago expecting hearts and flowers. When the breakdown of negotiations made it clear the city would force a confrontation, we knew only the bravest of our generation would answer the call.

I landed at O'Hare airport in Chicago in early August, dressed in a T-shirt, cowboy boots, beads, long hair, and carrying a suitcase full of disguises. As people stared at me I began to feel they already knew who I was and why I was there. There may have been ten other "hippies" in the airport.

My first stop was at the office of the Chicago *Seed*, the counterculture's voice to the Midwest street people. Editor Abe Peck and I had been working for six months to bring demonstrators to the convention. The local community organization, Free City Survival, had been bargaining with the city and their spirits were optimistic.

An elderly gentleman took me aside at the newspaper office and offered me a place to live directly opposite Lincoln Park, our prospective home during the convention. I accepted the lodging. The following morning in a tearful scene my host showed me a frayed *Saturday Evening Post* article concerning the Soviet spy Colonel Rudolph Abel.

"I turned in Colonel Abel," the man confessed, his hands trembling. Astonished, I sat there as the era of the Fifties played itself out before me. Head in hands, he told of the FBI coercion, how it had finally worked, and had not Abel been exchanged for Francis Gary Powers, anyway?

There was a yippie named Stew Albert, a big golden bear who had lumbered through the movement with the determination of an NFL defensive lineman after yet another quarterback sack. His bulk was excellent camouflage for the mind of a pro coach. Stew Albert was the yippies' Vince ("When the going gets tough, the tough get going") Lombardi. "You gotta move, Abbie. Once a turncoat, always . . ." Stew did not have to finish his thought. I had already packed my bag.

I soon found out my airport paranoia was justified, for I was followed wherever I went. After a couple of days of this I went up to my two constant companions and asked, "What's going on?"

"We're your tails," they said. "We're supposed to follow you twenty-four hours a day." I could ditch them when I wanted, but for the most part I didn't mind their following me around. I had little to hide. In fact, they sometimes were convenient to have right behind me. At one point a fellow organizer and I were driving around looking for a restaurant someone had recommended. We couldn't find it and I said, "Stop the car a minute," and walked back to my tails' car and asked, "Do you know a good place where we can get something to eat? We're hungry."

"So are we," they said and we all went together. Over lunch we discussed kids, sports, the Beatles, drugs, and the Chicago police hierarchy. I told them all high-level cops were phony liberals and full of shit and not to be trusted. They nodded and picked up the tab for lunch. I made their job easier for them, giving them lots of useless information for the reports they had to file. In turn, they kept me informed of their orders, giving me advance warning of their actions.

I talked them into driving me to North Beach one morning during the convention to see Allen Ginsberg. It was a cold, gray day, and people were sitting in a circle on the beach shivering and chanting. On the way back downtown one of my tails said, "That was a very weird scene. What's that all about?"

"A good politician always goes to church Sunday morning," I told them.

As convention week neared, organizers began setting up camp in Chicago. The *Seed*, realizing the confrontation was no longer controllable, began advising people to stay away. The coalition had been broken, but the momentum pushed forward at a rapid pace. The Mobe office on downtown Dearborn Street swirled with activity. While Dave Dellinger held the decision-making board together, the task of coordinating the activists fell to Rennie Davis. A tireless worker, Rennie was the calm at the center of all storms and crises. Rennie and I were counterparts, resource workers who got the leaflets printed, the workers housed, the money raised. Hayden and Rubin tended to be overall strategists who could direct a group toward a goal. All of us were experienced with the press, the courts, police, and politicians. All were veteran organizers.

A week before we were to begin activities in the park (August 20–28), the cat-and-mouse game of negotiations continued. We sent lawyers into court to try and force the city into letting us sleep in the park. Judge Lynch, a Daley appointee, kept things confused with picky legalities. I had my own way of negotiating with city officials; my tactic was generally to put them on the defensive. Putting my feet up on the table and calling them by their first names, I would say, "Do you want thousands of people like us wandering through the streets of Chicago with no place to stay? Use your fucking heads. You'll be creating a riot." At one point I joked that if they gave me a hundred thousand dollars I'd leave town. (Later this wisecrack was offered in evidence at the trial resulting in a huge *Chicago Tribune* banner headline, "Yippies Demand Cash From City." Abbie would have left town for a hundred grand.)

We staged a march to the precinct house nearest Lincoln Park to present the cops with peace offerings of apple pies. Packets of material were distributed to all out-of-towners. Jeff Nightbyrd, editor of the Lower East Side's *Rat*, moved his underground press to Chicago to put out a survival edition. *Ramparts* magazine published a daily wall poster. There were daily press conferences. At first, we did not attempt to dispel the confusion. To the contrary, we enhanced it:

REPORTER: How many yippies are in Chicago?

YIPPIE: Four (*holding up four fingers*), but we're bringing in four more (*holding up four more fingers*) on Wednesday.

An ABC reporter snuck us a kit of promotional material that listed the hotel rooms where all the delegates were staying. We printed the information, complete with floor plans of the hotels, and called it SECRET PLANS REVEALED. The response was panic—my God! Where did they get the secret plans? They're terrorists! They'll plant bombs! People were really convinced the information was secret. I got the idea from a *Chicago Tribune* article headlined: "Secret Yippie Plans Revealed." All the article did was quote from a piece I published in Krassner's *The Realist*.

I decided to label everything "secret." "Daring exposé—Top

Secret Yippie Plans for Lincoln Park," I headed maps and schedules. Together with the 20,000 buttons we had made up that read "Yippie Leader" and a recommendation to reporters to ask each and every yippie in Lincoln Park why they had come to Chicago, there was some confusion about our purpose, much of it intentional.

Infiltrating our activities didn't take much police skill. One afternoon I watched a volunteer lead a karate training program. There was something about the way he addressed the crowd that aroused my suspicions. It was more military than seemed familiar, and his karate technique went beyond the defensive. I walked up to him and said, "Let me see your wallet, Irv. You're a cop, aren't you?"

"The hell I am," he said. "You're just prejudiced because I don't have long hair." He continued to hang around. I didn't have time to worry about how many more of them were in Lincoln Park, although there was certainly a preponderance of two-hundred-pound lineman types hanging around who had mechanical expertise, understood walkie-talkies, police mentality, and spoke like military people. There was a limit to how much the average Chicago cop at that time could manage to look like a yippie.

The only infiltrator who succeeded in remaining undetected was Bob Pierson, who disguised himself as a scrubby biker and latched onto Jerry, acting as his body guard. It wasn't until a year or two later that undercover police appeared with long hair.

Our presidential candidate, Pigasus, a hefty hog, was nominated in a downtown ceremony and was quickly hauled off to the poky. That evening his wife, Piggy Wiggy, was set loose in Lincoln Park and after a merry, greasy romp was finally apprehended by Chicago's Finest. Mr. and Mrs. Pig were united in the animal shelter, prompting rallies outside demanding, "Free the pigs!"

"If the pigs are still in jail by convention time," I warned, "we'll run a lion!"

Jerry Rubin and I had a falling out over Pigasus. He didn't think the pig I had bought from a nearby farmer looked mean enough and I didn't think it was all that important. I was really pissed about him posing for the media more than organizing on the street and in the park. Between the pressures of organizing and the tensions of the times a little problem like pig aesthetics can kindle a major disagreement. This one lasted for months, but then, as on other occasions, we patched up our differences. We fought about the issues too; at that time I was much more of a hippie than Jerry, and I felt rock music, dope, the right to be in the park were *all* important issues. Everybody already knew we were against the war. Like the personality clashes in a marriage, fights among close friends under pressure are equally inevitable. But our relationship was totally public and we lived in a constant state of crisis.

One day we announced the yippies were considering putting LSD in the drinking water. Daley ordered thousands of National Guard to surround the reservoirs. When we said we were beginning "lessons" in snake-dancing (a vigorous parade movement that snakes through the streets offering some bodily protection to demonstrators), Mayor Daley, not to be outquoted, answered, "We're not worried about snake-dancing yippies; as for myself, I prefer an Irish jig."

Beneath the surface frivolity and the normal business of permits and court suits there were troubling signs. Daley had cancelled all days off for his police department. From now on each cop would work a tiring twelve-hour shift. Something we recommended against. In addition, the governor had ordered fifteen thousand Illinois National Guard on "combat alert." Army encampments were being set up on the outskirts of town. Television pictures of demonstrators meeting in the park were intercut with shots of National Guard convoys racing to Chicago. Several restaurants were refusing to serve obvious protesters. Building inspectors were harassing landlords who allowed tenants to house out-of-towners. The welcome mat was noticeably rolled up.

One night Ron Kaufman, my baby-sitter/guard, opened the door to find a man with a loaded pistol on the stoop screaming, "I'm going to kill that Abbie Hoffman!" Ron wrestled away the gun and turned the fellow over to my police tails. Next morning, after paying only three hundred dollars bail, the crazy was back on the street. A screen of reporters in the day, and disguises and evasive moves at night became my defense. I felt safer traveling alone and for much of the time lived underground.

The police command center was located in the Lincoln Park Zoo, quite a picturesque scene. An imitation farm was one of the main attractions, and every day, between the red and white barns, rows of police came marching to cadence down the center path flanked by baaing sheep, mooing cows, and oinking pigs. The pig analogy was becoming very real. The Chicago police were really huge. With their big beer bellies, triple chins, red faces, and little squinty eyes they really did look a lot like pigs, as did Daley and his city hall cronies. They all seemed hacked out of the same barnyard flesh.

On Saturday, August 24, the day before we planned to enter the park, I marched into the police command center wearing a karate jacket (I didn't know karate, but the jacket probably gave a few would-be mashers second thoughts), tipped my cowboy hat, and gave a little pep talk to the assembled constables. "Welcome to Chicago," I began, dispelling the myth of the outside agitator—I always tried to play the host wherever I was. "Now, you guys should go pretty easy. You're gonna see some strange things out there in Lincoln Park but we've got a lot of faith in Commander Linskey here, so let's not lose our cool. After all, you don't want to lose your jobs just like we don't want to lose ours, so just remember what you will see out there are just a lot of harmless funny people. Keep that in mind and we'll all get through this week. No one has any plans to fight with the police."

During my pep rally the cops just stood around, looking me over and banging their clubs into their palms. The night before police had killed a yippie, seventeen-year-old Dean Johnson, who they said had been robbing a store. "One last thing and I'll wrap this up," I said. "If you're coming after us, don't let the National Guard steal your thunder," unable to resist doin' the dozens on their heads.

The cops leafleted the parks: "Please cooperate," read their handbills. We countered with the following warning: "Beware: local cops are armed and considered dangerous."

In struggle, information is survival. Without it you can die. During the following days I used every information and communications tool in the arsenal I had assembled earlier to keep the lines open. I had the home telephone numbers of important city officials and social workers, the liberal wing of the city's establishment who were our buffers. I knew the police hierarchy, sympathetic local lawyers, the church centers, and all the resource people. We held regular yippie staff meetings to appraise the situation, but none of us had any reason to expect the kind of chaos the city was to unleash.

Keeping us out of the park made no sense, even if we didn't have a permit. There is a vast area between strict enforcement and looking the other way, which we assumed to be the city's policy. Our liaisons constantly assured us that it was. After all, the alternative was to make the streets of Chicago a war zone, and that made no sense at all. Nevertheless, that was what happened.

On Sunday afternoon, August 25, we formally announced we were entering the park. The city had given us permission to hold an afternoon rock concert, but everything was a hassle with the police. We got our music, but as the MC-5 were playing, random beatings by the police began. Stew Albert, singled out as a leader, had his skull cracked. As evening rolled in off Lake Michigan, park employees could be seen nailing up signs that read NO SLEEP-ING IN THE PARK. An 11 P.M. curfew was announced. I knew if we didn't establish a sleeping camp by that night we would have a hard time convincing more people to come, building up to the thirty to forty thousand we hoped to have by Wednesday. On the other hand, we didn't want to push a confrontation this early. Tempers were flaring and things were already beginning to get out of control.

At home America sat down for the evening meal and turned on the TV, expecting the background sounds of political Muzak that had become the hallmark of a decided convention. Instead, they were presented with the shock of helmeted police gassing and clubbing young people to the ground. The country was instantaneously plugged and plunged into civil war. Parents fought with their kids, some of whom left home, grabbed a plane, and joined us in Chicago.

Our determination to stay in the park became as firm as the city's to drive us into the streets. During the next two nights, the confrontation erupted with a fury. Barricades were erected. Tear gas clouds drifted from the park, as did the mass of demonstrators chased by police cars and flying wedges of cops. Like enraged bulls taunted by red flags, the men in blue charged in all directions.

Hugh Hefner got clubbed. Residents of Chicago out for an evening stroll got battered. Everything on the street was fair game. Then the police committed the unpardonable sin: they began to beat the reporters. Sandor Vanocur, then an NBC-TV reporter, later writing about these events in *Esquire*, would say that was the first time the correspondents covering antiwar demonstrations were to report the truth. For years, having seen demonstration coverage that read like police press releases, I couldn't agree more. News photos graphically told the story. An angry face capped by a police helmet, a club about to crash down on the camera. Illegally, the cop has taken off his badge to hide his identity. National guardsmen wearing gas masks holding their bayonet-rifles poised at the tires of a new compact. The television camera and microphone record the police menacing the driver. A peek inside the car reveals a middle-aged suburban woman at the wheel. The innocents are being ravaged by a blood-crazed army. Candid camera had become way too candid.

I didn't like the formal press conference approach and preferred to talk to the press in the park and show them the casualties. The cops had made a big deal over the barricades that were set up Monday night, making the action sound like the Battle of Lexington and Concord. When the television cameras focused on the twenty chairs and four park benches piled together in the middle of this enormous park, there was no need to elaborate on the absurdity of the police statements. But a helicopter shot was required.

The myth was that we dominated the news coverage coming out of Chicago. Actually our broadcast time—an hour and ten minutes in the week's ninety-six-hour total—was just a small percentage of the gavel-to-gavel coverage. And much of this was rerun footage. But while the convention droned on, everyone knew what was taking place outside the hall. When Senator Ribicoff remarked from the podium that "gestapo-like tactics were being used in Chicago," a shocked nation of lip readers focused in on Daley's angry namecalling: "You motherfucker Jew bastard, get your ass out of Chicago."

When police inside the halls hit Dan Rather, Walter Cronkite emotionally referred to them as "thugs." The Battle of Chicago raged. The politics of the street had in three short days become mainstream (or, more accurately, prime-time) life. Each night we gained a few more minutes past the curfew before the police came storming into the park. Each day we were assured by the city that we were going to be allowed to stay in the park and the police were just making a show. During one charge I went over to the nearest cop in charge and said, "What's going on? Your men are clubbing us and we've got two more hours." He apologized, called off his men, and in no time they regrouped and came back clubbing on schedule. I telephoned city officials, telling them, "What's the difference whether we stay in the park? We're already here so why can't we sleep here?" and they readily agreed that was the only sensible thing to do, but the cops still kept charging.

Running through the swinging clubs and the tear gas and out into the streets, I managed to lose my tails every night by jumping in and out of taxis, going through restaurants, in the front door of meeting places and out the back, taking buses and subways on my way to church cellars and the homes of friends.

I kept their telephone numbers on bits of paper separate from my address book, or committed them to memory. Calling them from a pay phone booth, I would ask whether they were going to be home that evening and could they leave their door open after eleven. I had a set of clothes in each apartment or home and changed constantly. My old college roomie, Manny, put me up one night.

There was a church directly across from the park that was a popular meeting place. As I walked past rows of police with my hair concealed under my hat, sometimes wearing a pasted-on moustache, I knew if they had recognized me they would have broken my bones on the spot. What they didn't seem to know about was the back door, from which I escaped out into the streets of Chicago and moved through the city. After the curfew a hippie walking the streets was about as safe as a Jew in Hitler's Berlin.

On Tuesday night I gave a speech to about four thousand people in a nearby auditorium. After the speech we returned to the park, only to be driven out again. I lost my tails and headed for an apartment on the South Side. After I arrived I got undressed right away, listening to the radio before I turned in. As reports of the latest police riots came over the air, I put on a different set of clothes and sneaked back through the streets, returned to the scene, and went back to work, getting the injured to hospitals, going to the precincts, calling lawyers. There was no need for sleep. The situation created its own adrenaline.

That afternoon over coffee my tails had told me I would be arrested the following morning.

"Why?" I asked.

"We'll think of something," they said.

Wednesday, August 28, was the big day, the culmination of all we had worked for that year. While the world watched, the Democrats would nominate a presidential candidate and the people who had come to Chicago to protest against the war would mass together and march down Michigan Avenue. That morning as I was getting dressed I took a lipstick and wrote the word "FUCK" on my forehead. I didn't feel like having my picture in the media that day. Walking out of the house, I tipped my hat and said to my tails, "Well, today's the big day! Are you ready?"

As Anita and I sat with Paul Krassner over breakfast, I kept my gray cowboy hat on to conceal the notorious word, not wanting to get the waitress upset. We were still eating when two cops came in.

"Lift up your hat," they said.

"I'm not done eatin' breakfast. I ain't goin'."

"Come on, take off your hat. We're serious."

"Did you call Inspector Rutherford about this? Here's his private number. I'm supposed to finish breakfast."

They took the slip of paper I handed them and had a conference. Then they left. They came back a few minutes later with six more cops. There were four patrol cars and a paddy wagon outside. I noticed the new cops were from the Eighth Precinct.

"You guys had better call Commander Brash," I said. "He told me if anybody tried to touch me they should call him first for instructions."

All eight cops started moving for the phone while I finished my juice. Then one of them said, "Come on—what are we doing?" and they all came back to the table, guns drawn.

"None of that stuff. Just take the hat off."

I lifted my hat and said "Bang bang!" and they dragged me

right across the table, through the bacon and eggs, across the floor, then threw me against a squad car, handcuffed me, and tossed me into a waiting paddy wagon.

I had figured after I was processed at the precinct I would be back on the streets in a few hours. Instead, the police moved me from precinct to precinct, cell to cell, for thirteen hours, without food, phone calls, or lawyers, while cops beat the shit out of me. I laughed hysterically through the beatings, I was so winged-out from not sleeping and all the tension. One of the cops shoved a bullet in my face and said, "See this? It's got your name on it. I'm gonna get you tonight."

"I've got a silver bullet with your name on it. I'm the Lone Ranger!" I never let cops get the last word. Every time I got in these situations, I played it like I was in my own private movie.

All day the cops kept telling me how they were "wiping the streets up with you hippie fuckers," but aside from the football talk they wouldn't tell me what was going on outside. All day they kept my exact location a secret from the lawyers frantically trying to bail me out. By the time I got to court I was so furious I ripped up my arrest papers right in front of the judge. The cops had kept me away from the Battle of Michigan Avenue.

By evening I was back on the streets. Surveying the parks and our church basement encampments was not unlike the scene in *Gone With the Wind* where Scarlett walks among the wounded after the battle of Atlanta. Miraculously there were no dead, but the street combatants were swaddled in bloodied rags. The smell of tear gas lingered in the air, and you knew some apocalyptic moment had just jolted history forward. Something on an inner level happened to many of us that day. I don't think I was much of a pacifist after Chicago.

Hubert Humphrey won the nomination. As the cameras rolled, he rose and kissed his wife Muriel. It was not his real wife, but a TV-screen image of her that his lips pressed against. Happy Hubert kissing a television screen would remain a symbol of what happened in Chicago. Democrats and Republicans alike knew it was the kiss of death. What had happened in the streets had destroyed any chances the Democrats might have had of holding onto the presidency.

Our battle in Chicago was not with the Democrats. Our battle was with those responsible for the Vietnam War. At Nixon's inauguration the following January we would turn out equal numbers of demonstrators and continue the struggle for the next four years. Nixon's first steps in office were to see that those events that smashed the Democrats would not be repeated under his administration. Having no intention of abandoning the war, Nixon made plans to destroy the antiwar movement. He took dead aim on those he considered leaders.

Even before Nixon got in on the act, various government agencies wanted their whacks. When I returned to Chicago, three weeks after the streets had been hosed down, I set a movement record by being arrested three times in one day. Apparently the Chicago police enjoyed having me around. During the next two years I was to see many of their best courtrooms and jail cells. Risking the heights of grand delusions, I'd venture to say they even grew to love having me around.

Chicago! Chicago! My kind of town.

Living with Lawyers

After the summer's clash, just about all the "names" the public associated with Chicago were preparing for a lengthy legal struggle. Everyone now faced a series of trials, and each new speaking engagement meant some local prosecutor could earn political points by nailing a big-time outside agitator. Immediately after returning to New York, I paid a visit to the offices of William Kunstler. Battling Billy was on board the movement train long before it gained fashion. Because he has extended his neck so far for so long, he is an easy target for those wishing to do chop jobs on idealists. Kunstler's philosophy stands refreshingly unique among lawyers, indeed among all professionals. He refuses to accept some of the basic house rules.

Our legal system, although pretending to function on adversary representation, is in fact more like a British gentlemen's debating club. The defense attorney is, literally, an agent of the court. His first loyalty, after putting on a jolly good show, is to the legal system itself. Just as a doctor owes loyalty to hospitals and the medical profession. Just as priests owe loyalty to the church.

If conflict arises between the patient, a lost soul, or the defendant and the institution, invariably the professional will sacrifice the individual or the ideal to protect the going system and his own career. In Washington, they have a great phrase for this brand of sellout. It is here, they say, that one learns to "rise above one's principles."

Kunstler rejects the house rule segregating professional from client. He does not dine with the prosecutor nor belong to the judge's country club. Kunstler gets high with his defendants. He defends only those he loves (defying another house rule) and makes no pretense about hiding his political feelings beneath some phony cloak of objectivity. He is the conscience behind every shyster out to make a fast buck, and he is not about to win any accolades from the American Bar Association until after he's dead. A handsome, defiant showman with a leaning toward the theatrical—always the romantic renegade—he remains *the* radical lawyer of our times.

I was not asking that Kunstler become my lawyer. He was much too busy to handle the piles of cases I saw coming after Chicago. What I needed was some young blood anxious to form a partnership whose purpose was to create havoc in the legal system, "Gerry Lefcourt. He's the lawyer you're looking for," answered Kunstler after I mapped out the strategy. "You'll make a good team."

Gerry Lefcourt didn't smoke dope. Then again, he was not a boozer. He was not a fellow prone to letting his emotions run amok in public (à la myself and Kunstler). Carefully groomed, a serious workaholic, betrayed only occasionally by the most mischievous of grins, Gerry answered my questions with remarkable patience. He had just been involved in an important case attacking the house rules. He had done exactly what I would have done had I been holding his briefcase. As a Legal Aid attorney assigned by the court to handle defendants unable to afford lawyers, he soon realized that Legal Aid functioned less for the protection of its indigent clients and more as a cover-up for yet another glaring fault of the system: no big money, no big defense. Even the most idealistic of Legal Aid lawyers would quickly be trapped by the overload of cases, trapped on the endless treadmill of securing the best deal regardless of justice or truth. Gerry decided to change things by organizing a lawyer's union and publicly making critical statements about the agency. A professional code demands no washing of the dirty linen in public. He was promptly fired. He counterattacked by instituting a court suit and was now just emerging from his own seven-month trial. The judge decided against Lefcourt, but within a year his efforts were bearing fruit through badly needed reforms.

A young activist lawyer, one who had jeopardized his slot in the system by placing ideals above career, was just what the doctor ordered. I explained my position. "I have no money. I wouldn't pay even if I did. There's one law for the rich and another for the poor, and I'm out to fuck that system. I work twenty hours a day at screwing around. You're the only one who's to know I'm serious. You keep me on the street. Is it a deal?" We embraced.

The next day our law partnership left for trial in Chicago. In question, the infamous four-letter word. Stepping off the plane we were greeted by six of Chicago's blues. Handcuffed and arrested on a charge of bail jumping, I was quickly waylaid to a makeshift jailhouse in the airport to be searched. "You were trying to trick us!" the cops said. "You switched airplanes." My lawyer and I had missed our scheduled flight and had radioed ahead to the people who were to meet us in Chicago. Apparently the cops had found this out and were very proud of their tremendous undercover work. Then they searched me and found a little penknife that is legal in every state in the union. By this time I was surrounded by about a dozen huge cops bedecked with their .45s, clubs, mace, and so forth. They were petrified by the discovery that I had been carrying a concealed weapon. They passed the little knife back and forth, and each cop tried to open it. When nobody could, they came to the conclusion that it was a switchblade. The photo in the *Chicago Tribune* that evening made the knife look about a foot long and just as menacing. I was arrested for possession of a dangerous weapon. Now there were three charges. A parade of cops and reporters set out to make the court rounds dragging their captive yippie along. "But your honor, but your honor," pleaded the young attorney, not exactly sure what to make of law Chicago-style.

Finally, emerging after a full day of successful maneuvers, we relaxed for a moment on some police precinct steps. Up popped two trench coats. "Are you Abbie Hoffman?" they baritoned. "You got him." "You're under arrest for crimes aboard an aircraft." The penknife again. Thoughtfully the feds let me sleep the night in jail. Next morning, after posting bond, we boarded an airplane for the trip back to New York. Once seated, the plane taxied to the end of the runway when the pilot announced there would be a slight delay. Three more trench coats boarded the plane and searched the aisles. Finding me, they opened a folder and announced I had been subpoenaed to appear before a hearing in the House Un-American Activities Committee.

In the following eight months, I would be arrested no fewer than seven more times. Everything from not fastening my seat belt (disorderly conduct) to possession of dangerous weapons and felonious assault. Few of the charges would ever stand up in court (the penknife, for example, suddenly "disappeared" as evidence) but the government and local law officials operated on a policy of systematic harassment. By forcing me to show up in some court or other weekly, by draining funds for bail, by restricting travel, energy had to be channeled away from organizing opposition to the war. In the end, thanks to Gerry's dogged perseverance, the forces of law and order scored few direct hits. Gerry kept me on the streets.

Revolution for the Hell of It

In a two-week period during the aftermath of Chicago I wrote *Revolution for the Hell of It*. With the exception of its more blatant sexism, I still stand by the book. Though the title reflects (deliberately) the flippancy of a brash kid, it embodies a view of the period, and of human nature, worth some emphasis. Activity not determined by deficiency replaces Freud with Maslow, Darwin with the Beatles, and possibly even Karl Marx with Groucho. The title attempts, up front, to demolish the critics who search for analysis in an unfulfilled childhood, negative traumas, or repressed libidinal instinct. There are "healthier" reasons to explain revolutionaries. I remember once during this period visiting old friends of Anita's, the Renzlers. She a writer on the rise. He a well-known psychiatrist. The whole evening was spent with them insistent on analyzing us. We had all come from the same backgrounds, so therefore society's imprinting had failed in some way. We were "immature," "passive-aggressive," "blocking," to name just a few professional judgments passed over the bridge table.

Near the back of *Revolution for the Hell of It*, I printed a list of eighteen yippie demands. Shockingly radical a decade ago, more than half have already materialized. The war in Vietnam is over. The draft has been abolished. The legalization of marijuana is just a few years away. Abortions are legal. Censorship restrictions have been eased. Freedom of sexual choice, through the efforts of the women's and gay movements, has gained wider acceptance. The environmental issues listed have become commonplace concerns for millions. Open-access media, through cable television, offset printing, CB radio, and lower-priced video equipment, has made possible greater participation. Home computers point in the direction of a society unburdened by the drudgery of "work."

Indeed "work," a yippie four-letter word, is slowly undergoing a transformation we helped initiate. In utopian terms we called for "total unemployment," insisting that machines do the slave work. That money be abolished. That art replace labor. Capitalism, as Max Weber wrote, was nurtured on the spiritual sustenance of the Protestant ethic. You got into heaven by working your ass off for the company. Eternal bliss was just another promotion. With Yippism the distinction between work and play collapsed. It blended fun with struggle.

I did not sign *Revolution for the Hell of It* with my real name. The publisher insisted the book would have sold fifty thousand more copies had I forgone that gesture. Instead, on the cover, I scrawled the most popular word in the English language. It is the only word, including *love, charity, equality, peace,* or any "ism"

that is noncorruptible. That word is FREE. The yippie political
program was built around FREE, and by using the word as my
pseudonym I wanted to say that the individual is not separate from
his or her politics. I dedicated the book to FREE and identified all
the photos of my friends as FREE.

Is all this gesturing the work of an egomaniac?

I reject the Freudian distinctions between id, ego, and superego
as oversimplifications designed merely to let us recognize the
existence of the unconscious. I reject the notion of "modesty" as
something invented by the WASPs to keep the Jews out of the
banking industry. Self-advertisement, including self-indulgence
and self-ridicule, seems to be an important tool of my trade. So I'm
a stand-up comedian and not a scholar? So sue me? Tell me one
thing Jesus said that was funny and I'll eat this chapter.

So Long, HUAC,
It's Been Good to Know Ya

In October, we finally got a chance to meet the House Un-
American Activities Committee. Recalling how I was drawn into
protest partly because of HUAC's activities in the early sixties, I
was anxious to personally thank the committee. There were old
debts to be settled. We knew of the history of U.S. repression that
had gone on before us, dating back to the Palmer Raids of the
twenties, the repression of activists such as Big Bill Heywood and
Emma Goldman, and the blacklisting of artists like Paul Robeson
and the Almanac Singers. Coming into existence just before World
War II, HUAC was determined to crush all leftists through scaring
the country into a witch hunt. All forms of social idealism were
tarred by creating an atmosphere that hinted there might be a
"red" hiding under every bed.

Jerry Rubin updated his previous appearance before HUAC as
an American revolutionary with a tasteful blend of international
wardrobing. Beret by IRA. Black pajama bottoms by Viet Cong.
Bandoleers borrowed from the mountains of Mexico were criss-

Blood brothers Gerry Lefcourt and tennis partner after yet another court victory.

Jerry Rubin attacks HUAC

crossed against the bare sexy chest of a yippie warrior—his body slashed with lavish swatches of red paint. Under his eyes were those black marks baseball outfielders smudge on to dull the glare of the sun. His scruffy hair and beard were so long and straggly that you had to guess he had a neck. He was barefoot and carried a very real-looking large toy M-16 machine gun in his hand. Deliberately he had not bathed in three weeks. God, was he ugly! The nightmare vision of all HUACs, past and present, rolled into one.

My act was low-keyed. I would follow Rubin's opening.

The inner chambers of HUAC presented a perfect stage setting for the skulduggery to follow. Behind a long table sat a row of inquisitors in business suits mouthing prepared patriotic speeches into microphones. In the spectator pews friends of the Committee mingled with our legal team, the demonstration "leaders," and reporters. Abby Mann, who had once been blacklisted by the Committee, had come to watch us finish them off, as had other HUAC watchers. After the opening speeches, things started to come alive. Nancy Kurshan, Sharon Krebs, and other yippies, dressed as witches, began circulating through the room. They busied themselves sweeping the floor, emitting eerie moans, and passing out incense sticks. Jerry began strutting up and down the aisle brandishing his toy M-16 at the Committee and snarling. Lawyers, objecting to points, politely raised their hands. I bounced out of my seat, approached the table, and interrupted. "Can I go to the bathroom?" I asked at the top of my most childish voice. Outside the door I bellowed "BULLSHIT!!" so loud I swear it shook the Capitol. Guards jumped me. "Take it easy fellahs, the fun's just beginning," I cautioned. Not sure of their orders, they backed off. The next day I would make my move.

I rose early for make-up call, and Anita carefully painted the Cuban flag on my back. Boots and buckskin pants of the early pioneer were topped by a red, white, and blue shirt. In exactly two hours I'd do more for the flag than anyone since Betsy Ross.

As our star-spangled retinue approached the hallowed halls of Congress, a detachment of police summoned to the scene quickly encircled us. "You are under arrest for desecration of the flag. Come with us." "Leave him alone," shouted Anita, pouncing on the cop's neck with the fury of a banshee. Instantly the steps became a swarm of cameramen, cops, and screaming yippies. As if an intruder had stuck a hand in the social beehive. I fought for life and shirt, swinging wildly. Rrrrrrrrrip! "You pigs, you ripped my fuckin' shirt," I screamed, transporting my consciousness back to the scene which got me thrown out of high school.

The hearings went on. Anita and I were carted off to jail. The next day I stood before the judge, bare to the waist. The tattered shirt lay on the prosecutor's table in a box marked Exhibit A. "You owe me fourteen ninety-five for that shirt," I mentioned. Bail was set at three thousand dollars. "Get out of here with that Viet Cong flag. How dare you?" the judge intoned. "Cuban, your honor," I corrected. A few months later this same judge started letting his hair grow long, called for the legalization of marijuana, and began speaking out against the war.

Volume 18, *United States Code,* Sections 700 and 711, protects the U.S. flag, the 4-H Club's cloverleaf, and Smoky the Bear from "defacing and defiling." The maximum penalty being one year in prison and a thousand-dollar fine. I was the first person arrested under the newly enacted federal statute. Even so, I find it just as hard as you to believe that "rational" men actually brought this about.

Gerry Lefcourt and I played the trial for all it was worth, basing our defense solely on the First Amendment. The judge deemed it his duty to find me guilty. "Does the defendant have any last words before sentencing?" he questioned, trying to imitate a movie he'd seen. I rose solemnly, trying to imagine myself about to be sent to the death house, and began to pace the floor while lecturing on free speech. I ended with one of my favorite court-room lines. Striking the proper defiant pose, I cried out, "Your honor, I regret that I have but one shirt to give for my country." "Bang!" went the gavel. "The defendant is hereby sentenced to thirty days in jail," boomed the voice high up there on the bench somewhere.

Eventually, at the appeals-court level, we overturned the conviction. By the time we had, over three dozen people had already been arrested for similar offenses. A vest in Virginia. A bedspread in Iowa. All with the familiar flag motif. In arguing for the government in defense of the law, Nixon's prosecutor stated: "The importance of a flag in developing a sense of loyalty to a national entity has been the subject of numerous essays.'' The first essay the U.S. government quoted was a lengthy passage from *Mein Kampf*, by history's most famous housepainter, Adolf Hitler.

Wrapping Yourself in the Flag

The flag and I became a good act. At a college speech in Topeka, Kansas, I had the audience at the point of climax when I shouted out an aside: "Where are the Wichita Minutemen?'' The Minutemen, a right-wing terror group of the period, had made a public threat to castrate me if I entered Kansas. A group of male spectators at stage left raised their hands. Walking directly in front of them, I said, "Your hatred is bad for my allergies. Ah . . . ah . . . ah . . . chu!'' I sneeze-pretended, yanking a flagkerchief out of my pocket to catch the imaginary snot. Their eyeballs did the Wichita Minuteman Shuffle. Apparently the gesture was so shocking they were stunned into immobility. The next day the newspapers announced that the Sheriff, summoned to the scene minutes too late, had issued a warrent for my arrest. It is still outstanding.

The flag shirt played a central role in my most heralded television appearance. That spring I was a guest on the Merv Griffin Show along with Virginia Graham, two hippie stars from the movie *Zabriskie Point*, and an obligatory right-winger, a writer for William Buckley's *National Review*. With me present he was necessary to fulfill the requirements of equal time, although that system never ever worked in reverse.

Virginia was first. She talked about her face lift and knocked the feminist movement. Next the *Zabriskie* hippies came on and Merv asked them embarrassing questions about sex in their Boston commune, and then I came out, wearing a suede jacket with long fringes. After introductions all around I said it was hot under the lights and would anybody mind if I took off my jacket?

"Go ahead," said mild-mannered Merv. When I removed my jacket, Virginia almost clawed off her new face lift in horror. Even Arthur (Fish'n Chips) Treacher managed to look genuinely appalled. Merv tried to pretend he didn't notice I had just unfurled Old Glory.

"I'm sorry this is just a copy of the one I got arrested in," I said politely. "The original is on its way to the Supreme Court for a decision." I then handed Arthur Treacher a joint and he spent most of the interview holding it up and examining it at a distance like it was radioactive.

Merv Griffin has these beautiful clear blue eyes, and as I talked to him I had the impression I could see right through his skull to an imaginary sky beyond. He decided to handle the shirt-shock with a little small talk. But eventually the topic turned from men's fashion to more serious matters. We had a little thrust and parry over the mandatory tough question, "How can you claim there's so much repression in America if you're allowed on my show?" I told him how I had just been given a thirty-day jail sentence, not for *wearing* the star-spangled shirt, but for the thoughts in my head; how Rickie Nelson, Roy Rogers, Dale Evans, Raquel Welch, and Phyllis Diller had all worn similar flag garb on television and in movies; how anyone could go to the fashionable boutique a few blocks from the studio where I had bought the shirt and get one just like it.

Then the right-winger came on, livid even before he sat down. "No one takes you seriously," he said, jabbing his finger at me across nervously smiling Merv, and launched into an incredible chop job. After he had spent himself I said, "Where did you get that tie? It's a nice tie," doing to him what Merv did to me. At least my shirt had some relevance, but I wanted to make a comparison on a fashion level, determined not to pay any attention to what this guy was saying. I wanted to let him hang himself by his own Windsor knot.

By that time Virginia had also recovered. "This is the Theater of the Absurd," she declared. She was furious and started sputtering about what her generation had accomplished in comparison to ours. "We've gone to the moon, we've made great movies, we put on terrific plays" (not only have things gotten pretty show biz oriented, but it's become we-we-we), "we've discovered cures for cancer—'' at which point I prostrated myself in front of her, kissed her feet, and said, ''My God! Virginia Graham has discovered a cure for cancer! Did you get that, *National Enquirer*?''

''We're out of time,'' said a now-desperate Merv, but not before I had the lucky hunch to make him the prediction that my appearance would be heavily edited, just like the incident with the duck on the David Susskind Show and all the other times I had been on television. Of course I didn't know at the time that the top CBS brass would prove willing and witless corroborators beyond my wildest dreams.

The next night we all gathered at our apartment, ready for anything, we thought. Right before the program was to begin a disembodied voice told us that there would be an important announcement preceding the telecast of the previously recorded Merv Griffin Show. Then the screen filled with the image of a very grave-looking man as the voiceover announced, ''Ladies and gentlemen, vice-president of CBS, Robert D. Wood.'' He looked as if he were about to tell us there had been an earthquake in California and all of Los Angeles was floating out to sea. Instead he gave us this caution:

An incident occurred during the taping of the following program that had presented CBS network officials with a dilemma involving not only poor taste and the risk of offending the viewers but also certain very serious legal problems. It seemed one of the guests had seen fit to come on the show wearing a shirt made from an American flag [not true; it was a shirt with a flag motif]. Therefore, to avoid possible litigation the network executives have decided to ''mask out'' all visible portions of the offending shirt by electronic means. We hope our viewers will understand.

The show began. First Graham, then the *Zabriskie* hippies, then me, and at the moment I removed my jacket our color screen went blue, a brilliant, glorious, Dayglo blue. Unknown to millions of viewers throughout the land, the talking blue blank then brought out a copy of Chairman Mao's *Red Book* and said, ''Merv, I'd like to open with a little reading.'' I opened up the book and started in, and he interrupted me, saying, "Oh, you people, you're all alike, every time you come on here—."

"Merv, what are you talking about?" I said. What *was* he talking about? I could have been from Venus. He'd never had anyone with radical views on his show, let alone someone who started reading Mao.

Then I pointed to Mao's picture and said, "Merv, I just wanted to show you this guy. You have all these writers that come on your show that sell books, maybe thirty, forty thousand copies. You know how many copies this guy's sold? He's sold close to a billion—this guy outsells the *Bible* twelve to one! Why don't you get him on your show? You can see by his picture he's a neat dresser and all."

By this time people all over the country had given up peering through the solid blue wall trying to figure out what was going on and started calling their local stations. In all, 88,000 people were angry enough that night to call and protest the censoring. In the following days stores all over the country sold out their stock of shirts bearing the flag motif, demonstrations were held at CBS offices in three cities, and Merv Griffin publicly apologized, saying he had not been told of the censoring in advance. In fact, I was offered two thousand dollars to sit in the audience the following night. I refused, knowing the incident would be laughed off and my personal appearance interpreted as sanction.

As a footnote, McLuhanites will be interested to know *The New York Times* reported my shirt was "blacked out," revealing they did not watch color TV. Audio censoring, of course, was old hat for the television industry as it blimped and blooped its way through the fifties and sixties, but my shirt entered that infamous back closet of TV's Hall of Fame, the one reserved for visual offenses, along with Faye Emerson's cleavage and Elvis Presley's pelvis. What I would give to have been able to eavesdrop on the conference meeting that decided my words could travel the coaxial cable but remanded my shirt to the censor's laundromat. Some fancy hair-splitting must have gone on.

Electronic masking was the phrase born that night, at least for the general public. "Electronic fascism," I countered, and demanded equal time with the talking blue screen, threatening to sue CBS for its other eye.

Nine years have passed, but my censored appearance on the Merv Griffin show is still talked about among television people as a major trauma. Last spring, Virginia Graham appeared once again on Merv's show and she brought it up. "What's 'Abscess' doing these days?" she said. She calls me Abscess. Apparently I'm a nine-year-old boil on her buttocks. Merv was kind. "Now, Virginia, I think he had a right to wear that shirt on the show, and he shouldn't have been censored for it."

There was one final note of irony. Right before the CBS brass came on that night with his warning there appeared a commercial for American Motors in which Uncle Sam, decked out in his Old Glory costume, simonized a gas-guzzler. Perfect lead-in. I couldn't have planned a better one and there was no way I could ever hope to top this appearance.

In December, HUAC resumed its public pillorying of the Chicago protest leaders. Its attack was seriously blunted by the official government study of the events which was to conclude that a "police riot" had occurred. I was not in attendance. As a result of that one-night stand in the D.C. jail I had contracted a serious case of hepatitis. The guards, against my will, had managed to jab a syringe into my arm to extract a blood sample. Eight weeks later to the day I came down with the illness and had to be rushed into the hospital. Doctors, explaining the eight-week period the disease needs to incubate, agreed that that was the incident responsible. We sued the government over the issue, and although we lost the suit, we uncovered a previously unreported hepatitis epidemic in the jail.

The debilitating illness, affectionately dubbed "the yellow peril," dragged on into 1968. That year proved to be a global apocalypse. During May of '68, French students succeeded in triggering a national strike affecting all schools and nine million workers. If it had not been for the meddling of the French Communist Party, the de Gaulle government might have been toppled by people from the streets. In Mexico City, on the eve of the summer Olympics, students assembled in Tlaltelolco Plaza to protest harsh government repression. Police and secret hit squads blatantly moved in and murdered hundreds of unarmed demonstrators. In Rome, Berlin, Frankfurt, and Tokyo, huge rallies attracting twenty thousand or more were organized outside U.S. embassies to protest the Vietnam War. As we prepared to go to Chicago, Russian tanks were summoned to crush a youth revolt in Prague. On army bases overseas and at home, soldiers were refusing military training and combat. An estimated fifteen thousand potential draftees fled to Canada and made it known they would not sacrifice principle to become common fodder in a war they despised. The cry of liberty was heard in almost every country, and in almost every case, opposition to U.S. involvement in Vietnam was the spark that ignited the protest.

If '68 had been great, '69 would prove almost equally fine. The crescendo of the past year's events would crystallize in what the ACLU announced would be the most important trial of the century. But before we move on to the Great Chicago Trial, we had best pause for a brief return to the cultural front and some words on a musical event not equaled since Joshua fought the battle of Jericho.

The Rise of Woodstock Nation

Throughout the spring and early summer of 1969, the growing militancy arising out of street confrontations moved onto the planning boards of movement gatherings and conferences. At an "underground" editors' conference in Ann Arbor, Michigan, Youth International Party activists from communities across the country gathered to map out a post-Chicago strategy. Increased police harassment of tribes and the vamping of hippies by right-wing toughs was so commonplace one could say a national pogrom against longhairs was in process.

Secretly, John Mitchell, the attorney general, through the FBI, was beginning the infamous "dirty tricks" campaign, while J. Edgar Hoover had already instituted a policy of infiltration and disruption on the left. Until Watergate, this policy—although clearly known to us, the targets—would for the most part be dismissed as "paranoia" by the press.

And so when we gathered in Ann Arbor to discuss all this, we came as a culture oppressed. Spirits were high, though. Repression had brought a certain unity between nationalist and socialist tendencies. We were a cultural revolution on the rise while at the same time we were a nation under siege. The hosts of the confab, the White Panther Party, a YIP affiliate, best typified the new stance. Their politics came from their experience on the street. John Sinclair, the chairman, had been sent to prison on a ten-year sentence for passing a lighted joint to an undercover narc. Sinclair had become our Huey Newton—an imprisoned leader. "Free John Sinclair!" became synonymous with militancy. What had happened to John Sinclair was occurring in other communities, and people reported on police forcing haircuts on hippies, gang attacks on communes, warrantless dope searches, pressure on distributors not to handle underground papers, and the banning of rock-n-roll music from public parks. In the past twelve months, something like 340,000 dope busts had gone down, almost all for marijuana. The killer weed has moved onto the center stage of protest. Young people smoked and experienced none of the traumatic effects their parents and newspapers warned against. In Vietnam, just about every soldier was exposed to grass and many, through smoking, came to identify with the antiwar movement. Marijuana subverted the army more than did the organized left. Smoking it made us all, as the Jefferson Airplane sang, "outlaws in the eyes of America."

In Berkeley, a raging street battle occurred. Young people had occupied some vacant lots protesting the university's connection to the war effort. Taking things further than the one-shot rally, they began transforming the lots into a garden-play area that earned the name People's Park. The crunch came when the university realized the park was fast becoming a counterculture institution. Real estate is money, and the university, being a business, forced the police to destroy the park. The people decided to defend their territory and street battles raged for days. James Rector, a young activist on the scene, was shot to death. He was the counterculture's first martyr to die in battle. He was, of course, unarmed.

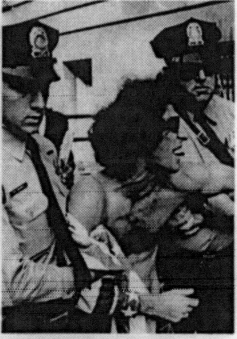

Three out of forty-seven bust shots.
See if you can pick me out.

Wide World Photos. Bob Parent.

The discussion at the conference centered on the need for self-defense. The slogan "Armed Love" expressed the consensual consciousness. YIP exhibited its New Nation flag. Black with a green marijuana leaf superimposed on a red star.

To underscore our new anger, the conference was raided by state police. In an early-morning coordinated attack, troopers wielding shotguns stormed out of the woods surrounding our camp. Kicking in farmhouse doors on the pretense we were training guerrillas, they roughhoused people. A few pot busts occurred, and we underwent the humiliating experience of being forced to line up naked under a row of shotguns. We left the conference determined to bring the war home.

Only two weeks before, I had attended another national conclave. In Chicago, SDS had held its ninth and what was to be its last conference. It had proven to be the most stormy left-wing parley of the decade. After the "shit hit the fan" in the Chicago police riots, SDS proved itself unable to contain the various strains of leftist thinking. Was youth itself a new class? What of conflict between class analysis and factors such as race and sex? Should local organizing be favored over national action? The faction known as Revolutionary Youth Movement I emerged in the leadership by walking out of the conference with most of the participants. The Progressive Labor faction, an anti-hippie, white-working-class-oriented group centered in Boston, was left with the initials and the mere shell of an organization. Under the leadership of Bernardine Dohrn, Jeff Jones, Bill Ayers, Mark Rudd, and others, the so-called action-faction established itself in Chicago. There were now two groups laying claim to the national organization. RYM-SDS became popularly identified as the Weathermen and much of its politics was similar to the Yippies. The Weathermen took youth culture more seriously than the rest of the left.

The Vietnam War was internalized by both groups as "our war," and convincing young people to avoid the draft, desert the army, and fight against imperialism in any way possible were our essential programs. There were, however, great differences. Weathermen could never make use of humor either as a weapon of ridicule or as a counterbalance to one's own fanaticism. Weathermen also saw its members, indeed all white youth, as guilty of "crimes against Third World peoples." This guilt, arising from "white skin privilege" could only be purged in sacrificial blood. White blood must flow to show blacks, Chicanos, and Vietnamese that white kids were serious. Weather politics, when translated into action, were apocalyptic. They burned too many bridges behind them. Kamikaze street fighters, soon to become underground bombers, the Weathermen were to quickly prove that it took more than a courageous few to topple a government.

In April, that spring, the U.S. government announced it was indicting eight antiwar leaders on charges of conspiracy to cross state lines to incite riot. I was privileged to be one of the eight. Jerry Rubin, I, and our yippie cohorts in New York greeted the news with a joyous pot party. When I had thrown myself completely into the movement, by going to New York, it felt like moving up to play big-league ball. Now, three years later, I had been selected for the All-Star Team. There were and would be other trials, but more often than not they were of "figures" such as Dr. Spock, Dan Ellsberg, or Angela Davis. The Chicago 8 was a trial of organizers. We were not known in other fields. We lived and breathed movement organizing. Our politics were based not on any quick conversion but on years of struggle. The Chicago demonstrations were not an isolated incident in our work, but one necessary action along a continuum of legitimate protest.

In recent Freedom of Information Act files J. Edgar Hoover described at length the significance of this showcase trial as a means of intimidating others. One early key memo, dated October 23, 1968, from J. Edgar Hoover to his key Bureau offices states that indictments will soon be brought against leaders of the Chicago demonstrations. He added, "A suggessful prosecution of this type would be a unique achievement for the Bureau and should seriously disrupt and curtail the activities of the New Left."

By targeting organizers, the government had openly declared war on the antiwar movement at a time when factional disagreements threatened our ranks. When we really had no idea what to do "after Chicago," our enemies in the Justice Department gave us a new issue around which to fuel the national forum on the war. Instead of just blaming "Chicago" on the Democrats and getting on to new business, Nixon and Mitchell made a fundamental miscalculation. They picked the wrong place, the wrong time, and the wrong charges. On Chicago we stood not guilty, and we were not about to let Nixon and the courts rewrite history. If a showcase trial was desired, we would be more than happy to oblige.

Looking Back on Woodstock

At the Ann Arbor Conference, everybody was buzzing about this mammoth rock festival scheduled for the following month in the East. "Yes, I heard about it." "No, it was not being held on Bob Dylan's farm." "Yes, I thought New York would allow it." Rumor built upon rumor until I realized something of the magnitude of Chicago was in the making—Woodstock, the small village two hours north of New York City, was about to be replaced by "Woodstock," the event. The New Nation politics evolving at the meeting needed a focus. When culture becomes a nation it requires an army. Our troops lay in that amorphous body of youth, which, especially during the summer months, roamed the land in search of itself. A huge rock concert lasting a few days presented an opportunity to reach masses of young people in a setting where they felt part of something bigger. Liberation. Freedom. Peace. Love. Whatever the song, it needed translation into the experience of a life-style under attack.

On returning to New York I immediately arranged a meeting with the Woodstock promoters. As representatives of the street culture we made certain demands—ten thousand dollars to community groups, two hundred free tickets, the right to set up booths and leaflet the crowd. We wanted to set a national precedent. Surprisingly, the promoters agreed. As it turned out later, they got a bargain. Prepared for a crowd of 70,000 tops, everyone was stunned when six times that number showed up. Neither the movie, the record, nor the book I wrote, *Woodstock Nation*, conveyed the experience of being out there in the woods with 400,000 other people. The myth we believed in was becoming reality. We were not alone. Acres of freaks. No cops. Not a single

The New York School, visibly upset over the indictment for conspiracy to interstate riot. From left: Battling Billy Kunstler, Abbie-Yoyo, Dangerous Dave Dellinger, and Jerry Rubin wearing the Lower East Side Button Shop. For good measure Abbie-Yoyo got arrested again that night.

Somersault. The trial as circus. Chicago Conspiracy proceedings, Fall 1969.

fight reported. New Nation's first test proved a huge success. The greatest musical gathering in history taught us we could be together. We could survive. We could triumph. What most people didn't realize, we were very lucky to pull it off and the Lower East Side "politicos" played a large part in making it happen.

During the first night, as Richie Havens cannonballed through one of his songs, buckets of rain began falling. The torrent continued nonstop. People ran for cover under trees, makeshift lean-tos, or just huddled together in human piles. Meadows and hills were transformed into mud slides as the first-night arrivals sloshed through the fields looking for lost friends and belongings. When dawn crept onto the site, all around were thousands upon thousands of people, wind-swept tents, garbage, and backpacks, covered with mud. Nothing stood on terra firma. Lighting structures, the twenty-foot-high stage, the cars, the people all started one giant slip-slide. On top of this the population was to double in the next few hours as an endless stream of music lovers trekked some fifteen miles to join us. Access roads had become so clogged with vehicles, people had abandoned their cars and decided to get there by any means necessary. "Woodstock or Bust" was the motto. State troopers had sealed off the New York State Thruway, turning away thousands more. Governor Rockefeller convened an emergency Saturday morning meeting of advisors and declared the area a "disaster site." *The New York Times* led the establishment dailies in attacking "this outrageous episode" (drugs, nudity, etc.) headlining it "Nightmare in the Catskills." Meanwhile, locked into the site, a determination to see it through took hold of the crowd. Their "nightmare" was our dream.

The movement folks did not come to just passively sit and listen. Some of the Woodstock bucks had been spent on a printing press we lugged to the festival. Quickly, survival sheets were circulating. We organized people into sharing food and blankets. We kept track of non-polluted water. A group of us ripped down the press tents and constructed an emergency hospital site. We commandeered walkie-talkies, a helicopter, and cots. A few dozen doctors we summoned from the Medical Committee for Human Rights were flown in from the city. We tended to the physical injuries as Wavy Gravy and the Hog Farm handled the bad trips and helped feed people. Within hours a complete field hospital with an operating room and supply depot was established. The pace was fast and furious. There were broken legs and acute appendectomies. There were births and there were deaths. One accidental, one heart attack. The condemning press would try to discredit Woodstock by pointing these out, forgetting the fact that for three solid days we were the second largest city in New York with an accident and death rate far below the average weekend in places a quarter the size. A music festival. An event. A city. And finally a symbol of hope. New Nation had a name, and for years we would be known as the "Woodstock Generation."

Early that Saturday morning I had decided to help make Woodstock a model of community sharing. The cultural revolution had to survive. I had a bullhorn, a box of walkie-talkies, and organizing skills. I printed a phony identification tag that said GENERAL COORDINATOR and took off on my little power trip. Those hours were among my finest, most gratifying, but on a crucial political level I failed, and it's difficult to discuss without making it seem like I'm self-advertising for the "Woodstock Good Guy" award. Let me explain. If you ever heard about me in connection with the festival it was not for playing Florence Nightingale to the flower children. What you heard was the following: "Oh, him, yeah, didn't he grab the microphone, try to make a speech when Peter Townshend cracked him over the head with his guitar?" I've seen countless references to the incident, even a mammoth mural of the scene. What I've failed to find was a single photo of the incident. Why? Because it didn't really happen.

I grabbed the microphone all right and made a little speech about John Sinclair, who had just been sentenced to ten years in the Michigan State Penitentiary for giving two joints of grass to two undercover cops, and how we should take the strength we had at Woodstock home to free our brothers and sisters in jail. Something like that. Townshend, who had been tuning up, turned around and bumped into me. A nonincident really. Hundreds of photos and miles of film exist depicting the events on that stage, but none of this much-talked-about scene. The reason the story got exaggerated and repeated so often in the rock world was because by this time I, too, had become a symbol. A threat to the idea of rock singers as unapproachable, infallible royalty. I was politics personified, and as most in that world like to say, "We ain't into politics." (One incident in this period stuck in my throat. Jerry Rubin was interviewed on the Dick Cavett Show. When he began speaking about the Vietnam War, Cavett cut him off with the line: "Politics bores my ass!" See, the "my ass" made Cavett appear hip, and prevented Rubin from outflanking him on the youth front. Later I pointed out to Cavett that he had numerous senators and congressmen on his show and never once remarked, "Politics bores my ass!") In the world of hip capitalism, the yippies *were* politics, because we threatened their pretense as rebels and leaders of the youth culture.

When it came time for the rock establishment to throw garlands at someone who "saved" the scene they turned to establishment figures like the farm owner who said hippies were okay and pulled down fifty thousand bucks for the rental of his land. The local doctor they hired, William Ambruzzi, became so well-known that he began a career out of lecturing and consulting big rock promoters on how to handle bad trips. A career which finally ended when the doc lost his license. In truth, before Woodstock, the doctor had never in his life witnessed a bad drug trip and he stood around with his hands in his pockets as Hog Farmers and movement radicals took care of those who bummed out.

Fred Weintraub, the Warner Brothers executive responsible for the Woodstock movie, told me they had made a conscious decision in the studio to "purge" anything that smacked of politics from the screen version of events. You weren't allowed to see the infirmaries or known radicals.

"Hey, Abbie, you don't like it? Why not go to Berkeley and cut the screen up—we can use the publicity," he told me. Fred was no dummy. He had fought in the mountains with Castro, even spent time in Batista's jails. Now he worked for Warner Brothers. Thus, while my book portrayed Woodstock as a battle cry to legalize grass, stop the war, and confront a decaying culture, the movie went on to extol the power of rock music and the righteousness of hip capitalism. Only ex-radicals like Fred Weintraub, Jann Wenner, who cut his teeth at *Ramparts*, and Bill Graham, who began by working with the San Francisco Mime Troupe, were clever enough that early in the game to realize rock music could play an important political role. Worthy adversaries in the battle for young hearts and minds, they easily triumphed in the Woodstock image war.

Of course, rock as revolution was one of the era's biggest put-ons. Its high energy got you wet all over. Got you all horny and angry. Made you feel a part of something bigger. But it was not a revolution. Revolutions are not engineered from the studios of communication conglomerates. That is called good business, and the *content* of revolution can never be good for business, only the form. Mick Jagger can sing all he wants about fighting in the streets; he's gifted and outrageous. But he probably inspired more young people to become millionaires than to overthrow the system. Only by making a lot of loot could they ever hope to share in the life-style of the Stones. Loving dope makes you an outlaw, loving rock music just makes you a good consumer. It was only "revolutionary" because we said it was.

Rock is now respectable. The story about the daughter bringing home her shaggy boyfriend whom the father regards as some hippie bum until reminded he makes a million dollars a year playing the guitar is now old hat. Today parents encourage rock-guitar lessons as much as they urge their children to be doctors or lawyers. Large festivals and outdoor concerts have pretty much gone out of vogue. Attempts to do Woodstock II never got off the ground. There is still a rebellious streak exemplified by punk rock. Reggae music, more than any form of rock, has utilized rebellion/revolution politics in the lyrics. There are the outlaw (ha!) country-western singers. The decadence freaks like Lou Reed and David Bowie. And the city rocker-rebels like Bruce Springsteen and Billy Joel. Even Kiss makes the teeny boppers snarl at adult society.

Sexism remains. Women are relegated pretty much to the role of singing canaries, seldom play instruments in groups, and never take part in decision-making. Racism is reemerging in form of the statements of British musicians such as Eric Clapton and Elvis Costello. The mood of the hour is disco. Elegant. Ruling class. Indoors. Expensive clothes. (I just saw a full-page color ad in *Rolling Stone* for diamonds!) Music not exactly designed to promote community or kindle the passion for social change.

It all seems pretty dull. Pretty predictable. After twenty-five

years of rock-n-roll, the establishment has learned to differentiate
bark from bite.*

A Trial to End All Trials

Fugitives travel light. Two suitcases limit what I carry, but I've
managed to save the letter my father sent me the day before the big
Chicago trial began.

September 22, 1969

Dear Abbott,
   On this, the eve of your coming trial, I hope and pray that
you conduct yourself in a respectable manner. For, after all,
the courts of our land are still our way of justice, and when
they lose their respect, what have we left. After all is said and
done, this is still a God given land and as one who has lived
through two atrocities of man's inhumanity to man, this
country has exemplified itself in more ways than one.
   Please stop to realize that your manners and conduct in the
court room will both act for and against you. I am not trying to
be a preacher, but just trying to give you a little advice. As a
parent we still love you and wish you the best.
                                                    Dad

   My father and the U.S. government were the only people who
ever called me "Abbott."
   What's interesting about my father's letter is that he instinctively sensed what the trial was all about before it happened. Sure,
there would be testimony about all the great issues that brought us
to Chicago in the first place, but what made this trial different from

---

*This was written before I witnessed the successful and visionary MUSE (Musi-
cians United for Safe Energy) no-nuke concerts in Madison Square Garden, the
most significant cultural/political event since Woodstock.

other political trials would be our willingness to go outside the accepted form of courtroom behavior.

Once it was demonstrated that we neither feared the court's power nor were impressed with the pomp and circumstance of tradition, all hell broke loose. The Chicago Conspiracy Trial became, among other things, the greatest comedy of manners ever to occur in a courtroom.

If you're ever arrested and put on trial, the first thing the lawyer will tell you is to dress up and keep your mouth shut. It is the public signal that you accept the authority of the court—that you're willing to play the game. Even further, it testifies to your sanity and gives evidence that you belong in society and need not be ostracized. Just before the Chicago demonstrations in '68, I had appeared before one Judge Lynch in an effort to force the city to grant us an assembly permit. "Your dress is an affront to this court," he announced, even before I began the arguments.

There was never any question about changing our dress and general conduct. Is that alone contemptuous? Nothing I've ever read suggests that it is. What the vain, cantankerous judge daily demanded was that we pay him homage. Homage as a symbol: as someone selected to wear the black robes of justice and sit on the bench of what he continually referred to as "the highest court in the land." He deserved our respect because he was "your honor." And he also demanded personal homage as an elderly millionaire-member of the upper class; as a German Jew who had risen to acceptance by the gentile community of Chicago's Gold Coast.

So as the trial proceeded or disintegrated, it became our job to attack the unnatural attitude that persons condemned to prison should respect the system about to deny them their freedom. Put more bluntly, we were supposed to kiss the ass of the ruling class.

By now some twenty books have been written about the trial. There have been several plays, one currently playing in Los Angeles. BBC-TV staged it as a lengthy television drama, which was the most popular show of that year in England. It is a record album. CBS-TV has just announced it will present a three-hour prime time re-enactment of the trial, directed by Jeremy Kagan, in the fall of 1980. Just about everybody had an opinion one way or the other. During the trial, support for us came from all around the world. When we were finally convicted, after nearly six months of toe-to-toe legal/psychological warfare, half a million demonstrators took to the streets making "Free the Chicago 7" one of the most celebrated slogans of the sixties.

It was probably the first political trial in which the defendants (at least some of them) went the nonlinear route of communicating through symbols, gestures, and other means to a television audience. We didn't exactly stage the trial for television, but one could not be unaware of its lurking presence. Millions of viewers saw us, not as we actually were but as cartoon figures sketched by day and flashed every evening into the nation's living rooms. As organizers trying to convince people that their government's policy was in error, we had to realize the limits and advantages of this mode of communication. Television is simultaneous and spontaneous. Cartoons are graphic, exaggerated, and action-oriented. Yippie politics could scarcely conceive of a better means of expressing ideas.

We wanted to reach young people. We wanted to "show" we were different from those prosecuting us. We wanted to present a synopsis of the issues dividing the nation, thereby elevating our cause to equal footing with the government. We could never hope to accomplish this power struggle with arms; we could only begin to manage it with imagery. An imagery designed to force those in between to choose sides. Once involved in the trial, most people quickly allied themselves with either the defendants or the prosecutors (the judge and prosecutors merged). There were, of course, society's guardians, institutions like *The New York Times* and the American Bar Association, which tried to remain aloof by casting a plague on both our houses, but in general we divided the population to a far greater extent than had any trial in U.S. history. It brought us one step shy of armed civil war and proved a fitting summary for a decade of confrontation.

Of all the material I've read dissecting the trial, none captures my own attitude better than a book not specifically about those events but one which views them in the larger context of the Jewish struggle with modernity. The book, called *The Ordeal of Civility*, by John Murray Cuddihy, makes its main thesis in its view of the battle between the two Hoffmans: Julius the judge and myself. Cuddihy fastens on something I said in court after being sentenced for contempt. ("When decorum becomes repression, the only dignity free men have is to speak out.") Cuddihy shows the inevitability of a powerful clash once a Jew like Julius is invested by the state with the authority to put a Jew like me in prison. I could not recommend Cuddihy's book more. It's amazing how well he understood it all, having neither been present nor having met either Hoffman.

I threw every ounce of my being into the trial. Prison? Assassination threats? Really, none of this mattered. What did matter was winning the case before the jury and convicting the government before the world. Right off you could see these were somewhat contradictory. No one who walked with us into the large hall from which the jury was to be selected could say, by any stretch of the imagination, that these people would make up a jury of our peers. That's just so much nonsense. Someone had called a joint meeting of the Rotary Club and the First Baptist Choir, and from this assemblage we had to select our jury. We drew up a list of forty-four interesting questions that would point out the incongruity: Who is Janis Joplin? What do you think of women who don't wear bras? Have you ever tried marijuana? Do you display a "Support Your Local Police" sticker? Of course the judge allowed none of this. In the words of a *New York Times* reporter, they were "Overwhelmingly white, middle-class, and middle-aged." (These words were quoted not in the *Times* itself, but in *Barnyard Epithets and Other Obscenities* by *Times*-man Anthony Lucas.)

The best we could do was to place one person our age on the jury. One day into the trial her family received a mysterious note we were convinced originated with the FBI that said, "We are watching you, The Black Panthers." On examination it turned out that she had no knowledge of such a note so the judge read it to her to make sure she did. Then he proceeded to convince her she couldn't make a fair judgment, and she stepped down. We replaced her with another young person who, as things turned out, had an enterprising boyfriend who not only worked for Mayor Daley but had arranged a ten-thousand-dollar contract with the *Chicago Sun-Times* for her exclusive story right after the verdict (not guilty—no story). John Schultz in "Motion Denied," his investigative report in *Evergreen*, extensively explores the jury's reaction after he had interviewed many members. Four of whom, by the way, felt that they were manipulated by the judge and by a "loaded" juror to bring in a guilty verdict, despite the fact that they believed in our innocence. "We convicted these men for speeches not a single word of which could any of us recall," stated one sympathetic juror after the trial. But aside from all this, the median age of the jury was twenty years our senior, and in 1969, with the country in the throes of generational warfare, how can anybody in their right mind claim we were tried by a jury of our peers? That was our first handicap.

I want to say one more thing about juries—and this jury in particular. Everyone knows we spoke out in court all right. They could hear us in Afghanistan. Under our system of law the jury is perfectly free to ask questions. To question defendants, lawyers, the judge. Many of the posttrial interviews showed the jurors' confusion about the law and what took place in the court, yet for six months they made no attempt to clarify things. It's safe to say of the thousands of juries sitting in the country today that they all sit in silence. They are intimidated by precisely that rigid decorum demanded by the judicial system. The jury is paid lip service as some sacred institution, while the real power passes to the judge. That brings us to our second handicap.

Of course, it's a bit unfair to label his honorable Judge Julius Jennings Hoffman, age seventy-four, millionaire token Jew of Chicago's legal establishment, a handicap. Sure, the judge's reputation was summed up in his nickname "Hang-'em-High-Hoffman." Sure, he ran the court like my grandfather ran his candy store; if you came in the door you were there to buy, said my grandfather, and likewise the judge regarded defendants as customers there to buy fines and time in prison. You think I'm exaggerating: Of the twenty-four trials that preceded ours before Judge Hoffman—twenty-four guilty verdicts had been returned by the juries.

In the course of the trial, our legal team probably raised something like two thousand objections. To the best of my recollection, not a single one was recognized by the judge. On the other hand, virtually each and every prosecutorial objection was sustained. And it's important to point out that of the one hundred and thirty or so decisions in which we felt the judge had made a serious reversible error (any one of which could be grounds for a mistrial) the appeals court agreed with us on *every single count*. The judge didn't need us to goad him into being outrageous. He was outrageous from the opening day on; in fact, his whole judicial history was pretty far out. Again, Freedom of Information Act files reveal serious collusion between the FBI, the judge and the prosecutor. A motion is now pending in the federal courts to punish the judge and prosecutor for their unlawful collaboration.

What's of interest, given the strongly worded reversal of the case, is looking back to see how the media conspired to make it seem that everybody was wrong. For example, the judge often screamed at us, but newspaper editors changed their reporters' accounts. In the newspapers, the judge merely "said," whereas the defendants "shouted." Our lack of civility was measured against the judge's intolerance. Just as we were to politely accept Mayor Daley's decision not to permit us to assemble and protest, just as we were to politely go along with HUAC's attempt to red-bait us and with Attorney General Mitchell's persecution campaign, we were now supposed to politely accept a biased judge. "Don't worry," we were told, "the appeals court will set you free." But the prisons were loaded with inmates waiting for the appeals court, and history is filled with the stories of political defendants unfairly railroaded by judges just as biased as ours. We could no more passively accept the injustice of this court than we could have passively accepted the war we were determined to stop.

But, of course, in his outrageousness and by unwittingly playing the cartoon character (he looked and spoke like Mister Magoo) the judge allowed his racism, his vanity, his isolation from the real world, and his cruelty to breach the surface of his personal decorum. We defrocked him of his sacred black robes (Jerry and I even wore judges' robes for one day) and exposed him for what he was—a schtunk (just one of the many Yiddish insults I threw his way). Now those are harsh words, but they are *not* my personal feelings about the judge. Those are (and were) my public-personal feelings.

Viewing the trial as a theatrical experience, I had great respect for the judge. He was witty, filled with his own sense of drama, and committed to his role with a furious passion. On one tape in our lawyers' possession, the judge, in chamber, is listening to TV news. Cronkite announces that the defense attorneys doubt they can get a fair trial. "I'll show them how prejudiced I can be!" He had forgotten the court stenographer was with him and her tape recorder was activated. The part did not call for a Solomon because the law stunk. We needed a yippie judge who could play in a real-life political version of "The Flintstones." Julie was our man, and together we made it happen. The proof of our collaboration—and it's surprising that no one seems to have commented on this—was that either of us, the judge or the defendants, could have closed down the trial at a moment's notice but chose to see it through. Jail was never a final deterrent for most of the defendants, and our attacks (probably the most flagrant in judicial history) obviously didn't push the judge into ringing down the curtain. Although we defined the play in different terms, all sides decided that the show must go on.

Here's further proof of the judge's conspiracy. By the time we had all assembled in Chicago for the trial, there was only one person in the country who could have controlled us—and that person was Charles R. Garry, the person who was then attorney for the Black Panther Party. To realize this would have required a lot more insight into the inner workings of the left than any outside critics had at the time, or any insiders cared to admit. Judge Hoffman made the whole trial happen when he would not allow a six-week delay because Garry, our chief attorney at the time, required a gall-bladder operation. From my point of view, that gall bladder was a god-send. None of us wanted Garry. At our first meeting he passed us a bill for $375,000, which I folded into a paper plane and winged at Rennie Davis. It wasn't money. It wasn't personal feelings. Garry came from another school of legal defense where defendants weren't supposed to go around up-staging the lawyers. An old-liner, he was, like most of those who preceded us on the left, a cultural conservative. Garry would have kept his distance from us, demanded decorum, and changed the entire dynamics of the trial.

Garry only had one advocate among the defendants. That defendant was Bobby Seale. Seale's inclusion in the indictment was a shocking surprise to us all. He had been in Chicago for just a day and in no way was involved in organizing any phase of the demonstrations. He gave two short speeches as a last-minute

substitute for Eldridge Cleaver, and only one of the other defendants (Jerry) had ever met him before the trial. The only evidence
against Bobby was three or four fire-and-brimstone lines from the
speeches and an airplane ticket proving he crossed a state line.
That you can get ten years in prison for something like that comes
as a surprise only to middle-class white people. It's difficult,
without knowledge of conversations between Mitchell, Hoover,
Nixon, and the gang, to figure out why Seale was included.
Perhaps they included him knowing the evidence wouldn't hold
up, so that when he got acquitted and the rest of us got sent to jail
no one could say the judicial system was racist? Maybe it was
assumed that his "menacing" appearance would help convince
the jury of our guilt? It could have been that the boys in Washington just wanted to get rid of "one more bad nigger." Probably all
these reasons and more went into the decision.

Looked at from our point of view, as organizers trying to bridge
the gap between the races, the indictment of Seale was an added
bonus. It was also good for Seale, because at the time he was
facing a far more serious charge (conspiracy to murder) in New
Haven and exposure in Chicago would build support for that case.
Seale was facing the electric chair, and any decision he made as to
lawyers or general conduct of the trial had to take precedence.
Even if he had not been in that predicament, black movement votes
got multiplied by eight—making the vote 8–7 for Garry. Bill
Kunstler swallowed his big ego long enough to agree to play second fiddle at what would have been Garry's wedding.

The judge, in refusing the delay, not only committed the first
major error that was cause for reversing the entire decision, but he
set the stage for the New York crowd (Kunstler, Rubin, Dellinger,
and myself) to dominate the defense. Garry never dropped out of
the case though. He had to defend Seale in New Haven, and as
chief counsel for the Panthers he couldn't let things get out of his
control in Chicago. Huey Newton and Charles Garry forced the
situation that resulted in the chaining and gagging of Bobby Seale.

Seale, like the rest of us, did not want to push things to the point
where the judge would have to close the curtain, but he decided
that it was "correct politics" to go along with the idea. The
Panther Party, for a variety of reasons—not the least of which was
competitive ego rivalries—wanted Bobby separated from the trial.

It was more complicated than simply personality clashes though, and a lot had to do with black-white relationships in the American struggle. In other words, movement politics. But no one was motivated by these not-so-noble impulses alone. A black man chained and gagged because the court refused him the lawyer of his choice, then refused to let him defend himself, needs no interpreter. Nothing in our trial or in all the political trials of our time could match the power and truth of that moment. What always struck me as particularly interesting was that the prosecutor (and I suppose the government behind him) consistently attacked Kunstler as the manipulator of events and accused us of "using Seale as a puppet." In fact, the controls were entirely opposite. The Panthers controlled the defendants, the defendants instructed the lawyers. See, in the government's head whites control blacks, professionals control clients, but inside the movement, and in reality, the exact opposite was true.

Once Bobby had made it clear he was going to continue interrupting the procedure until the judge allowed him to defend himself, we all knew it was just a matter of time before the judge had to act. Because of the prison threat, outbursts like this were fairly uncommon and not much precedent existed on the books. Federal judges rushed to convene at hastily assembled panels around the country. There were rumors bandied about that we would all be locked up in soundproof glass booths, or that special cells would be constructed behind the court and the trial broadcasted to us. Mostly we assumed the judge would order Bobby bound and gagged, which is what he did. Of course the judge added the right touch of drama by ordering the federal marshals to "take that man out and do with him what must be done." Suspenseful. Ominous. Binding and gagging a human, as it turned out, seemed near impossible and three or four different methods proved unsuccessful. At first it was a simple folding chair with handcuffs and a towel gag. Child's play for Bobby—and he struggled loose within a minute, stood up, chair and all, and screamed, "I demand my rights." Each time the chains got heavier, the gag and bindings more elaborate. Yet each time, no matter what the muzzle, a faint voice demanded to be heard. It was the most remarkable testimony to the human spirit I've been privileged to witness.

Finally, after two or three days of this medieval torture and international embarrassment, the judge had to admit a certain defeat in that he had failed to intimidate Bobby Seale. He sentenced him to four years for contempt and severed him from the case. The Chicago 8 became the Chicago 7, but what happened to Seale was far and away the most significant episode of the trial.

There was much criticism from the left that the white defendants did not protest more vigorously. Even Dellinger wrote of his later regrets. This was Seale's show though, and in the conferences we held each day together, Bobby insisted that we do nothing to sabotage the entire trial at this point. As it was, we accumulated eighteen months' worth of contempt citations for battling the guards and shouting out protests. The tension was so strong it just became impossible not to act. But it was Bobby Seale's willingness to push things to the limits that broke the trial wide open.

This is one of the trial's greatest ironies, because as we prepared to go to trial the Black Panthers were scolding us (Jerry and me in particular) to refrain from creating situations that could get Bobby jail time. They expected us to mock the court, and that expectation was quite justified.

Here's how I came to Chicago to stand trial. It was September. Both Chicago ball clubs were strong and surprising pennant contenders. The first order of business was to establish ourselves as the hometown team. Baseball was the first framework we used to turn the trial into imagery. "The World Series of Injustice," I called it. In New York I contacted Michael O'Donoghue, Chris Cerf, and George Trow, a bunch of wild and crazy guys who were later to start the *National Lampoon*. Terrific satirists. We brainstormed a baseball program (we called it "the official pogrom") and even got the cartoonist who does the Mets' scorecard to design the cover. The Chicago Conspiracy versus the Washington Kangaroos. Rather than deny the conspiracy outright, we attempted to defuse its menacing image by pointing out its derivative meaning—"to breathe together." A good thing.

So we had programs. We made pennants and sweatshirts with the baseball transformed into an anarchist's bomb. I flew to Chicago with a group of twenty-four yippies. Some of us dressed as ballplayers, some women carried cheerleader pompons. Our guerrilla theater began right in the airport. My opening line, of course, was: "It's good to be home." Home? Three weeks before, Ron Kaufman and I had spent the day surveying all the buildings surrounding the federal courthouse where the trial was to occur. If there was a sniper taking aim we wanted to get an idea where the shot would come from. At the beginning all of us believed someone would try to kill us. If you had listened to some of the call-in radio shows or read our mail, this was not an unwarranted fear. So this play-acting, the baseball caps, the pompons, passing out thousands of free tickets on street corners to come and see us, all had another purpose—to allay the fear that we, personally, were a threat to the people of Chicago. It worked terrifically. Not only were we never once physically attacked, we were accepted as local celebrities. People recognized us in restaurants and bought us dinner, cabbies would turn the meter off and wish us well. Any animosity created by the disruption at the convention was blown away by our theatrics.

On the first day of the trial, before entering the ground-floor doors, I did a full-front-flip somersault. I used to be real good at backyard acrobatics, but by then I fell on my face more often than not. This time I was right on the money, landing firmly on two feet. A photographer snapped a picture while I was in midflight, and it was in every paper in the country. The trial was circus—the photo proved it. Later I would be asked about somersaults in front of the judge and standing on my head. Myth. People provided closure and the somersault got moved up twenty-three floors into the court. You get the right story with no concept. Good move, Kid.

My next gesture came as the prosecutor introduced us to the jury. I followed Hayden. He had risen and saluted the jury with a raised fist. The judge jumped on it, cautioning the jury to disregard the menacing fist waved at them by defendant Hayden. Tom argued, but he was not really a match for the judge on this level. When I was introduced next, I rose and blew the jury a kiss. "The jury will disregard the kiss blown by defendant Hoffman," intoned the judge. Of course, one of the courtroom's biggest jokes is when the judge tells a jury to disregard something they've seen or heard. (I can still see the twelve gaping mouths and twenty-four bulging eyes staring at Seale chained and gagged before the jury and the judge instructing them not to notice.) The kiss, by the way, was a real gentle, playful kiss. Hand held horizontal to the floor, below the puckered lips. It was blown across the room. The TV cartoon that night had a string of valentine hearts streaming toward the jury.

There were more gestures. On Bobby's birthday we marched in with a cake. We opened one morning by placing two flags on the defense table—one American, one of the National Liberation Front in Vietnam. This produced a tug-of-war with the marshals. We wore black arm bands to publicize the current National Moratorium. The lawyers wore them too, prompting the prosecutor to accuse Kunstler of being a "mouthpiece" for the defendants. Prosecutor Thomas Foran, a stock villain in our little drama, was straight out of Chicago's past era. He snarled his words like Edward G. Robinson in *Little Caesar*, had a Dick Tracy jutting-jaw which he nervously snapped back and forth. He was the tough police lieutenant always warning Sam Spade he was going too far. In his summation speech he called us "evil men," giving credence to his middle name—Aquinas. It was clear that for the Catholic Democrat Foran this trial was an inquisition. He had a locker-room mentality, and when the trial was over he preached about how we were losing our children to the "freaking fag revolution" and referred to us with antiquated slurs like "scummy" and "faggots."

Schlepping after Foran was another German Jew, the brains of the prosecutorial team, Richard Schultz. What can I say about Schultz. He looked like a kid named Yale Newman that everybody picked on in my grammar school because he was always trying to brown-nose the teacher. Thick glasses, slightly uncouth, with pants that always looked like there was a load hanging in the back. The bathroom debate remains my sharpest memory of Schultz. See, we had to organize around the trial while we were on trial eight hours a day, and we would rotate leaving, on the pretense of going to the bathroom, so that we could make telephone calls and confer with staff workers in the hall. Sometimes we'd just slip out to get stoned. The prosecutors objected to this, so the judge insisted that we go to the bathroom in a jail cell adjacent to the courtroom. Jerry fastened on this issue and at one point whispered (we sat but six feet away) to Schultz that he was about to pee-pee on his foot. Schultz jumped to his feet. "Your honor, the defendant Rubin just threatened to doo-doo on my foot.'' Like I say, the class brown-nose. A tattletale!

Our table was an important prop in our presentation. It was a sprawling mess of letters, books, newspapers, vitamin bottles. We had hundreds of letters delivered to us each day in court, and during the more boring moments we spent the time reading them. Once I got a bulky letter hard to open. I tugged and ripped until it tore open and deposited an ounce of grass right in the middle of our table. We dressed no differently than we dressed in the streets, and all this was a great visual contrast to the prosecutor's table, behavior, and dress.

One of the biggest affronts to the power of the court was our refusal to rise when the judge entered the room during the shackling of Seale. The judge went red with rage over this silent protest. (I think the appeals court eventually agreed with our contention that such an act was protected under the First Amendment.) It was one of the few times we acted in unison. On the baseball scorecard we were all listed as quarterbacks, and even the jury threw out the conspiracy indictment. Asked if we were a conspiracy when I was on the witness stand, I remarked, ''Conspiracy? We couldn't agree on lunch.''

This was not *my* trial by any stretch of the imagination. In an autobiography the pronoun ''I'' is bound to pop up a lot, but one of the great joys of the trial was working with such a great gang. Did you see *The Magnificent Seven*? It's funny because that Western was a remake of the ''Eastern'' *Seven Samurai*, and if you saw us as a contemporary midwestern version of that movie you'd get an idea of how I saw things. Each of us brought a certain personality and skill to the battle. So before going further let me introduce the other guys in the band.

Jerry Rubin you've met. When it came time to begin in Chicago Jerry was a prisoner in California's Santa Rita penitentiary and had to be driven halfway across the country in chains and under guard. What bugged Jerry the most was the haircut prison guards forced on him. We concocted a publicity stunt to draw attention to this gestapo-like practice being used in prisons around the world. Lee Weiner and I posed in barbershop sheets and allowed locks to be snipped off. Behind us, a huge banner announced THE YIPPIE WIG CONTEST, as we called on sisters and brothers throughout the land to vote with their hair. They could, we suggested, send a lock to either Jerry or Julius (our judge) depending on which yippie they favored. Jerry received mounds of hair in the mail, out of which he fashioned a wig. We could only guess whether the bald judge did as well.

Dave Dellinger had a difficult role. He was some twenty years our senior and the only "absolute" pacifist in the group. He consistently took the most principled positions and advocated everything from defending ourselves to going voluntarily into jail to protest. Rennie Davis was the movement's most capable administrator. Blessed with an even-keeled temperament, he knew how to balance the various factions and keep things going. When it came time to present our defense, only Rennie and I would be selected to testify. Rennie would play the good scout, the kid next door who unselfishly mowed your lawn in the summer. I, the neighborhood prankster. A minor nuisance whose neck you'd like to wring but not someone you'd send to prison for ten years.

Lee Weiner and John Froines did not figure that prominently in the trial. There was practically no testimony against them, and in the end they were acquitted on all counts. From the beginning the general feeling was that they had been added in case the jury deadlocked. In such an event Weiner and Froines could be used to bargain for guilty verdicts on the rest of us. They did not alter the power balance within the group since they balanced each other temperamentally and politically. Within the movement it would have been to our advantage if these slots had been filled by women. Kathy Boudin and Judy Gumbo would have done nicely. Tom Hayden was the only central figure who claimed he did not want to be on trial. He considered his work more important and made it clear at the beginning that he would not go off speaking or raise any money for the defense. If all of us had that touch of arrogance needed to be activists, Hayden had a double scoop. He made me thankful there was more than one foxhole on our side of the barricades. He had a movement reputation for sending others to face the cops while he ducked out the back door. He avoided all collective decisions where he could be outvoted. He was absolutely without humor. Tom and Jerry fought like the cartoon characters that shared their names, with the rest of us shuttling back and forth to hold our fragile unity together. I wanted to see us harness all the focus and energy directed toward the trial into an all-embracing left organization. Everyone but Tom more or less favored the idea, and he effectively torpedoed all efforts at unity. During the most climactic moment of the trial, the judge, upset over a newspaper account of a Dellinger speech, ordered Dave's bail terminated. As Dave got dragged off to jail, pandemonium broke out in the courtroom. Later that night we held our most important strategy meeting. Jerry and I argued strongly for standing with Dave and not letting the trial proceed until he was released. Tom's position was that since Dave was a pacifist, he wanted to end up in jail anyway and we shouldn't interfere. His reasoning was as cold-blooded as any I had ever heard. Later, after the verdict and when we were all in jail, another incident demonstrated Hayden's ability to turn fellow comrades into objects. The hour was approaching for our ritualistic haircuts. In my presentencing speech I had alluded to this symbolic act. "Tonight the guards will shear our heads and sell the hair outside the prison walls," I had said. Now that prophecy was coming to collect its truth. I fought them every inch of the way, kicking, spitting, cursing. Two guards had to drag me, handcuffed and in leg irons, down four flights of stairs. Tom was so blasé. To him the counterculture was a joke. He hated grass and rock music. He wore his hair long for "political" reasons. They brought in more guards for me. They stretched me on the barbershop floor. I kicked and screamed. The barber, himself a convict, had tears in his eyes. It was a powerful scene. Tom was happily fixing his assimilated hairdo in the mirror. He kept saying that I shouldn't make such a fuss, just let them do what they had to do. Both prisoners of war, we had opposite ideas about how to cope with the situation. (The sheriff, by the way, proudly displayed our "shaved head" mug shots that night, to the wild stomps and cheers of the county Republican dinner. I assume this was followed by Salome's veil dance.)

Hayden, Davis, and Froines made up one force within the conspiracy; Rubin, Weiner, and myself the opposing tendency. It's no accident the two factions broke on religious grounds. There were other divisions. Our faction was composed of dopers; they drank liquor. (Rennie was a swing vote on this issue.) We were the hairy, hedonistic hippies, they the tough-nosed, intellectual politicians. It was also interesting that Dellinger was seen by much of the country as Jewish (he even got a few anti-Semitic letters), and he enjoyed puffing a little grass with us every once in a while. We even split on eating habits. For them roast beef rare was exotic, for us every meal seemed like the last and we indulged. In psychoanalytic terms, they were anal retentive, we were orally fixated. Murray Kempton once wrote that "There were two kinds of people, those who liked Hayden and those who liked Hoffman." I think these were some of the differences he meant. In its way, the split served to keep the whole show afloat. Like perfectly balanced see-saw mates, the differences afforded us the ability to reach different kinds of people, and we became a kind of political version of the Beatles, each framing the events from his own perspective and producing a total "gestalt" in the process.

Lenny Weinglass was the trial's unsung hero. The workhorse, Lenny had been a strong running back in college, then had channeled his energy into storefront community law in Newark. He was close to us in age, had strong movement politics and a tough legal mind. He was a good balance to Kunstler. When Bill and the judge went head-to-head, psychically it was a fair match up. Somehow, though, it always looked like the judge was picking on Lenny, lecturing him professorially. On at least a dozen occasions he made a point of addressing Len by the wrong name. "Now Mr. Weinruss," he would admonish. Or Weinstein, Weinburg, Finestein, Weinrob, Weinramer, or Fineglass. It was as if the judge were unconsciously dredging up all the Jewish nose-pickers holding back the Tribe's assimilation and laying them on poor Lenny. Once in the elevator, Nicholas Van Hoffman, a reporter covering the trial, overheard the judge remark, "Now we are going to hear from that Wildman Weinglass." To burlesque the judge's obvious antipathy we drew up a placard that said MR. WEINGLASS, and once when Julie did the wrong-name number we held up the sign and paraded around the table.

There were four other lawyers who deserve mention. Michael Kennedy, Michael Tiger, Dennis Roberts, and Gerry Lefcourt. All of Len's generation, any would have functioned well in the trial. They all worked on pretrial hearings but withdrew from the case. The withdrawal, made by telegram, did not follow rigid procedures, although it was a routine practice for out-of-state lawyers.

Right off the bat, on opening day when Seale demanded Charles
Garry as his attorney, the judge picked up on this oversight and
ordered federal marshals in different cities to arrest the lawyers.
This being done, they were escorted back to Julie's court, ad-
monished, and stashed in the slammer. The judge, peering over the
bench, bellowed, ''Mr. Kunstler, the keys to their freedom are in
your hands.'' What he meant was that if we dropped our demand
for Garry he would release the lawyers. Three hundred and fifty
attorneys from all over the country flew quickly to Chicago and
picketed the federal building in protest. It was the largest demonstration of its kind ever held, and it earned Julius national animosity among young lawyers. Although he also got a free trip to the
White House and a slap on the back from Richard Nixon for his
refusal to polycoddle lawyers.

The defense relied on one other lawyer—Arthur Kinoy. A
Rutgers Law School professor, Arthur was Mr. Impossible. There
was nothing the defendants came up with too outrageous for
Kinoy. He figured how we could get Howard Zinn on the stand to
draw historical parallels between our trial and others going back to
the revolution. How Frank Bardacke could explain the relevance
of People's Park. We tried to relate all contemporary events to the
defense, using the witness stand, the galleries, and the press
conference as platforms. We even tried (unsuccessfully) to get one
of the Vietnamese My Lai survivors on to testify. We did manage
to draw attention to the cold-blooded murder of Fred Hampton, the
Chicago Panther leader, which took place while the trial was in
progress. Kinoy helped us plot many of the more creative detours
that fashioned the defense into an experimental workshop for
future political trials.

Of course Kunstler was the central figure in the court. He was
fearless and quick on his feet. His passion knew no limits and he
roared with laughter or wept with tears as a legal system he really
believed in crumpled in chaos around him. The trial changed Bill.
For the defendants it was the events in Chicago '68—the riots in
the streets—that had seemed to sever our connection with the
system. That confrontation made us radicals; the trial made a
radical of Kunstler. How the events registered on him and how he
responded made up one of the trial's greatest dramas. Only Brando
could do Kunstler justice. Someday Bill will write of those times.

He'll have the last (and the best) word, if he can resist the temptation of paying too much homage to left rhetoric.

All our courtroom efforts relied on a very active staff of organizers, law students, fund raisers, and shit workers. At the end of each
day we'd return to our headquarters around the corner and map out
the strategy for the next few days and arrange our speaking schedules, mailings, and other forms of publicity and fund raising. We
screened witnesses and movies to be used in the defense but tried
not to let the trial separate us from our activities in the antiwar
movement. At every opportunity we seized the time to boost
morale and attendance at rallies and demonstrations around the
country. Five or six hours sleep at night was a lot for me. I have
been gifted with a camel's ability to go long stretches with little
sleep. Besides, barring illness, the Russians have proven that
humans can function normally on four hours sleep per night.

The government's case was pretty cut and dried. Mostly it
consisted of the testimony of Chicago city officials, police, and
FBI undercover agents. In all, seven government agencies sent
undercover agents to testify—everything from the Cook County
sheriff's office to Naval Intelligence. They included a TV news-
man from San Diego who doubled as an FBI informer, a wire-
service photographer from New York working with the feds, and
good old George Demmerle, a John Bircher who somewhat successfully infiltrated the New York yippies.

"Infiltration" has a much heavier ring to it than what actually
happened. We were not operating out of underground cells but
were an open democratic movement. Infiltration often meant nothing more than attending a speech or a meeting. All an infiltrator
had to prove was that he or she was in close proximity to a
defendant. As far as the testimony against me—it was fabricated.
My speeches were public and well recorded, but no recording of
any of the things I supposedly said was presented. Even if I had
said things like "Tomorrow we're going to storm the Hilton and
not let the blank pigs stop us," that type of speech is protected in
the Constitution. (If it isn't, how come I wasn't charged under the
tougher state laws against inciting riots?) When it comes to informers, it's your word against theirs—and if they don't return

with some evidence they didn't do their job. There was no hard evidence, like, say, a cache of Molotov cocktails or printed leaflets. The prosecution failed to offer up even a single "dupe" (that is, a demonstrator who was one of us but ran to the police because we were criminals). But, given the asinine, untested law, there really wasn't that much to prove.

Our defense ran the panorama of movement activity. We threw in everything, hiding nothing. From Quaker pacifists to lovely Linda Morse, who told of practicing with her M-16 rifle in the hills of Berkeley because of what happened in Chicago. We presented testimony from singers: Phil Ochs, Country Joe MacDonald, Judy Collins, Arlo Guthrie, Pete Seeger. We tried to work the tight, restrictive questioning into a line where they could end up singing. This often led to riotous situations. Judy Collins closing her eyes, letting loose in full voice, "Where have all the flowers gone. . . ." The judge ordered the marshal to clap his hand over her mouth. That's a nice cartoon for the evening news—Judy Collins with a federal marshal's hand over her mouth. She was gagged in another way. A few days later, on "The Dick Cavett Show," she was prevented from talking about the trial because it could influence the jury. A phony excuse—the jury had been sequenced since the opening day of the trial and was not allowed to watch television or read newspapers. My favorite trial-singer episode was the repartee between Arlo Guthrie and the judge as Kunstler pushed for "Alice's Restaurant" and the judge agreed to allow it. "Be brief," he lectured, unaware that "Alice's Restaurant" was a shaggy dog story-song lasting some twenty-five minutes. The judge quickly got the point, ordered Arlo to talk the rest, then to summarize, and finally to be quiet. At every occasion we had to twist and bend the testimony to conform with the Q and A format of the courtroom. We brought in poets, playwrights, comedians, eyewitnesses, even a member of the British Parliament. Hundreds of people volunteered to be witnesses, but we couldn't accommodate everybody. We even turned down a liberal congressman—Allard Lowenstein—who begged to be allowed on the stand. We felt he wanted to use the occasion to further his own career. Not many defendants turn down a congressman.

Ralph Abernathy, Martin Luther King, Jr.'s successor, arrived fifteen minutes late and the judge refused him permission to go on.

Wig contest to see if Jerry or Julius Yippie could receive more locks. Hair today, gone tomorrow. The guy with the glasses is Lee Weiner.

Chicago Sun-Times photo. Reprinted with permission from Field Enterprises, Inc., September 26, 1969.

The Full Chicago 10. Inset—Bobby Seale. See if you can identify My Hero, the Architect, Rosencrantz and Guildenstern, the Mouthpiece, the Comedian, the High Priest, the Candidate, the Workhorse, the Sex Expert. Some of us were guilty, some were not. Label each.

United Press International. Wide World Photos.

Ramsey Clark, who had been attorney general of the United States
when the demonstrations occurred, was also refused. This was
probably one of the judge's most outrageous decisions. Even *The
New York Times* busted his balls on that one. Imagine barring the
country's chief prosecutor, the person who knew most about the
intelligence reports, about negotiations. Of course, it was public
knowledge that Clark did not believe we should have been on trial
and held the Chicago police responsible for the riots.

Here's the opening of my own testimony:

DIRECT EXAMINATION OF DEFENDANT ABBOTT H. HOFFMAN BY DE-
FENSE ATTORNEY WEINGLASS.

Q. Will you please identify yourself for the record.

A. My name is Abbie. I am an orphan of America.

. . . .

Q. Where do you reside?

A. I live in Woodstock Nation.

Q. Will you tell the Court and jury where it is.

A. Yes. It is a nation of alienated young people. We carry it
around with us as a state of mind in the same way the Sioux
Indians carried the Sioux nation around with them. It is a
nation dedicated to cooperation versus competition, to the
idea that people should have better means of exchange than
property or money, that there should be some other basis for
human interaction. It is a nation dedicated to—

THE COURT [Judge]: Excuse me, sir, read the question to the
witness, please. (*Question read*)

THE COURT: Just where it is, that is all.

THE WITNESS: It is in my mind and in the minds of my brothers
and sisters. We carry it around with us in the same way that
the Sioux Indians carried around the Sioux nation. It does not
consist of property or material but, rather, of ideas and certain
values, those values being cooperation versus competition,
and that we believe in a society—

MR. SCHULTZ: This doesn't say where Woodstock Nation,
whatever that is, is.

MR. WEINGLASS: Your Honor, the witness has identified it as
being a state of mind and he has, I think, a right to define that
state of mind.

THE COURT: No, we want the place of residence, if he has one, place of doing business, if you have a business, or both if you desire to tell them both. One address will be sufficient. Nothing about philosophy or India, sir. Just where you live, if you have a place to live.

Now you said Woodstock. In what state is Woodstock?

WITNESS: It is in the state of mind, in the mind of myself and my brothers and sisters. It is a conspiracy . . .

Q. Can you tell the Court your present age?

A. My age is 33. I am a child of the 60's.

Q. When were you born?

A. Psychologically, 1960 . . .

. . . .

Q. Can you tell the Court and jury what is your present occupation?

A. I am a cultural revolutionary. Well I am really a defendant—

Q. What do you mean?

A. —full time.

It went on like this for days. Once the judge ordered me to answer a prosecutor's question and I took the Fifth Amendment. "It's nothing personal, judge, I just always wanted to do that. Something for the Rosenbergs." Somehow this threw things out of kilter and I had to take back the Fifth. Feigning compliance with the judge's instruction that I must answer the question, I remarked, "In all my years on the witness stand, judge, that's the worst ruling I ever heard."

Another time, dueling with Schultz on the cross-examination, the prosecutor read some lines from *Revolution for the Hell of It* (which he always menacingly termed "your handbook for revolution"). I had described a visit I made to an abandoned apartment building near Lincoln Park and how if rains came we could have occupied it. I guess that's intention to illegally trespass.

Schultz was pressing on my state of mind:

Q. And what were your thoughts at the time?

A. I'm not sure what you mean by thoughts. Is that like dreams?

Q. Yes, like dreaming.
A. Well Mr. Schultz this is difficult. I've never been on trial for dreaming before.

Much of the trial consisted of us reacting to some off-the-wall remark by the judge, such as the time he questioned a prospective black juror who stated that his wife had worked for the prosecutor. "Oh, was she a domestic?" he inquired. She had been a legal secretary—and no more racist remark could be imaginable. One of us or another would comment, not letting many of these insults pass. Once Dave rose and addressed the judge as "Mister Hoffman," explaining his democratic tendency not to address people with formal titles. I remembered something Saul Alinsky once told me about negotiating with government officials and how on occasion you could undercut their power advantage by using their first names. Following Dave's lead-in, when it came my turn to yell at the judge, probably during the Seale chaining, I called him "Julie." From that point on, he and I fashioned our own little battle—the war of the two Hoffmans. Later, when he addressed me as "defendant Hoffman," I informed him that no longer was that my name and that I had dropped it as it had been disgraced. To the press I announced plans to legally change my first name to Fuck. When the judge sent Dave behind bars in the final days of the trial, I really exploded. "You're a disgrace to the Jews. You would have served Hitler better," I screamed. "You *shtunk*!" And then, in the sharpest thrust of all, I called him a "*shanda fur de goyim*" which roughly translated is a Yiddish expression meaning "frontman for the gentiles."

His reactions were very strange and ambivalent. With a mixture of sadness and resentment, he still seemed to regard me as his wayward grandchild. He ended up giving me only eight months for contempt, the shortest time of all the main actors—even though, with the exception of Seale, I was the most disruptive. There were some days when Jerry and I would commit what seemed the same outbursts. Rubin would draw six months, I but a few days. It was only one of the many mysteries surrounding a trial which ten years later is still being argued in the courts, and will for some time to come be debated in law schools and dramatized on the stage. I have seen recent statements by Jerry Rubin saying that we were guilty, but he's just being sensational in order to make some philosophical points. We should never have even been indicted. One of the time twists was that by the time we were on trial in Chicago, we often were indeed intent on inciting riots and disrupting the system by any means. In fact, we used the trial to organize a coast-to-coast riot on the day after we were found guilty. It was not true, however, that we originally came to the convention with those intentions. In my closing speech I quoted from Lincoln's famous inaugural address of 1861:

> When the people shall grow weary of their constitutional right to amend the government, they shall exert their revolutionary right to dismember and overthrow that government.

Then I said, "If Abraham Lincoln had given that speech in Lincoln Park, he would be on trial right here in this courtroom because that is an inciteful speech." I believe that to this day.

Now the trial is a part of history, but the participants have been persistently tracked as signposts in a changing world. Foran and Schultz are still a team, carrying on a successful law practice in Chicago. The prosecutor who followed Foran and tried us on the contempt charges is now the governor of Illinois. His predecessor was Daniel Walker who authored the government report terming what had happened in 1968 a "police riot." One of our press liaisons, Don Rose, just engineered Joan Byrnes' upset victory as mayor of Chicago and is currently active in the Barry Commoner campaign for president. Mayor Daley, Hubert Humphrey, Lyndon Johnson, and J. Edgar Hoover have been subpoenaed to that Great Courtroom in the Sky. I hope they all have good lawyers. Richard Nixon was run out of the presidency in disgrace, and everyone in his administration responsible for our trial went to jail.

The judge, as peppy as ever at eighty-four, still occasionally sits on the bench in the twenty-third floor courtroom that served so well as a stage for our trial and has become one of Chicago's tourist attractions. I am told Julius speaks fondly of me, and he should know my feelings are likewise. Tell him I said all those nasty things about him just to sell books, he'll understand. The stenographer made several hundred thousand dollars selling transcripts of the trial and, later, of not one but two tape recordings. Len Weinglass is part of a movement law commune in Los Angeles. Bill Kunstler continues to defend unpopular political causes even in an era when it has become unfashionable. Bobby Seale ran a close race as Black Panther Party candidate for mayor of Oakland in 1974, then left the party but continued as an activist/writer living in Philadelphia. John and Lee work in Washington for the government. Dave is now a coordinator for Mobilization for Survival and as active as ever in movement politics. Jerry wrote an extremely honest dissection of his movement life, *Growing Up at 37*. In fact, he was a bit too tough on himself for my taste. He's now happily married and has finished a book on male sexuality with his life-partner, Mimi Leonard.

Rennie Davis is learning economics for a Denver-based insurance company. He underwent a conversion to the kid from India who's supposed to be God (and what kind of God does America deserve after Vietnam?). Hayden desperately scrambles to deny his radical background in his current rush to join the mainstream of Democratic Party politics, taking as much of the anti-nuke movement with him as he can manipulate. I have nightmares in which he and Prosecutor Foran share a bottle of scotch and reminisce about those "scummy faggots" who had no respect for the system.

As for myself, in a way I got lucky. Forced to be an outlaw, I never had to face the life crisis confronting my comrades. Either that or I had to face it in such totality that the anxieties of the seventies passed overhead. It's as if being underground helped me escape the radioactive clouds of neurosis polluting the atmosphere. The government solved my identity problem by insisting that I become someone else if I was to survive. They should know I'm surviving and then some.

The Road Show

During the trial we were swamped with invitations to speak on campuses, at rallies, and at benefits. With a little seed money I set

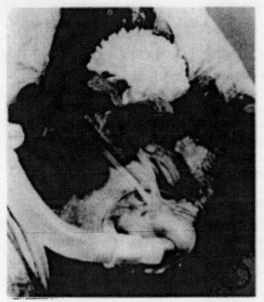

These hospital photos are interesting. The top is Yippie Pneumonia. A hoax. Judge Julie refused to give us a long Christmas week so when called as a witness, I got instant pneumonia. Yippie doctors snuck me a phony culture to convince the government quack it was real. Two days later I made a miraculous recovery. The tube is filled with laughing gas. The lower photo shows the result of a nose job performed by the Washington police in a back alley. It was the fastest, cheapest one I ever got. It was real and it hurt.

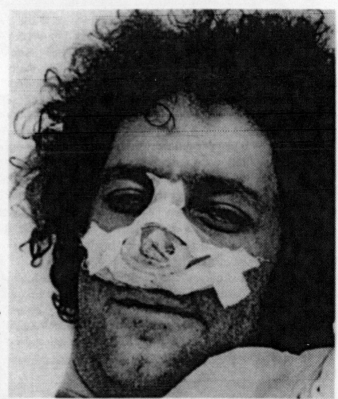

up something called the Movement Speakers Bureau. It followed my notion of alternative distribution. I wanted to spread out my "drawing power" to help get more exposure for lesser known folks who had something to say. It worked pretty well until one day I picked up the paper and saw that everyone running it back in New York had been busted on a bank-bombing charge. They were caught *en flagrante* shall we say, Molotov cocktails held high. I knew absolutely nothing about such carrying on but sweated things out for a while. The bureau's office was in a ground-floor pad next to the precinct house on 5th Street. The same night I was arraigned on the Chicago Conspiracy charges, I got a late-night call that three people crashing there had just been taken next door and arrested. I pulled on my boots and went over to investigate. Bang! "Sorry, Abbie, but you're under arrest."

"What the hell for?" I responded.

The story turned out to be something like this. A guy walked into the office with a suitcase and asked if he could store it under the desk for a few hours while he got a bite to eat. Half an hour later the neighborhood coppers were pounding on the door. Surprise! Inside the suitcase was a collection of guns, silencers, grenades, and heroin. Everyone was busted. I wasn't there. The apartment was leased in Anita's name. A dozen people had keys. I had never even seen silencers and heroin before. One of the phoniest of the phony busts I ever took the pipe on, all charges were summarily dropped in pretrial hearings. The judge even warned the arresting officer that something fishy was happening on 5th Street. How do you think my parents reacted to those headlines? Grenades. Heroin. Silencers. I did add a nice touch though. When they led us away in chains from precinct house to paddy wagon, I managed to pull my jacket over my head, blocking my face from the TV cameras. You know, Mafia style. Even Bill Jorgensen, who hadn't cracked a giggle during the marijuana mail-out caper, laughed at that gesture.

A few months later another strange scene took place there. This sharp-lookin' dame came in, offered me a joint, and before not too long was making what we lustily used to refer to as "improper advances." A glance? ESP? Who knows? I grabbed her handbag, yanked it open, and there whirling away was a little tapey-tapey machine. Talk about ripped-off sex object! I was furious. Teary-

Anita, Nancy Rubin, and Tashia Dellinger burn judicial robes in defiance of court's ordering us to prison, February 20, 1970. Wide World Photos.

Anita and I: tearful reunion coming out on bail, Chicago, February 1970.
Wide World Photos.

eyed, she confessed that she was researching an article on what it was like "to do it with him" for one of those pulp mags. I really suspected "cop" but didn't know how to explain the incident—given women's liberation and all. Prying secrets loose with sex and dope. Have they no shame, I ask you?

So the office/pad had a history of surveillance, and it was a long way from paranoia to think that the place had been wired for sound and was not too ideal for planning a bank bombing. The Movement Speakers Bureau folded when the staff went off to prison. I threw in with a national campus agency and soon was crisscrossing state lines left and right, bringing word on the trial and resistance to the Vietnam War.

My speaking style was suited to the mood. It was a far cry from the style used in the teach-ins of previous years. "Free speech," I once remarked, "is the right to shout *theater* in a crowded fire." Halfway between performance and lecture, I spoke "talk-rock" and paid attention to the rhythm as much as the lyrics. Fire leaped from the tongue. Theory. Organizing tips. Some factual stuff on the war and news about the counterculture. What's generally referred to in the popular press as "rhetoric." I'd juice it up with cuss words, slogans, timely jokes, info on the local movement, and calls to action. Spontaneity sprang both from the stage and the audience as the boundary between the two became less distinct. Often I would sit in the audience and come up to the stage unannounced to speak as "one of the crowd." A hand microphone allowed more mobility. During the question period (renamed "answer period") I would roam the aisles and at the final applause would clap and cheer the audience as was the custom in socialist countries.

I tried never to play on the audience's guilt, and instead appealed to feelings of liberation, a sense of comradeship, and a call to make history. I played all authority as if it were a deranged lumbering bull and I the daring matador. Well versed on the legal limits, I'd plant the sharpest banderillas I could dream up, reaching straight over the horns. I got nicked and whacked a jolly-good number of times but if you saw me, you would have said, There goes someone who loves his work. Impulsive and outrageous, the message was disruption. "There are over seven million laws in this country— We aim to break every one of them. . . . including the law of gravity.''

I remember standing on the stage at a college on the border between Ohio and a neighboring state. "Over here," I said, pretending to be in Indiana, "you can get five years for smoking pot, but over here [in Ohio] you can get forty years." Of course, I wouldn't just say it. I'd walk it out, puffing on a joint. Three thousand people in the auditorium were generally more protection than even a sharp New York lawyer. But not always. I gave a speech at St. Joseph's College, and when it was over the Indiana State Police drove me to the border with the warning that if I ever returned I'd be arrested on sight. At Rio Grande College, a cat with my name on it was hanged on the campus before I arrived. In upstate New York, I spoke at Adelphi College—the American Legion had asked everyone in the town to display the flag as kind of a mid-American purification rite. I drove down the main street in an open convertible, waving like an astronaut running for Congress. After the speech I was driven to the next college, Genesee, but en route our car was stopped at a roadblock. Police yanked me out of the back seat, pounded me, and said I'd be dead if I talked that way again. I gave the same type of speech that night, pointing directly at the cops who had roughed me up. When I was finished I asked everyone to accompany me to the nearest airport. A convoy of a few hundred cars escorted me to safety.

Often a sponsoring group had to fight the administration to permit me on campus. There were dozens of sit-ins, expulsions, firings of faculty, and such which preceded or blocked appearances. I was denied permission to speak in my hometown of Worcester until finally, under pressure, Holy Cross College relented. Hometown boy makes bad. Six thousand people crowded into the field house. The conservative alumni were furious and the school lost a million and a half dollars in canceled pledges. In many cases, the school administration laid down the condition that the student lecture committee, in order to get me, had to agree to invite a right-winger as well. William Buckley and Lester Maddox were my shadows. They got several speaking dates because administrators forced them on the student body. Both the Merv Griffin and Dick Cavett shows I was on were also forced by management to include a conservative spokesman. The opposite, naturally, never held true. I knew no case of a left-winger being given a speaking date to "balance" a program or schedule.

I was once invited to the University of Alabama to debate Governor Wallace but was prevented from entering the state because the state legislature had passed a law keeping me out. Instead a telephone system was rigged up that would allow me to be present. While Wallace was speaking, a coffin was brought up on the speaker's platform. It was labeled FREE SPEECH and sported a wig. All of a sudden my voice came out of the coffin, challenging Wallace from the grave.

I was banned in several other places. Thirteen state legislatures, primarily in the South and West, actually passed resolutions forbidding me to speak. In Oklahoma the ban was fought by the ACLU. It took two years and cost some five thousand dollars but was ultimately successful. I finally spoke in Oklahoma, and the speech served as the basis for a federal indictment. New Hampshire tried to ban Dave Dellinger, Jerry Rubin, and me from speaking at the university. The students fought it with a strike. The governor was facing an insurrection and finally relented—a move which cost him the next election. At the airport in Boston, state officials posing as students tried to escort us to New Hampshire to speak in the afternoon. Some alert students had followed them and managed to monkey-wrench their plans by tipping us off. The actual student rally was scheduled for that night. The officials had planned to trick us into speaking to a small daytime crowd and then to hustle us out of the state before nightfall. Our speeches that night sparked a statewide college and high-school strike against the invasion of Cambodia. The students who arranged our talk were kicked out of school. At Colgate the ROTC members and fellow jocks had surrounded the campus chapel where I was to speak. Attacked by members of the football team, I ended up stabbing myself in the ass with some old dagger Paul Kantner (who had come with Grace Slick to hear me speak) had slipped me for protection. I managed to get through somehow, and the show went on. The blood was running down my leg and I lowered my pants to do a little first aid. I delivered part of the talk while holding the wound closed with my ever handy flagkerchief. Next day the local prosecutor tried to arrest me for attempted murder, indecent exposure, and flag desecration. Gerry Lefcourt, however, managed to convince him to do otherwise, on the promise I'd never return.

I gave two speeches in Canada and was promptly banned from the country on grounds of "moral turpitude." Which, although it sounds like something old men get charged with for looking up the dresses of schoolgirls, is a Canadian legal version of Catch 22. We later had a facedown on the border.

I went to the University of Miami to speak. When I was in college, Miami was one of those schools that had a reputation for being a top party school. It hadn't changed. They actually offered courses in basket weaving. The scene on the campus was so far out, it looked like we ourselves had planned it and then discarded it. The CIA and the Secret Service were everywhere, for the summer White House was about four miles away and Tricia Nixon was there with the measles. The crowds were full of paid Cuban *provocateurs*, and on the sidelines the jocks were screaming, "Love it or leave it, love it or leave it," and two or three hundred movement people were lined up in front of the crowd, shoulder to shoulder, shouting, "Power to the people, power to the people," while about five thousand spaced-out Miami students milled around, not understanding anything that was going on.

Meanwhile, Anita and I were up on the stage dodging tomatoes and other flying objects and people were coming up and beating the newsmen and in the midst of all the craziness I was making a speech. While I was telling them about my acid trip in the Fontainebleau Hotel a middle-aged woman, dressed Florida suburban-chic, came up on the stage and started hugging me. "I'm your cousin Eleanor!" she said. "I haven't seen you in twenty years. How've you been?"

Later repercussions included thirty arrests and the firing of the Miami TV news director. Through some fluke, he had allowed the nightly news round-up to include three thousand students chanting "FUCK THE JUDGE!" They said the oranges fell off the trees that night.

At Georgetown University, I was threatened if I appeared at a student rally. I brought along a bullwhip for protection. Before I spoke, I asked for a volunteer to come on stage and sure enough this mellow-looking hippie fellow all in white obliged. I propped a

cigarette in his mouth and stood back. *Crack! Crack!* Don't ask me
how, but I plucked the cancerette right from his lips—clean as a
whistle. I had never tried anything like that. The Georgetown
headstompers got the message and refrained from charging the
stage. At Queens College I spoke protected by forty or so helmeted, club-bearing students standing guard against some hardhat
platoons.

Unfortunately the FBI so far has denied me access to the several
thousand pages of surveillance and harassment files which must be
revealed under the Freedom of Information Act. Several research-
ers are now in the process of documenting that period, but it would
have been apparent to anyone accompanying me that the feds did
everything they could to prevent me from making speeches anywhere but at the more liberal schools. As soon as it was learned that
I was scheduled, the local FBI office would notify campus officials
that they would be in attendance to record every word. They would
try to scare the schools into canceling me as a "threat to the general
safety and well-being of the community" with tales (mostly false)
of riots that followed in the wake of my appearances. They were
forever knocking on the door of the Boston lecture bureau that
handled me.

Often there were provocative incidents that had a phony ring.
They often requested information on the student leaders responsible for inviting me. One time at the University of Kansas, black
militants disrupted my talk and attacked all "honkies" with such a
broad barrage of unreasoned arguments that it appeared something
was behind their provocation. Often local reporters were "tipped"
as to "factoids" about me that wouldn't look so good in print. And
on one swing through the Detroit-Cleveland area, each school,
radio, or TV station had been sent a smear sheet on me beforehand.
Only my lawyer and the federal court system (a parole require-
ment) knew my exact schedule. Obviously the federales had a
finger in this dirty trick.

I have heard one story, from released FBI reports researched by
Stew Albert, that you might enjoy. At the University of Buffalo, I
mentioned casually that I had among other things that week
"fucked Kim Agnew," the vice-president's teenage daughter. It
had just the right edge because at the time she was dressing in

semi-hippie garb, into the ecology movement, and being photo-
graphed with Indians. Interdepartmental memos show the FBI
debating how to handle this rather delicate piece of intelligence.
Everyone knows what happens to the messenger who brings bad
news to the emperor. At first the FBI agents consider destroying
the tape, but that's rejected because another department is sifting
through the words to see what can be worked into a federal case.
Then someone offers an idea to circulate the speech to other
government branches anonymously. That, too, is rejected. Finally
it's decided to hand-deliver the tape to Spiro, let him hear it first
and decide how to proceed. Of course, no one wants to make the
actual delivery. Eventually, something or someone called the
Liaison Division is given the assignment without being told what is
included on the hot tape.

Right after this episode, Papa Agnew exploded with a rash of
references to me. Now, any public-relations adviser would tell you
the vice-president of the U.S. ought not to refer *by name* to some
street agitator whose professed aim is to overthrow the government. But there was Spiro berating "Abbie Hoffman and his ilk,"
chiding me to take a bath, or suggesting that I be chased with a
butterfly net rather than a television camera. At the time, of
course, I had no idea it was the remark about Kim that lay at the
root of the attack. I responded by publicly challenging Agnew to a
golf or tennis match, the two sports he favored. I added that if he
beat me, I'd shave my head, and take back everything I said about
him and Nixon. If you want to know what really happened between
Kim and me, you'll have to wait for *her* autobiography.

In spite of all these obstacles, I managed to speak at scores of
rallies and campuses in places few radicals had ever ventured.
West Virginia. Iowa. Arkansas. Northern Florida. All in addition
to the traditional stomping grounds of the Ivy League colleges and
big-city schools.

The wildest tour of all took me through the heart of Texas. I
spoke at an antiwar rally in Dallas while a coalition of right-wing
groups paraded around with welcome signs saying nice things like
KILL THE COMMIE JEW. In Austin, the largest crowd in campus
history, some twelve thousand, crowded into the gymnasium,
spilled into adjoining buildings, and massed on the lawn outside.

A huge photo of Agnew was hung upside down from the rafters. Cowboys ran across the stage, pulled their pants down, and "mooned" the crowd. People lit up joints, ran into the aisles to set their draft cards on fire, stomped, cheered, and threw their stetsons high in the air. "A hoopin' 'n' a hollerin' " I think they call it there. Later a sorority girl on a national talk show compared me to Hitler. "Why, everythin' ah believe in cam apahrt when that man spoke on ah campus. I had tears in mah eyes for Texas," she said.

The climax of the Texas tour was Houston. "Don't go to Houston," everyone said, "you'll never come out alive." The papers had been filled with warnings every day. A week before, the underground FM radio station had been bombed for its leftist politics. G.I. organizers trying to get soldiers to form a union had been ambushed by rifle fire as they drove in from the airport. I had been invited to speak at Rice University. When the student council made it known, the Klan firebombed the student union. Alumni spokesmen put on the pressure, and the president took it upon himself to cancel the invitation. In retaliation, students had swarmed into the administration building to engage in the school's first sit-in. The president, caught between his liberal inclinations to let me speak and financial pressures, resigned. A conservative organization, meanwhile, went into court and secured a restraining order prohibiting me from setting foot on campus. The police had made it clear they would not be responsible for my safety.

"Jeff, are you sure this is necessary?" I asked my old comrade. Jeff Nightbyrd was solid Texas. He had first been a national leader of SDS, then moved to the Lower East Side where he founded *Rat*, the gutsy underground paper. When the women's movement led to a staff revolt, Jeff went home to Texas.

"Yeah Abbs, we got it pretty well covered. You can't back out. The local movement's countin' on it," he answered. The local people had arranged a large antiwar rally in a downtown Houston park and a talk that evening at a night club in the black ghetto. The night club's owner had made the committee agree that there could be no advertising the event until three hours before I spoke. We flew to Houston. As I got off the plane I was quickly surrounded by twenty longhaired folks carrying shotguns. Two guys in karate outfits were introduced as personal bodyguards. There were no police in sight. Quickly I was rushed to a waiting van and instructed to lie face down on the floor. The windows had been blackened out. Vans took up positions on each side, and on signal we began our little parade to the downtown rally. A reporter from the bombed-out station kept trying to get a microphone under my face. "So how do you like Houston?" he asked. Everyone seemed to be taking all this matter-of-factly. The vans drove right up to the stage, the doors flew open and I jumped out, grabbed the microphone, and sang a few bars of "Midnight Special." ("If you ever go to Houston, you better walk right / You better not stagger, you better not fight.") And gave a funky antiwar rap. Then we were off again. At a stopover at the underground newspaper, a carload of Klan types whizzed by and let fly a steel-tipped arrow from a crossbow. Thing came right through the damn window and imbedded itself in the concrete wall. Whoosh!

Next stop was the Holiday Inn. The committee had rented three rooms. Me and the squadron of bodyguards were checked in and the whole floor was sealed off. Half an hour later we got a call saying the next arrow was going through my head. Someone went out for some Big Macs and then it was showtime. Off we sped to the night club.

I was ushered through a back entrance to avoid the head stompers who had quickly congregated in the front. I spoke behind a line of bodyguards. Jeff introduced me by presenting the steel arrow someone had managed to pry out of the wall. "A memento of your trip to Houston," he cracked. Halfway into my rap, a Neanderthal struggled to his feet and managed to yank a rather large Luger out of his pocket. I was quickly thrown to the floor and people threw themselves on top for protection. The karate team flew off the stage and disarmed the loony before he could get off a shot. I was starting to realize why Jackie Kennedy never went back down there.

Next morning I walked onto the campus in violation of the court order and gave a short impromptu speech. "I really hate to leave y'all, just when I was startin' to feel like ah was homefolk," I drawled. I ended with the motto of the Texas Rangers: "Little guy'll whup the big guy, long as the little guy's right and keeps on a comin'."

Rags to Rags

During this period, I became something of a "brand name." That is, if someone performed a particular type of act, someone else would write that it was "just like Abbie Hoffman." My hairdo, or rather non-hairdo, became, like Gloria Steinem's glasses and Bella Abzug's hat collection, an object of national concern. It was imitated by both men and women, and at one point a national barbers' association offered a reward to any member who could coax me into submitting to a haircut. (Reporters' most persistent philosophical inquiry seemed to be, "Who did your hair?" "Oh I just lay down on Second Avenue and let a truck run over it.") I was voted one of the four sexiest men in America by *Mademoiselle* magazine and was winning all sorts of popularity contests on the radio. In addition to all the adjectives you'd expect to read in the daily newspapers like "shrewd," "cunning," and "dangerous," I was probably the only professed revolutionary ever referred to as "cute."

Now there are those among you who will say I deliberately played to the gallery, and if it makes you feel any better I'll go along with that. Once I met a psychologist at the University of Miami who had been hired by the government to "analyze" Jerry Rubin and me. "What did you come up with?" I asked. "You're an exhibitionist," he replied. The study cost twenty-three grand and I would have gladly saved the taxpayers' money by admitting something like that right up front. We tried to build a popular movement. By definition we projected ourselves into the public eye just like politicians, clergymen, artists, actors, and athletes. I really doubt there's ever been a society that craved entertainment to the extent ours does. Maybe the later days of the Roman Empire with its circuses and orgies could match us, but even then there seemed to be more direct participation, fewer vicarious thrills. There's something about glossy magazines and color television that demands "personalities." I never agreed with Andy Warhol's much repeated dictum that soon we'll all be famous for fifteen minutes. True, with a Polaroid camera most Americans can take a decent snapshop of themselves, make Xerox color copies, and send them to friends. Only a very few people, like Andy, are ever going to earn millions of dollars at it, and only a small number in any society are ever going to get even their fifteen minutes' worth of fame. The reason Warhol's pronouncement rings true to him and his crowd is because they all *are* famous for fifteen minutes or more. Café Society *is* café society whether it's tuxedoed or blue-jeaned. Radical chic or fascist chic. Fame is for the "beautiful people," with beauty of course being rigidly defined—usually by some fellow traveler like Truman Capote. Fame is for the "talented," yet that, too, is dependent on the mood of the marketplace. Just about the only constant seems to be money. Fame and riches go together like Princess Grace and Monaco. If you're rich, it's relatively easy to make yourself famous—and if you're famous, it's just as simple to become rich.

I never tried to turn fame into dollars and neither did any of the other movement celebrities I knew. The opportunities that existed were among the most inventive contradictions any capitalist society ever contrived. It is indeed possible in the good old U.S. of A. to be wanted equally badly by the FBI and Universal Pictures. I did sell the screen rights to *Revolution for the Hell of It* for sixty-five thousand dollars (a decent price ten years ago) but the day after I got the check, Jean Genet guilt-tripped me (in another language no less!) into giving most of it to the Black Panthers. I donated twenty-five thousand to their bail fund and it vanished along with one of their members on trial. That was the most money I ever had in my life. The Infernal Revenue Service grabbed off twenty thousand and what didn't go to agents and lawyers ended up in my lap—about twelve thousand total. Most of my speaking fees went for trial expenses or were given outright to groups. The IRS stalked us with unrelenting perseverance. I was audited on an average of twice a year, and Nixon used the IRS most effectively during those years to recoup the bucks we managed to shake loose from colleges and publishers. Their harassment was highly selective and politically motivated. A few years ago Jerry Rubin received a letter of apology for IRS "dirty tricks" and shady tactics during that time.

I'm sure if I was above ground I would have received the same letter.

If I had desired though, I could have become a millionaire in 1970 with surprisingly little effort. Here were some of the more bizarre offers for doing little more than signing on the dotted line: There was a novelty item gaining some popularity at the time—a box that did nothing but laugh for three minutes. If would lend my name to the gadget, the manufacturers would allow me 1 percent of all gross sales—an amount my lawyer estimated at "six figures." Two other manufacturers wanted to do an "Abbie Doll," and one even wanted to market it as part of a set along with a policeman doll. Get it? The Abbie Doll always gets busted. I was offered ten thousand dollars to allow a researcher to compile a "Dear Abbie" collection of letters I had been receiving. I would have actually gone through with this but a women's staff strike against the prospective publisher caused me to cancel the deal. A Robin Morgan gut-check. There was a twenty-thousand-dollar offer to let this same publisher reprint my trial testimony (which was public information anyway), but again I said no.

One day a Humphrey Bogart type in a trench coat cornered me with an offer to "process" me into the highest echelon of Scientology. He didn't try to hook me on any spiritual arguments, but rather made it clear it would be worth my while financially. Leacock-Pennebaker, the filmmakers who did the Bob Dylan documentary *Don't Look Back*, offered me fifty thousand dollars up front plus 35 percent of the profits if I would let a camera crew follow me around for only three weeks. There were several poster offers.

Right off we're talking maybe half a million without me even doing much. Then came the offer for "talent." Movie roles, records, and, of course, books. I could just about "name my price" for a book on the trial. Random House, which had done very well with *Woodstock Nation,* regarded me as the "house freak." Not only did I write okay, in their minds, but I had showed them how to design and market my book for less money and in half the time than were standard. It was suggested that I head up a counterculture section of the company.

At one point, my lawyer felt I should at least consider going the commercial route, and he arranged a secret meeting with a vice-president of the William Morris Agency. Step-by-step the marketing plan was spelled out to me, the potential new "multitalented property." It was a plan guaranteed to put me in the "top tax bracket." The thinking behind it was not that much different from what goes into any other packaged celebrity. You have to remember that there was a culture explosion going on that had caught big business by surprise, and old-line firms were desperately trying to be hip. Discotheques such as the Electric Circus were offering seminars on the counterculture to executives. Ad agencies were climbing over each other to corner "freaks." I even recall one dinner at Max's Kansas City, our favorite watering hole, where execs were given love beads and other psychedelic paraphernalia to fondle. Attending were representatives from such blue chippers as ITT, Dow Chemical, Chase Manhattan Bank, and the U.S. Army.

The people who sponsored this dinner offered to back a newsletter I would edit/write. It was to keep subscribers (at a hundred bucks a whack!) abreast of "things happening in the youth scene *before* they happened." I mean, they were suggesting that I actually become a spy on the counterculture I was helping to create!

Given today's attitude toward personal gain, it may seem hard to imagine, but I accepted none of these offers and told Gerry Lefcourt to hang the "not for sale" sign in the window. Self-righteous you say? Perhaps, but again you have to remember the times. Thousands of people rejected the money lure. A crazy heir to millions, Michael Brody, became a national folk hero when he announced (where else but on "The Ed Sullivan Show") that he was giving away all his money. There even existed the notion of "the righteous dealer," someone who gave a large percentage of his take to the community. All the activists turned away from round-the-clock groveling for the dollar and wore that rejection as a badge of honor.

There were some "legitimate" uses of the "name" that deserve mention. Soldiers being sent to Vietnam were routinely given a ten-thousand-dollar life-insurance policy. By filling in my name (or that of another known antiwar activist) as beneficiary, their departure was inevitably delayed and in some cases they were actually kept stateside. A young sailor stationed in Maryland once wrote me that he had second thoughts about it all and no longer wanted to be shipped overseas. Could I help? I called him up and we worked out the following scam. I wrote his commanding officer a letter that went something like this (the envelope was formally addressed to the rear admiral):

> Dear Frank:
> It's been a while since I saw you in New York. Hope you enjoyed those free tickets to *Hair* and had a good time with the girls from the cast. I'd like to ask you a personal favor. You have under your command one Ensign ————— who is about to be shipped to the Far East. Everyone in New York is really upset because he is a key person in this LSD ring we have working down there in Maryland. It would really hurt all we are trying to do if everything got screwed up just because some dumb bureaucrat saw fit to transfer the guy. I'd appreciate anything you could do, and I'll be at your service next time you come aboard the Big Apple and need another good time.
>
> In solidarity,

I signed it with my name and dropped it in the mailbox. All's fair, so they say. A week later, the ensign called me. "Fantastic!" he bubbled out. "All hell's breaking loose down here. They had me up before a panel of inquiry and I got thrown out of the navy." He couldn't stop repeating that he was eternally grateful. I don't even think it was illegal, but in any event, I never heard from the rear admiral or the navy about the matter.

Just about the same time, I got a message to call Gracie Slick from a safe phone. I did as instructed and Gracie, all excited, ran down one of the wildest dating proposals I had ever received. "How would you like to take me to the White House?" she asked.

"To the White House, Gracie? What the hell you smokin'?"

"No, I'm serious," she continued. "See, I went to this fancy school, Finch College, and guess who was a classmate? None other than Tricia Nixon herself. Seems she's invited all of us over for tea, and I thought we could think of something if you came as my escort."

I readily accepted and we agreed to rendezvous in Washington the night before the caper. I got my funeral suit out of the closet, and with a combination of water and hairspray I was able to mat down my mop and fashion it into a style acceptable to Nixon's White House. A little trimming and I was what my parents would have called "halfway presentable." When it was time, Anita and I grabbed the shuttle down to Washington and checked into a hotel. Once we were all together, I laid out a plan. "When we get inside, let's start rearranging the furniture. I'll unwrap this Woodstock Nation flag I've secreted around my body and we'll hang it on the wall. We'll just announce the new government's taken over and we're movin' in."

"Is that all?" responded Gracie, somewhat unimpressed.

"What you got in mind?" I queried.

"Look, an opportunity like this comes down the pike once in a lifetime. I see myself as a member of the ruling class. It's assumed I can be trusted. You know the history of the Russian Revolution—when it came time to storm the Winter Palace there had to be someone on the inside to unlock the gate. I'm that someone," she offered. I could see she had given this escapade more thought than I. "So what I say we do," she continued, "is douse the bloody fuckers. Douse 'em, I say!"

"With LSD?" asked Anita.

"Exactly!" she said, pulling out a vial and emptying the orange powder on the table. "Owsley's finest, damn it, but it's worth it," she exclaimed. "We'll push it under our fingernails, anyway. Just let's get it in the punch bowl."

A silent hush came over us. Paul Kantner interrupted the silence, "See, I've got my chauffeur outfit. We'll rent a limousine and drive over in grand style. It will be the dousing of the century." Anita and I answered in chorus, "Far fucking out!"

The next morning we drove to the proper gate. Gracie and I, invitation held high, stood in line for the processing. Uh-oh! Snafus. Seems so many classmates have responded that only the women are being allowed in. Gracie starts to argue with the guards. Next Pat Nixon's press secretary is there and rules that Gracie's see-through blouse is unacceptable attire. More shouting. "Isn't that . . . !" shouts a reporter, and the jig is up. I quickly pull the flag out from under my shirt and start climbing the White

House fence until I can fasten it to the top. Guards pull me down.
Sometimes the best laid plans of mice and rock queens go awry.
Ah Finch!

Steal This Author

One of the reasons I was keeping my distance from all those out to
package me was that I had had my own idea about a project for
quite some time. Ever since I had written and distributed the
survival handbook called *Fuck the System*, street people had gone
out of their way to keep me up to date on the latest rip-off scams.
When I was a teenager that was the sort of information I loved to
hear and pass on. I remember one summer at the beach when we
listened attentively to some traveling guru as he demonstrated how
you could fashion a clothes hanger into a tool that when pushed
correctly into a telephone coin slot released any money deposited,
giving you free calls. When I brought the idea back to my local
pool hall, someone showed me another trick. "Watch this," he
said, pulling an oversize thumbtack out of a box he carried in his
pocket. Expertly he pushed the point through the telephone cord
and rubbed it against a nearby metal pipe. Magically the dial tone
signaled that the phone was engaged. Of course, both these
techniques were, by the late sixties, outdated. The phone company
keeps abreast of all these schemes and spends millions researching
foolproof phones. The same goes for shoplifting, free travel rip-
offs, and any other form of thievery. Both the bank and the bank
robber have to keep up with the times, with the prize going to
whoever stays one step ahead. Morality seems to enter the picture
only when individuals interact with each other. It's universally
wrong to steal from your neighbor, but once you get beyond the
one-to-one level and pit the individual against the multinational
conglomerate, the federal bureaucracy, the modern plantation of
agro-business, or the utility company, it becomes strictly a value

judgment to decide who exactly is stealing from whom. One person's crime is another person's profit. Capitalism *is* license to steal; the government simply regulates who steals and how much. I had always wanted to put together an outlaw handbook that would help raise consciousness on this point while at the same time doing something about evening the score. Besides, there was the challenge of testing the limits of free speech.

Jason Epstein had been my mentor at Random House. A smart guy who popularized, if not invented, the "quality" paperback. Jason knows just about everything there is to know in the publishing racket. He was in Chicago every day, writing a book about the trial. "What's it about?" I'd ask him. "Oh, it's irrelevant," he'd explain, lamenting the fact that Western civilization was rapidly drawing to a close in the rice paddies of Vietnam. He knew that no interest really remained out there in the marketplace for carefully reasoned thought. The era belonged to the action freaks. It was under his and his wife Barbara's suggestion that the *New York Review of Books* diagrammed a Molotov cocktail on its cover. A certain despair had gripped the Eastern literati, and he personified it. A brooding man who offered living proof that intelligence is often a curse. Someone who has learned to rise above his principles.

Jason leaned over his bow tie and asked what I planned to write next. "Jason, I'm going to write a book no one will publish," I said. He was laughing uncontrollably. "Abbie, you could piss on paper and some publisher would lick it up," he said. Jason and Random House had already given me the title. *Steal This Book*. I had put the same three words on the back cover of *Woodstock Nation*, and when the first hundred thousand copies went into the stores, the booksellers hit the roof. "Tell 'em to steal from the banks, tell 'em to steal from the phone companies, tell 'em to steal from anybody, but don't tell 'em to steal from me," they chorused. On the second printing Random House removed the troublesome slogan. This violated our contract, and I let them know in no uncertain terms. Back went the phrase and back came the bookseller complaints. The book went through nine or ten printings, some had the slogan, some not, depending on which

side yelled the loudest. The battle whetted my appetite for trouble.
No one could censor a book title. So I began the new book with a
title and a challenge.

Enter Izak Haber. Young Mister Haber offered his services as a
bodyguard and legman for a book project based on an expanded
version of *Fuck the System*. He and his girlfriend arrived with ·
shotgun in hand and moved into our small rooftop apartment. He
was unwanted by society. I was his hero—he said he would take
the first bullet. His "original" research turned out to be material
copied verbatim from existing texts. He had simply collected and
typed it all up as "his" work. I confronted Haber. "Nobody will
know. Who reads that stuff?" was his reply. My opinion of the
gentleman was rapidly deflating; besides, Anita couldn't stand
having them sleep in the kitchen. I sensed a fight brewing and had
him label all the pages. Across each and every section he penned
"taken word for word from ILS Handbook" or "the complete
mini-manual by Marighella." In the end, less than twenty pages
were original, and even those ideas had come from an ad I placed
in underground newspapers requesting suggestions. He got a
lawyer. The notes were examined and all agreed Haber deserved
no more than a small percentage as a researcher. I would continue
the research and write the book. We signed a contract. Exit Mr.
Haber. He had been around less than five weeks before he left for
Europe. A year of writing and research lay ahead.

I traveled cross-country interviewing doctors, fugitives, dope
dealers, draft dodgers, private detectives, country communalists,
veterans, organizers, and shoplifters. Every time I met someone
living on the margin I asked about a good rip-off or survival
scheme. People love telling how they screw the establishment.

Some of the research was original. One day while turning on
with the Video Freex, a New York media collective, I asked if it
was possible to pirate an image onto network television. Curiosity
flickered faster than a strobe light. Equipment was bought, tests
made, and one evening while David Brinkley was analyzing the
news, a couple fucking appeared on a number of sets in the Soho
area of downtown Manhattan. Eureka! It worked. The Video
Freex freaked, gathered up all the equipment, and hid out. "But
we saw the fingers of the monster move," I pleaded. It was no use;

their equipment and license were more precious than jewels. The technique lived on, however, in the pages of *Steal This Book*. (Later this group managed to tap into the cable going from Madison Square Garden to a control center and steal a complete video print of the Ali-Frazer "fight of the century." The plan was to broadcast the fight over regular network facilities after the sign-off but again they feared repercussions. We ended up showing free screenings at the local bar.)

One night a pale shadow of a fellow found me on the streets. He whispered into his cuff that he had something to show, someplace cool. In a nearby movie theater, he produced from his pocket a two-inch ivory plastic cube with four prongs sticking out of one side.

"So?"

"It's a device."

"A device for what?"

"When you put it on your phone, incoming calls are free."

"What's your name?" I asked.

"Just call me Bell, Dave Bell, I'll be in touch."

It wobbled in the outlet but it worked. We bought a hundred devices for movement groups throughout the country. Finally I talked Bell (half the phone phreaks adopt the name Bell) into giving me the wiring diagrams, which I printed in the book. This was the outer world's first peek at phone-phreaking.

Notes for the underground chapter were provided by fugitives, living out the trip. Most of the sections, however, had to do with legal activities. How to run a cheap farm, set up a newspaper, organize a demonstration, perform first aid, hitchhike, equip an apartment with furniture. I invented many of the survival techniques, although most were revisions of street lore. It looked strange seeing rip-off scams, generally passed by word of mouth, catalogued. In part, the book was a tongue-in-cheek parody of America's appetite for how-to manuals. It was rewritten several times, trying for more simplicity, greater clarity. I wanted it to be a book young kids would like. Something for people who never read books. Finally it was finished. Nothing like it had ever been written. Chris Cerf was my editor at Random House. He championed the book to the top of the house but the house said *nyet*. Bennett Cerf's son quit as a result. Random House would do the book only if I agreed to several changes. I remember the scene in Jason Epstein's office. "But Jason, you're censoring my book," I complained. Jason got all red and puffy. "Random House does not censor books!" A hush came over the room as we played liberal scrabble looking for the right word we could all live with. Jason broke the silence. "We edit, that's it. Random House edits books."

Thirty publishers rejected it next. Oh, there were offers. Change this, change that. Mostly change the title. One offer of forty thousand dollars up front if the proper changes were made. You had to be crazy to refuse. I was definitely crazy. Publishing companies felt the phone company or the government would stop the book's distribution through lawsuits (they never materialized). All agreed the book would make money.

Enter the Rev. Thomas King Forcade. I approached Forcade in December of 1970, just before I entered jail in Chicago for a few weeks' rest. Forcade offered to arrange publishing and distribution of the book. He had some minimal experience, being the founder of an underground news service. My two weeks in jail were spent finishing the book's introduction. When I returned, Forcade had concluded that a distribution system outside the mainstream was impractical and that he couldn't fund such a venture. He wanted eight thousand dollars for two weeks of editing. "!@%@/!" I replied. "I'll sue," he said, rejecting a take-it-or-leave-it offer of fifteen hundred dollars. Exit Mr. Forcade. Temporarily.

Enter Grove Press. If I could raise the money to publish the book myself, bring them one hundred thousand finished copies, and bear all legal risk, they would serve as distributor. On fifteen thousand dollars borrowed from friends, I founded Pirate Editions. Layouts, designs, more loans, typesetting, and paste-ups were arranged. Ads were composed and sent out. Rush, rush, rush. Finally one hundred thousand books packed in cartons labeled STEAL THIS BOOK began making their way around the country. As head of the publicity department, I sent copies to reviewers. Zero reviews. As head of public relations I gave away two thousand books to movement groups. Every underground newspaper was sent a signed letter authorizing them to reprint the entire book and sell it locally as a fund raiser. British rights were given free to an Irish civil-rights group. "No go," said Scotland Yard and banned the book from England. There was a pirated Spanish edition. A French-Canadian edition free. The Japanese bought the rights for just one hundred dollars and sold some fifty thousand books.

Back in the U.S., half the distributors refused to carry the book. Cartons were being shipped back and forth. Many were disappearing. The Benjamin News Company in Montreal was raided by the Royal Canadian Police with a search-and-seizure warrant. Four thousand copies of *STB* were confiscated. For the first time in history, Canada had banned the importation of a book for other than porno reasons. The Mounties always get their book. Campus stores were a wasteland—Yale, Michigan, U. of California, even my alma mater, Brandeis, refused to carry the book. The Harvard Coop refused. The *Harvard Crimson* scolded them. The store revised its policy and agreed to carry the book if it was kept in the manager's office and sold on request only. Libraries across the country banned it. In Coldwater, Michigan, Richard Rosichan put it in the stacks. He was summarily fired. In Rochester, New York, the library battle raged for months. Angry meetings, with over seven hundred people attending, were held. The libertarians won. The book stayed. Similar battles were fought in Indiana, Connecticut, and Iowa. In Lansing, Michigan, the police caught two guys running from a vacant building whose door had just blown off. A copy of *STB* was found on them, and the police tried to indict me on a conspiracy rap. In Granada, a small island in the Caribbean, the prime minister arrested opposition leader Maurice Bishop on a charge of illegal possession of ammunition. When the police kicked in Bishop's door they found a copy of *STB*. The government charged that this was proof of foreign involvement in a plot to assassinate the prime minister. This year Bishop took over Granada. (Hey, Maurice, remember the tunnel of love, if you read this, how about asylum?)

In Oklahoma, some watchdog of the faith filed a class-action suit for four million dollars against me for "corrupting the youth." The director of corporate security for AT & T tried to get "fraud perpetrators" to confess they had come under the influence of *STB*. He blamed me, personally, for a ten-million-dollar increase in the number of phony credit-card calls! William Buckley's *National Review*; Jarvis Tyner, head of the Communist Party Youth Division; and Frank D. Register (*sic*), executive director of the National Association of Retail Grocers; all accused me of contributing to inflation because shoplifting raised prices. How's that for consensus!

The Department of Interior called a press conference and denounced the book, saying they no longer gave away any free buffalo as reported. They had received over three thousand requests. The R. T. French Company announced they no longer lent out a free film on parakeets. They had to hire a full-time secretary to answer letters. Henry Kissinger's home phone number was typeset inaccurately. Some poor bloke was getting weird calls at night from would-be political groupies. He sued. We settled. Mr. Bloke was two grand richer. I got letters that began, "Well I followed your advice and got busted—please send me bail money." Assemblyman Robert E. Kelly of Brooklyn introduced a bill making the publication of *STB* and similar rip-off materials a Class A crime. The bill breezed through the New York state legislature. Twenty-seven states passed laws, as a result of the book, restricting the publication of information about ways to cheat the phone company. Proving the movie *President's Analyst* was more fact than fancy, AT & T spent over a million dollars lobbying for these bills. As far as I know, none has been tested in the courts. Corporations petitioned the Federal Communications Commission and the Federal Trade Commission to stop the book, with no response. E. J. Korvettes' security manager told the *London Times* that the shoplifting section was mandatory reading for its new employees. AT & T told *The New York Times* that "a team of lawyers was researching ways to stop the book."

With the exception of a small radio station in Boston, everyone rejected a radio commercial I made for the book. Many, including WCBS and WNEW in New York, hid behind supposed FCC regulations. The FCC issued a statement saying the stations misinterpreted the rules, but they still refused all ads. With the sole exception of the *San Francisco Chronicle*, no daily newspaper would accept an ad. *The New York Times* acceptability department wrote me that the *Times* would refuse to advertise a book that advocated illegal activity. I received the letter during the week the *Times* was busy reprinting the Pentagon Papers! The *New York Post* rejected an ad even though the book was listed for eight weeks on their paperback best-seller list.

Grove estimated that half the books were being sold in New York City. In Pittsburgh, no stores would carry the book. In Philadelphia, only one store would—and it charged a dollar more than the cover price. No books could be found in Boston when I took reporters on tour. None in the San Francisco Bay area either. The entire Doubleday chain of bookstores was boycotting the book. A Doubleday vice-president said, "We don't want to tell people to steal. We object only to the title. If it was called 'How to Live for Free,' we'd sell it." Grove reported that half their outlets refused to carry the book. They said that no book since *Tropic of Cancer* had met with such a boycott.

Then we got a break. Dotson Rader wrote a glowing review of the book in *The New York Times*, in which he chastised the *Times* for refusing the ad. I clipped the review, wrote a check, and sent it to the *Times* as a new ad. They rejected their own review! The review did, however, shame a few stores, and some buckled under customer pressure. People actually started boycotting stores not carrying the book. As head of the promotion department, I criss-crossed the country appearing on talk shows and giving inter-views. I would take a reporter to a bookstore and engage resisting owners in a dialogue. In Boston, *Globe* reporter Bruce McCabe gulped when I ran out of a store lugging a huge art book that I stole because they refused to stock my book. A Judge Liebowitz tried to pressure a New York afternoon television show into canceling me as a public menace. He failed. In Baltimore I taped a show with two shoplifters, but management refused to air it, prompting some of the staff to quit.

Experiences with *STB* taught me remarkable things about the media. I hired a clipping service to keep track of the publicity campaign. The distortions and lies were astonishing. In Boston, for example, I was asked what I would do if someone stole something from me. I responded, "Well, I certainly couldn't call the local constable, could I?" That's how it read in the *Boston Globe*. The Associated Press translation read, "I would call a cop, of course." The translation was a big hit and hundreds of news-papers ran stories saying "Abbie Would Call a Cop." Editorials followed, "See, We Told You So. . . ." I collected scores of

clippings and compiled a newspaper account of me made up
completely of fabricated stories which I read to the first More
Media Convention in New York. It began, "Six-foot two-inch,
blond-haired Miss Abbie Hoffman, age forty-two, leader of the
Communist Party, left his fashionable East Side Manhattan penthouse. . . ." The whole media image of me as a swashbuckling
radical millionaire was just incredible. At the time, we lived in a
$135-a-month, two-and-a-half-room railroad flat on one of the
worst blocks on the Lower East Side. I owned no property. Not
even a car. Never invested a penny. Never had more than a few
thousand dollars in the bank and three children I was struggling to
support. In the press, I was constantly seen with movie stars I
barely knew in fashionable uptown haunts I'd never been to. One
account had me wearing a four-hundred-dollar suit in a Chicago
bar and drinking with Eisenhower's press secretary. I had only met
the guy on a TV show, never frequented bars, and aside from the
funeral suit all my other suits were in the courts. It was nothing to
pick up a newspaper and read about how I was playing tennis with
Mario Puzo even though I never met the man.

Aside from this, there were other hassles. I was categorically
refused any credit on general principles. The local supermarket
assigned a special salesclerk to follow me up the aisles. Airline
officials took me into little booths for examination. Foolishly I
stated in the book that I knew two foolproof ways to fly for free but
couldn't mention them. I got two hundred letters that began, "You
can trust me never to tell anyone." In all, I got about fifteen
thousand letters, most of which said *STB* was the letter writer's
favorite book or asked how to get a copy.

It was about this time that Izak Haber returned from Europe, and
a few days later I heard a rumor that *Rolling Stone* was about to
publish a story by him as to how I stole *his* book. I called *Rolling
Stone* and offered to show them all the notes, my several hand-
written manuscripts, and our contract. They said they had decided
not to run the piece, but a week later it appeared on the newsstands.
It was the pits of jaundice journalism! *Rolling Stone* said I could
have equal space, which on closer examination meant I could drop
a note to the letters column. You know, the part of the paper that's
in microprint. I offered to let them take pictures of the fabled

penthouse they talked about. The whole apartment would have fit
in Jann Wenner's bathroom! Meanwhile every newspaper in the
country echoed the story. My favorite hero was turning into
everyone's favorite hero sandwich. Naturally, all the talk of lawsuits was ridiculous. Haber and I never spent a moment in court.
He never wrote anything, then or ever. In fact I later learned he
hadn't even written the *Rolling Stone* piece! Reenter Forcade.

Well, Forcade's threat to sue *was* carried out, but I got the idea
we should have a people's court with agreed-upon arbitrators to
settle our differences. It was mutually agreed on, of course, but the
headlines read "Abbie Accused Before People's Tribunal." On
with the hearing. Tom wanted the eight thousand bucks. I re-
offered the original fifteen hundred. After three weeks of arbitration the people's court reached a decision. Abbie to Tom—one
thousand dollars plus the right to print, at his own expense, ten
thousand books and the right to try to sell them in places other than
bookstores. Forcade rejected the book offer and the people's court
reconvened and awarded him fifteen hundred dollars in total. It
was exactly what I thought his services worth, and I was delighted.
The press verdict the next day read "Abbie Guilty!" It was even
announced on national television. They assumed since Tom was
awarded any money at all that he had won and I had lost. On WBAI
and in a small magazine called *WIN*, the arbitrators insisted that
this was not true and that I was being burned in the media.

Forcade wasn't satisfied with the decision and rejected the
arbitrators. He went on the radio and accused them of being my
puppets. We had to repeat the battle at the American Arbitration
Association where I had to duel with Forcade's two lawyers. He
got another thousand dollars for his effort.

Then began a lengthy battle with Grove Press over the terms of
the distribution contract. I was fed up with everything that had
happened, so I ordered the book out of print and closed down my
publishing firm. At the time the book was selling about eight
thousand copies a week. A year later it was being bootlegged for
ten bucks—five times the cover price. Today I'm told a copy can
cost as much as twenty dollars. I have no idea how many finally
ended up in print. I have seen a blue-cover edition which was
printed illegally and by-passed me *and* Grove Press. I ended up

with about twenty-six thousand dollars as author/publisher. Peanuts really.

The original manuscript of *Steal This Book* wound up in the Columbia University library while I was still on probation from charges involving the 1968 riots there.

Two years later, Lancer Books, a now-defunct publisher, signed me to do a sequel. It was to be everything *STB* was thought to be but actually was not. A book for graduate students of the street. I met counterfeiters, jewel smugglers, car thieves, lock pickers, experts on phony I.D. A steady stream of outlaws made me a father confessor. They were more than willing to discuss in detail their particular hustles.

On Second Avenue one day, a strange bird who called himself "Agent Thirty-seven" told me how he was the first yippie bank robber. He showed me a newspaper clipping describing a bank robber with long hair. "See, that's us! We're in every field," he exclaimed, proud to have broken yet another equal-opportunity barrier. I talked him into giving me ten thousand dollars in cash, which was passed on to people living underground. Three months later I saw his face on a *Daily News* reward poster with a slash across it that read APPREHENDED. Good Luck, Agent 37!

I met all the great phone phreaks. An extremely strange group of people. After spending most of their lives talking in phone booths or huddled in basement labs, all had skin paler than a cue ball. People's engineers, they wracked their brains devising schemes to screw the phone company. By pirating their way into little-known circuits, using special access signals and codes, they were able to explore the secret world of high-level communication.

One phone phreak took me into a pay phone where he produced an eight-inch black strip of stiff electronic tape. Next he inserted it into a portable Sony, lifted the receiver, and held the machine up to the mouthpiece. Signals beeped out a message. Pause . . . "Here, listen," he coaxed me, holding up the phone. What I heard was a monotone voice reading off names and telephone numbers. "Top secret," explained the phone phreak. "We've just tapped into the government's secret GS Red System." I think that's what he called it. We were listening to a computer bank read-out. It was very spooky, there in the phone booth, listening to the voice of a government computer. I copied down Attorney General Kleindienst's home number and gave it out late one night over WBAI. I had, of course, seen every conceivable type of blue box, black box, red box, and cheese box imaginable. Little gadgets that in one way or another allow you to call anywhere free. I used phone scramblers and was shown how to tap and detect the tapping of phones. Later we joined together, sponsored a conference, and put out a newsletter with up-to-date info on the whole field. (Lancer Books had lawyers willing to battle the phone company and the new laws, and all these instructions and diagrams went into the sequel to *STB*.)

The greatest phone phreak by far was (and still is!) the legendary John Draper. Better known to the world as Cap'n Crunch. It is generally conceded that he invented the blue box. He had managed several feats of telephone wizardry, not the least of which was to call himself round the world for free. He was a dedicated anarchist. Probably the most dangerous man to the corporate state I've ever met. Crunch gave me reams of data to include in my new book. During the late summer of '72 we were talking, phone booth to phone booth, when I heard him yell into the receiver, "This is it! They're here!" Then I heard scuffling. Next day I learned that Cap'n Crunch had been grabbed by the feds. Charged with fraud by wire, he was fined one thousand dollars and put on five years pro. We had been discussing how blue boxes, used by people who understood a method known as "stacking," could tie up the entire phone system of a small city. I really get a warm feeling about humanity knowing the Cap'n is out there in some phone booth experimenting with his latest beeper-box. Our answer to Thomas Edison. Gad-zoots! Just learned the Captain got nailed in San Jose and is doing a year's stretch. The judge has forced him to make a public statement that he is no longer a phone freak. Ugly! Ugly!

The new handbook, consisting of some 475 pages, was without rival. The complete outlaw's manual, a dazzling display of how-to techniques on all aspects of what you might call non-violent, victimless crime. A week after I handed in the book, Lancer went bankrupt. A month after that, I was busted on a coke rap by one of the undercover dealers I had met while researching the book. That was back in August of '73. Five months later I went underground, using my own writings as a guide. Karma, huh?

There's one publishing tidbit I forgot to include. When I wrote

Revolution for the Hell of It, I used a jacket photo of myself with
the word "FUCK" on my forehead. Without consulting me the
publisher changed it to "FREE." On both *Woodstock Nation* and
Steal This Book I slipped the word by. If you have access to either
book, look closely in the shadows and wrinkles for the subliminal
message. My private little war on publishing censorship. Excuse
me, editing.

Bringing the War Home

The war in Indochina reached another climax during the late spring
of 1970. Nixon and his partner-in-crime, Kissinger, had been
forced to change strategy. They began cutting back on American
troop strength but escalated the bombing of North Vietnam. Also,
the secret B-52 bombings of Cambodia and Laos, which had begun
as early as May 1969, were daily, round-the-clock occurrences by
1970. (Speak of a free press! The existence of the world's largest
airport, based in Thailand and used for raids, went virtually unreported for two years.) While publicly proclaiming that they supported disengagement from Vietnam and de-escalation of the
fighting, Nixon and Kissinger were in reality carrying out a policy
of trying to bomb Indochina back to the Stone Age.

In the three years following Nixon's inauguration, figures released by the Library of Congress reported 469,000 fixed-wing air
missions and 20.8 million helicopter flights. All totaled, 3.6
million tons of bombs were dropped, 20,000 more Americans
were killed, and 110,000 were seriously wounded. This is what
Kissinger referred to as "winding down the war."

As troops returned, the slaughter of Vietnamese passed, in large
part, to robots of death. In far-off jungles, Doctor Strangelove
fantasies concocted by the Pentagon were turned into reality.
There were "smart" bombs guided by built-in television cameras,
heat-seeking missiles, needle bombs, mines triggered by remote-
control buttons, electronically wired battlefields. Defoliants and

Three thousand persons gather at New York's Columbia University, March 13, 1970.

New Haven, Connecticut. Members of the Chicago Conspiracy opened the May Day Rally with speeches in the Center Church on the Green, 1970.

other forms of chemical warfare had decimated the rice paddies and poisoned much of the water supply. One-fifth of the land mass had been reduced to sand and bomb craters—a veritable moonscape of inhumanity.

In the North, much of the city of Hanoi was leveled, including factories, homes, and hospitals. In an attempt to ruin croplands and cause widespread famine, North Vietnam's dike systems were bombed. Aerial photographs and on-site inspection by Americans (including a yippie women's delegation) and Europeans documented the tragedy, but the administration persisted in its denials, claiming the photographs and reports were fraudulent. In the South, billions of dollars' worth of American ammunition and arms continued to support the corrupt regime of President Thieu. "Vietnamization" of the war meant Nixon would do all he could to see that Asians died instead of Americans.

Nixon and Kissinger's public-relations campaign was surprisingly successful. Most of the bombing was beyond the range of the television crews, hence unknown. Once negotiations began in Paris, most Americans accepted the government line that "these things take time." To the great shame of our country, during the early seventies, while the war was held in general disfavor, the majority of people accepted the idea of substituting bombs and dead Asians for American blood.

Social movements, like water, seek their own level. Frustrated by an inadequate public response to the escalation of bombing and by the sheer passage of time, many in our ranks felt the need for more militant tactics. I was one of those advocating such a policy. I believed in making the domestic situation as chaotic and uncomfortable for the warmakers as possible, anyway.

I never believed in unrestricted violence. Nothing during those years warranted the taking of a single life by participants in the antiwar movement. But *violence*, just like *nonviolence*, is a rather imprecise term. Saying the world would be better off without violence has always struck me as one of those ritualistic mouthings void of real meaning. When it comes to abstracts, justice is far more essential than peace, because too often "peace" simply means the oppressor has successfully controlled the aspirations of the oppressed. A protest movement means "conflict." It requires "force." Participants must learn to "fight." The status quo is "disrupted." That is both the language and the inner emotion of social struggle and resistance. In one respect non-violence made sense; you got hurt less in situations where you gave up a size and number advantage. Pacifists too often elevate themselves to a higher moral plateau, that in my mind isn't always justified or effective.

By 1970, the Youth International Party had branches in some seventy cities and towns, even in Europe. It sponsored hundreds of guerrilla-theater acts not originated by those of us in New York. The counterculture press documented all this. Two I remember as particularly original. One occurred in Disneyland. The amusement park had persisted in denying admittance to longhairs, and its executive rank was a training ground for the Nixon administration. Richard himself had cut the ribbon opening the park. To say that those who created Disneyland also created Vietnam is really not that ridiculous. Some five hundred yippies organized by the San Diego YIP chapter stormed through the gates of Disneyland. Catching guards by surprise, they managed to plant the Viet Cong flag on top of the plaster of paris Mount Matterhorn. Scenes of helmeted police guarding Fantasyland from the hairy horde inspired other disruptions. The YIP chapter in Vancouver, British Columbia, organized several hundred Canadians, declared war on the U.S., and stormed across the border into Blair, Washington. Not since the days of Pancho Villa had anyone tried that!

There were also scores of smoke-ins organized in just about every state. Gathering in Washington, D.C., on July 4 to puff your head off became a tradition which still lives. Mostly, though, YIP chapters organized antiwar rallies and street marches. Wherever there was a gathering place for street people you could always find yippie agitators, the New Nation Flag, scores of rock bands, the Viet Cong flag, the pungent aroma of grass, posters, buttons, underground papers, and antiwar leaflets. The blending of Mao and marijuana created a new kind of American revolutionary, but no one should doubt that the war lay at the heart of all this. Cultural disruption was the meat and potatoes of yippie antiwar strategy.

After Chicago there was very little of the old-style civil disobedience. The ritualistic sitting down or standing up in violation of police orders was simply no longer acceptable to the majority of participants. Pacifists dreamed of the day thousands would peacefully block the war machine, get carried off to jail singing "Give peace a chance," refuse bail, go on hunger strikes, and through moral persuasion increase their ranks until everyone—including the generals in Vietnam (on both sides)—joined them. That was the pacifist vision. Everyone needs a vision. Many leftists dreamed of the unions joining our ranks, or of black people rising up, or of antiwar candidates going off to Congress to break the grip of the old guard, or of the Arab world cutting off oil supplies. Others thought the new cultural consciousness alone would create a climate in which the male mystique could no longer be used to manipulate armies. Different visions created different tactics. History, stubbornly refusing to repeat itself in exactly the same way, doesn't offer a precise prescription for social change. Mostly it's a catch-as-catch-can affair, and the activists who can best judge the mood of the times will always be the most effective—regardless of what philosophy or tactic they put forth.

By 1970, my "plan" to stop the war was to disrupt life on the home front. I did not see going to jail as the best use of my time. My vision was May '68 in France—strikes (especially in the armed forces and universities), street demonstrations, occupations of buildings, the blocking of recruiting centers, burning of ROTC offices, sabotage in defense plants. You get the general picture. We called it "trashing." It was, I might add, what happened.

Trashing in the Streets, Bombing in the Toilets

There was no real history we could turn to for guidance. To some extent, peaceful means of protest, such as picket lines, rallies, and teach-ins, would always be effective. So would sit-ins. And throughout this period it was the rare ROTC building that did not at one time or another find its hallways and offices clogged with sprawling bodies attempting to halt recruitment for the war. Never-

Abbie and Gracie trying to get
into Tricia Nixon's tea party,
1970. Notice Gracie's see-
through blouse and the LSD
under her fingernails.

Abbie and Anita perform
electronic voodoo on Nixon's
TV image as it appears before
the nation. This excorcism was
performed in Washington
before 30.000 TV freaks. May
9, 1970.

theless, frustration was building among the ranks of protesters. By now any group that had at least one nationally known spokesperson and had managed to raise a few thousand dollars for leaflets and newspaper ads could call an antiwar rally in Central Park and attract from twenty to forty thousand people, depending on the week's news and the weather report. Attendance became ritual and the speeches seemed to drone on endlessly.

During the Chicago trial, Weatherpeople descended on the Windy City for a national confrontation billed as "The Days of Rage." At first all of us defendants endorsed the idea. I, in fact, had come up with the name. It was inspired by the title of a documentary about John Kennedy called *Days of Lightning, Days of Drums*. Tom Hayden spoke to those assembled in Lincoln Park, with Froines standing next to him; as was his style, he quickly left the scene. I was in the crowd. Jeff Jones gave the signal to move out of the park and head for the upper-class "Gold Coast" section of Chicago. There was no beating around the bush. People pulled out pipes and chains and began smashing anything they came across. Cars, store windows, police. It was an indiscriminate rampage. Later I wrote an article critical of the action. It was, I felt, suicidal to openly challenge the police and I castigated the street-fighters for smashing the windows of Volkswagens and mama-papa grocery stores. I did not, however, disapprove of trashing as a tactic and urged the Weatherpeople to move their act to Washington and rampage through the halls of government buildings.

The Days of Rage triggered riots throughout the nation. For the following two years running through the streets was practiced by hundreds of thousands of participants. Mostly it was unplanned as people would congregate at a rally site. When police moved to stop someone who went beyond the limits of the situation the crowd would swarm. The majority just seemed to run, but many engaged in vandalism at preselected targets. Often attempts were made to barricade streets and create liberated zones. Seattle, Berkeley, Cambridge, Madison, and the Lower East Side were the most developed enclaves of resistance. Demonstrations in these places were weekly occurrences. In Berkeley, at times 5000 people would attack the ROTC building hurling rocks and bottles. In

Harvard Square, rioters burned police cars and smashed bank windows. No fewer than forty-one fires were set during one night of uprising in Madison. During a weekend of disturbances in Kansas City, an estimated two million dollars in property damage occurred. The American Council on Education estimated some 9,408 protest incidents on campuses during the 1969–1970 school year, with extra police and/or national guard required on more than seven hundred occasions.

In addition to this unstructured violence, clandestine revolutionary cells formed and carried out several acts of sabotage against symbols of the war or establishment power. Army induction centers were bombed. Banks were burned. These types of violent incidents, rather common in Europe, were practically unknown in the States. The antidraft riots in protest to the Civil War and the wave of anarchist militance in connection with union organizing in the 1890s were the only historical precedents for what was now happening. Neither of those periods, however, could match in scope the opposition to the Vietnam War during these years. Estimates on property damage ran over a hundred million dollars. The number of guerrilla-style bombings depends on whose statistics you trust. *Scanlon's* magazine, a short-lived outgrowth of *Ramparts,* published a detailed survey in January of '71 and catalogued 546 acts of sabotage occurring in 1970, or roughly ten a week. Extrapolating from another survey by the Alcohol, Tobacco, and Firearms Division of the U.S. Treasury, the weekly average comes closer to forty-two actual bombings or incidents of arson that could be traced to political origins. Kirkpatrick Sale's objective and detailed treatment of this period in the book *SDS* gives probably the best overall sense of what was transpiring. Sale estimates that close to a million people were involved in these acts of violence and that they were supported by as much as a fifth of the total population, perhaps an additional forty million more. I am only emphasizing these facts, because many of the books written by antiwar activists felt obliged to deny this reality and make it look like we were all little darlings.

"Violence," Rap Brown once remarked, "is as American as cherry pie," but violence as a political weapon directed against established institutions was quite a new experience. Especially so for white liberal-arts majors like myself who had never been through the army. (I was, by the way, deferred because of children, but burned my draft card anyway.) Guns and bombs were something completely alien to anything in my background. But mine, I was greatly surprised to discover, was a minority attitude. Many kids, especially from rural areas, grow up with a working knowledge of guns and a basic understanding of how explosives work. What seemed foreign to me was second nature to many contemporaries. Dynamite can be legally purchased over the counter in many regions of the country with just a signature. You can make a sizable (albeit unstable) bomb by mixing chicken shit and kerosene. Making Molotov cocktails requires no expertise. Assorted technical manuals providing anyone with lessons on sabotage are available from printing companies (Paladin Press in Denver is the largest). Some of the best texts are published by the U.S. government and can be read in the Library of Congress. More sophisticated weaponry and explosives can be easily procured on a thriving black market. I was approached by several arms dealers during this period with offers of hand weapons, machine guns, plastiques, bazookas, mortars. "You name it," one dealer said, "I can get you a tank, even a jet!" Although I never arranged any deal, I was utterly fascinated by this secret network. Obviously others did not shy away, and there was a constant buzzing on the street about secret bomb-making classes. Where there's a will, there's a way. Fuses were time-rigged, the bombs were wrapped in plastic bags and deposited in toilet tanks or secreted in doorways. The explosions went off at night and damage ranged from a few hundred dollars' worth up to two or three million. As time went on, no one could enter a federal building without submitting to a search, and yet people still somehow managed to set off explosions in both the Capitol and the Pentagon.

In most instances, the symbolic damage was far greater than the physical destruction. The power structure was no longer viewed as an impenetrable fortress. The Weather Underground, although responsible for just a small percentage of bombings, maintained an extensive support system that publicized their actions (propaganda of the dead) and enlarged their myth. Their greatest contribution, it seemed to me, was the fact of their own survival. Hundreds of agents tried to track them down. Large bribes and offers of legal deals failed to work. An up-coming trial and lawsuit of FBI officials will reveal the extensive illegal means agents used in trying to apprehend revolutionary fugitives. Unauthorized wire tapping, burglaries, and illegal breaking and entering have already been mentioned in the indictments.

Even though I was critical of the Days of Rage and much of the polemics of the Weather Underground, I saw great value in their myth and was a part of their support system. Anita and I both met often with people living underground, sometimes using disguises under the most complicated of security conditions. We were proud to actively aid and abet any and all outlaws. Of all above-ground groups (until Prairie Fire Collectives formed in the mid-Seventies) YIP had the closest association with the underground and many of its communiqués were first announced at yippie press conferences.

Our first contacts came right after the townhouse explosion in Greenwich Village on March 4, 1970. Three Weather people were blown to bits, several others were injured but somehow managed to escape in what was the great tragedy of the underground's development. Tragedy that it was, it hid a blessing in disguise. All groups have factions, even underground groups. The small faction that removed itself from the planet by its own suicidal impulses was gearing up for terrorist activity. Those bombs were to have been used against Columbia University in what could have been the most bloody insane act of our history. No one wins a revolution through hatred and intimidation of the general population. People are flesh and blood, not symbols. I agree with the notion that property has no inalienable rights; no revolution has occurred without destruction of property, especially symbols of power. "One cannot make an omelet without breaking some eggs," remarked Lenin. This attitude, however, is a far cry from the terrorism of deliberately taking innocent lives, be they in a classroom, an airplane, or an apartment building.

Not only is this kind of terrorism an unworkable strategy, it is one which could only replace one heartless system with another. The townhouse explosion saved lives in the long run because it wiped out terrorist tendencies in the Weather organization. From that point on no one was even injured in a Weather bombing. Leading that struggle away from terrorism into "constructive destruction" were Jeff Jones and Bill Ayres, who, in my opinion, were the most brilliant of the underground leaders. I always had a certain amount of respect for Bernardine Dohrn, but she too devoutly worshiped at the church of the left. She was responsible for much of the strident catechism echoing in those interminable twenty-page single-spaced communiqués emanating from the underground to guide the "untutored" masses. Jones and Ayres represented more of its creative tendencies, and were most adept at blending new culture with international socialist politics. Talking about the Weatherpeople is, of course, extremely difficult, even today. I knew one of the townhouse victims, Terry Robbins, quite well. After the explosion I helped organize a memorial service in front of the rubble, and it was about a week after that my contacts with the underground began. They were obviously dedicated and courageous, but a little out of touch.

I feel very close to them and would have those feelings even if I were above-ground.

The Weatherpeople guessed wrong about the course of the war and the antiwar movement. Had history taken another turn they might have led us down another more militant road. Today, it is fairly easy to write them off as some romantic misguided footnote to a chaotic period in history. The fact that they constructed an underground network and carried out guerrilla strikes (they did not, by the way, come under my definition of a terrorist group) while avoiding capture will be appreciated by the next antiwar movement that will appear in protest to the next (and inevitable) foreign war.

Then came May 4, perhaps the blackest day in the history of American colleges. Some two hundred unarmed demonstrators gathered on the campus of Kent State University in Ohio. A national-guard contingent, without warning or provocation, opened fire, killing four students and wounding nine others. Emotional shock waves tore through the country. Over five hundred more universities joined the strike as close to five million students refused to attend classes or take final exams. *Scanlon's* documented seventy-five bombings during the first week of May and a number of ROTC buildings were burned to the ground.

Throughout the strike, campus groups set up rallies and workshops to discuss tactics to force the withdrawal of troops from Cambodia and an end to the war. The majority of colleges were now being used to organize antiwar protest as organizers began visiting local high schools. The attorney general's office in Washington seized the initiative and urged all campuses to close down, hoping the students would then disperse.

Without doubt this was the period of greatest struggle and tension of the era. It was "All for Vietnam" and "Avenge the Kent State Four." At Pace College in New York, a clearing center for strike information had been established. I remember that night well. Returning from a round of speeches, I was picked up at the airport and sped to the strike center. A grim tale unfolded. That afternoon truckloads of hardhats carrying meat hooks had descended on a demonstration at nearby Foley Square. Swinging madly, the vigilantes had torn into students. Using walkie-talkie communication, one band raided the campus, destroyed equipment, and beat up strike coordinators. It was the closest thing to the movie *Z*. I received several death threats that night and stayed away from our apartment. The next day I spoke at Queens and Brooklyn colleges under armed guard, and again truckloads of vigilantes appeared. But this time hundreds of students carrying baseball bats confronted them, and the raiders did nothing more than wave flags, shout right-wing slogans, and speed off.

Through rallies like these we got out the message to gather in Washington on May 15 to "bring the war home to the warmakers." What promised to be the most explosive demonstration ever managed to turn into just another large protest outing. Once again it was the same old speakers warning Nixon about what was going to happen *next* time. Rally coordinators had spent the week cooperating with administration officials. One hundred thousand people were effectively contained by a wide circle of buses, police, and parade marshals. Something more militant was demanded. Not trashing—because it was a mixed crowd, including old people and very young children. This was exactly the moment for orderly civil disobedience. A hundred thousand people sitting down in front of the White House and refusing to leave would have been effective and forceful. (And the participants were willing.) It would have immediately encouraged similar actions at U.S. embassies throughout the world. It would have brought badly needed coordination to a movement already fragmented. And without doubt it would have hastened the conclusion of a bloody, evil war. That night a few thousand frustrated participants ran through the streets. Some five hundred were arrested. But there is a time to run, a time to fight, a time to be silent, a time for every tactic the imagination can dream up, I suppose. This, however, was the time to sit down and refuse to move until the war ended. Unfortunately, that good an opportunity never came again. Petty bureaucrats you never heard of and need not be mentioned carried the day. All the Chicago defendants were off speaking two, sometimes three, times a day right up until the morning of the national action urging people to drop everything and head to Washington. I, myself, had collapsed in exhaustion after speaking in one day at Syracuse, Queens College, and NYU. By the time we had all convened in Washington, the people who "man the office," so to speak, had taken control. People who lack imagination, who failed to modify their tactics one iota during six years of protest, and who for all I know are still carrying out the same rally, with the same list of speakers, on the same corner of Union Square today. Leftwing moonies! The sort who probably take over socialist revolutions after the inspired leaders have been dead and canonized.

The Algerian Connection

We returned to New York completely fed up with the mobilization in Washington. Nixon had walked among the demonstrators and gone back to watch a football game on television. Later the USIA would show a film of that rally overseas as an example of how free America was, of how orderly we had all been when we gathered to petition our government. Some groups on the left, for example, the Socialist Workers' Party, a Trotskyite group, saw their role as little more than training marshals to prevent others from taking to the streets, and members worked day and night to keep militants like me from speaking to the crowd. They were the cops of the movement, and this time they had managed to control the situation. That rally, and that group in particular, created a polite safety valve which was later regretted by the majority of participants who seemed to want "something more."

That summer Anita and I traveled through the West. I spoke at several schools and for the first time in our marriage we started to relax. We earned our mule-skinner certificates by schlepping up and down the Grand Canyon in a mule pack train. At the fabulous Circus-Circus Casino, Anita, who had never before touched a pair of dice, got lucky and made fourteen straight passes. Yippie! We netted about twenty-two hundred bucks, but a few heavy bettors scored ten times that. Guards made her roll up her sleeves. Shooters were yelling, "Let the lady shoot! Come on lucky lady!" It seemed to last forever. Complete euphoria! When the roll was over, strangers pressed hundred-dollar chips into her hand, hugged her, and thanked her for bailing them out. It was a great time, and Las Vegas earned its private place as our favorite city. Next day we met secretly in the desert with leaders of the underground. We split our Las Vegas winnings, smoked some dope, slept under the stars, and talked of the battles to come. I can still remember the expression on Delgado's face when he said, "All I ever want to do is smoke dope and make revolution." There was no reason to believe any of this would ever end.

About a month later word came that Timothy Leary, with the help of the Weather Underground, had broken out of San Luis Obispo Prison and was being hunted all over the country. I flew immediately to Oakland and asked Huey Newton to arrange with Eldridge Cleaver, himself in exile, for Leary to enter Algeria.

To the outside world it may have seemed that all of us were close friends, but that was not the case. I had never met Newton before and had just said hello to Cleaver once in a hotel lobby. I didn't even know Leary that well. (New York City was my beat.) They were all symbols to me, far more than friends. The way I pictured the next year (judging from what had happened in the spring) many people were going to be forced underground or into exile. Yippies, Panthers, Weatherpeople, and who knew who else. Half the FBI's most-wanted list were now political fugitives. For the first time, the top ten wanted was expanded to sixteen. And this was far from the only enemies list Nixon and Hoover had drawn up.

If a fugitive colony could be established in Algeria, not only would it help to bring the various tendencies of the U.S. movement together but our cultural revolution might come to be more accepted by other liberation movements around the world. I was always conscious of how poorly we must have translated globally.

It's a lot easier dealing with symbols like flags and buildings than with human beings. What followed was strictly high movement comedy.

We sent Stew Albert off to "explain" Leary to Cleaver and hoped they could work out some way of explaining him to the Algerian government. This was a lot more complicated than you might imagine, and we kept trying to "invent" a political background for Leary that somehow didn't come out sounding like L-S-D. Unannounced, Leary and his wife, Rosemary, popped in to the Panther Headquarters before all the negotiations could be worked out. He was not your most disciplined fugitive. Finally it was decided to pass Leary off as a black university professor fired for his antiwar views and being hounded by the government. Everyone stressed the appellation "Doctor," and the Algerians were starting to regard him as an American Frantz Fanon.

When Stew came back to New York, he filled us in on the situation. "They want us to send a delegation over. They're going to hold a press conference and announce it to the whole world," he reported. Anita would go. So would other yippies. Marty Kenner, who doubled as a key fund raiser for the Panthers, and Jonah Raskin, who was trusted by the underground. (Jonah's detailed account of these events can be read in his admirable book, *Out of the Whale*.) Jennifer Dohrn (Bernardine's sister), who had been infiltrating a bra factory in Los Angeles trying to unionize Chicana women, would go. So would Brian Flanagan. During the Days of Rage Brian had been running in the streets when Chief City Council Richard Elrod threw a tackle at him, missed, and broke his own back on the curbstone. Brian was charged with but acquitted of attempted murder in the incident. He then ran as a YIP candidate for sheriff of Cook County. Elrod rode the sympathy vote to victory. I wanted to go, but bail conditions ruled out travel to Algeria. I did, however, get permission to see my Italian publisher. Anita and I decided to push off a week ahead of schedule so that we could get in a little sightseeing before we all met in Rome.

This was a heady moment in the history of the Youth International Party, for we were about to realize the second word of our title and forge an important link in the global chain of liberation. Jerry Rubin, Nancy Kurshan, and Gus Reichbach, a yippie attorney, were to meet us later that month in Paris, where Jerry and I planned to speak at a rally and fan out through Europe building the party. Our fall program for the year was geared to go international.

Well, things went down a lot different than planned all right. Anita returned to Paris a week ahead of schedule and was fit to be tied. "Egomaniacs! Leary. Cleaver. Two nuts!" she kept yelling. "It'll never work. I escaped. Can you imagine, I had to escape!" It seems that Leary and Cleaver had planned a press conference, and when the press had heard a Ms. Dohrn was going to be there, they assumed it was Bernardine—at the time the most hunted fugitive in America. Scores of reporters flocked to Algeria, and the government started to take a closer look at all this international intrigue taking place under their noses. When they found out Leary was no "Frantz Fanon," they forced Cleaver to cancel the press conference. Leary had meanwhile smuggled in twenty thousand hits of LSD and had plans to turn on all of Africa. After just a few days, he and Cleaver started fighting. Anita felt Leary was just a little kookie, spouting off rhetoric he didn't believe. She saved her worst venom for Cleaver. "He keeps Kathleen a prisoner!" she exclaimed. "I wasn't even allowed to see her! Can you imagine, he parades around with a teenage mistress he's picked up over there. He ordered the women to stay locked in their rooms. We weren't allowed to speak. I'm no Algerian!" Eldridge and Huey spent hours on the phone screaming and threatening to kill each other. Anita accused others on the trip of being weak and not backing her up, and she said Cleaver openly bragged about shooting people who disagreed with him and burying them in the desert. During one of Cleaver's moods she had sneaked out a window, hailed a ride to town, and beat it out of Algeria as fast as she could. "Leary went off on a tour of Palestinian guerrilla camps to prove his revolutionary zeal," she said. "There's going to be trouble there, mark my word."

Anita paid a price for having the guts to protest Cleaver's one-man tyranny and for her escape. For quite a while she had been having a rough time. After the trial made me famous, people climbed all over me and ignored her. We'd be talking together at a party and someone would just step between us with his back to her and start talking to me. The fame game burned every relationship we'd known. Just before going to Europe we had traveled to upstate New York to investigate a small town we considered moving to and living underground. Partly to get away from police, partly to escape the movement groupies. Anita's passion for the revolution had been cooling for months and we were, among other things, trying to have a baby. The experience in Algeria had crystallized all her resentment about hypocrisies and ass kissing in the movement.

Then Jerry Rubin arrived. He and Nancy had broken up! He was completely wrecked. She had run off with an organizer from Kent State and Jerry was angry with all women. He refused to hear what Anita was saying. When the others returned we huddled. Cleaver wanted us to come under his leadership. Jerry and I were to raise money for him and Leary. He wanted us to buy him a car. Anita just laughed out loud. "He's a pig and you're a bunch of sexist hypocrites," she yelled.

Well, I stood by her. She was not only my wife, she was my best friend. Besides, she was right. Everybody went off to London while Anita and I stayed behind. What the heck, Paris is a good place to make a baby, we figured. Later, when we journeyed to Germany to meet Daniel Cohn-Bendit (Danny the Red), we refused to screw. We found nothing romantic about Deutschland.

We kept the Algerian drama to ourselves when we got back. I never spoke much about our great international achievement. In a few months it didn't matter because word came that Tim and Rosemary had been placed under house arrest by Cleaver. I was approached again to help get the Learys out of Algeria. First in, then out. We arranged for him to get asylum in Denmark but once again he screwed up the plan, got off the plane in Switzerland, and was promptly arrested. I always thought it funny that the country that had given the world clocks and banks had also given the world LSD. The Swiss didn't think it funny, though, and they threw Leary in the can. The rest is in his book.

The Last Round-up

Through the winter of 1970–1971 Anita grew radiantly pregnant. The bad aftertaste of Algeria remained. Worse, movement women began attacking her for having a baby. "There isn't time for that sort of indulgence," she was told. It was counterrevolutionary, sexist, and selfish. Even someone as flaky as Germaine Greer castigated her for turning herself into a baby-prisoner. "Like a cow!" she exclaimed. A large portion of the left seemed to go through life childless. Left-wingers were to be cloned from the mind, not produced from the womb. It seemed anything was grounds for personal attacks.

Both Anita's book and mine came out, and we toured the country together promoting them. I still went on speaking engagements to campuses but the summer of '70 seemed to have sapped the energy of students. The most tumultuous month in college history that May had forced the closing of hundreds of campuses, but by the following autumn all was calm. The invasion of Cambodia ended and troops kept returning to the States. There was a general feeling of intimidation. After all, at Kent and Jackson State six students had been killed. I spoke at Kent State and met with activists. According to the state reports the YIP chapter had been at the center of the confrontation, so several key organizers were now facing charges. Some heads had to roll, and as often happens the victims of brutality were blamed for the "provocation." Many schools were now heavily infiltrated with informers and *agents provocateurs* who encouraged factional fights. Mostly there was just the frustration that arises from seeing no choices but electoral politics or armed struggle, which in this period meant bombings. The underground was cheered. On most campuses you could see T-shirts with the rainbow-lighting insignia of the Weatherpeople and posters announcing "Bernardine Welcome Here." A big problem with bombings was their effect on

activists who regarded them as the only legitimate expression of
militancy. Once that idea came to roost, the existential dilemma
became, "Why am I not with them?"—followed by the perfectly
reasonable position that it wasn't worth the personal risk. Hundreds of activists were caught in that mind-crunch, and once there,
retreated from *all* activity, convinced that they lacked *real* commitment.

Fashions were changing. The "New Nostalgia" was in the air.
In the introduction to the paperback edition of *Woodstock Nation*,
I wrote (disparagingly) about the fifties revival, the self-analysis,
the new religious fervor, body drugs like smack and Quaaludes
(which helped you escape it all—as opposed to the effect of mind
drugs), and the absorption of the counterculture into the mainstream. Any call to idealism was greeted with choruses of "We've
heard all that," and in a way I had, too.

I kept active, though, and even found myself in the streets of
Belfast one week battling with British troops. A merry adventure, I
had come to observe and ended up donning the uniform of the IRA
(a World War II army jacket and beret) in defiance of a law making
that gesture a crime. At night, the women would clap garbage-can
lids together as cymbals, calling the faithful to rumble in the streets
at the approach of British patrols. At that time, the troops were
using rubber bullets in what I thought a rather gentlemanly approach to colonialism. The McCann Brothers, leaders in the provo
wing of the IRA, became my guides, explaining that the Irish were
the "white niggers of Europe." Outside the sprawling Belfast
Shipworks, brother Brendan bragged, "Our granddaddies built
the *Titanic* in there," knowing full well that no Irishmen from the
bogs had gone down to Davy Jones's locker on the ill-fated luxury
liner. Catholic unemployment ran four times that of the Protestant
Orangemen, with most of the work in unskilled jobs going to the
womenfolk. "How's your pa, is your ma still workin'," was how
the boys greeted fellow comrades in the streets and bars.

I was taken along a cemetery trail, behind a waterfall, to a secret
tavern—The Belfast Felons' Club. An honor they said, since only
those who had served time fighting for Free Ireland were members. Dope-smoking teenagers played darts with their whiskey-
drinking grandpas. I learned that the nuclear family was the

cornerstone of the Irish movement. I now had second thoughts about further encouraging the idea of generational revolt. (I, by the way, was then thirty-five.) After I left (I was warned that the U.S. courts were about to revoke my bail and declare me a fugitive if I was not back on U.S. soil within twenty-four hours) several of the European activists I had met in Ireland were arrested and charged with a fabricated plot to blow up Queens College in Belfast. For weeks the British press trumpeted my visit as proof of an international anarchist plot. There was a story in US newspapers, more fancy than fact, that I had slugged a British soldier who had attacked a kid. Scotland Yard escorted me out of the country, and I was forever banished from British soil. Back in the States, I lectured and helped raise money for the Irish cause. Word came that the McCanns turned their trial into a Belfast version of Chicago. Next a message that Jimmy, the youngest brother, had tied sheets together and gone over the wall of the Belfast prison. "Abie," he had called me—"Abie's Irish Rose." I love ya laddie, Jimmy; keep a runnin', keep a fightin'.

The bombing in Vietnam continued, but I no longer organized rallies or demonstrations. Bombs went off in the Capitol and in the Pentagon. Dave Dellinger went into the hospital. Jerry moved to California. Tom had some factional quarrel in Berkeley and was temporarily out of touch. Rennie Davis threw in with a Washington, D.C., collective called the May Day Tribe and issued a call for mass disruption that spring. Mobile tactics were to be employed in an attempt to block traffic. Thousands of police and national-guard troops were used to round up protesters from the streets and parks—usually before things had a chance to really get underway. They just arrested anyone who looked suspicious. Twelve thousand demonstrators were arrested in the police round-ups. Neither side now paid much attention to legalities. The courts would later dismiss every one of the arrests, castigating Mitchell for "taking the law into his own hands." A few years later the courts would award demonstrators a hefty twelve million dollars in a damage suit. No one believes any money will actually ever change hands, but it stands as an unemotional judgment of how the authorities failed to carry out their responsibilities and became the lawbreakers.

For me it was the last round-up. Running through the streets, a little slow in the legs now, the coppers caught me separating a bus from its distributor coil and chased me into an alleyway. I fought them with all I had. Swinging. Kicking. Clawing madly. My Irish comrades would have been proud. Visions of James Mason in *Odd Man Out* danced in my head—the doomed revolutionary fights on. "Fuck you, you bastards. You'll never take me alive. Fuck your father! Free your mother!" Like a cornered rat I crazily slugged it out with a bevy of big-bellied blues, each twice my size. Finally two got the arms pinned back while another, snarling, administered the crushing blow—a billy club, full force, straight across my face. I could hear the bones crack under the blow, and I knew my street-fighting days were over. More Cyrano than Samson, my strength had always been in my nose and not in the fright-wig hair.

Tossed into a bus, I woke up in a makeshift concentration camp, along with thousands of other demonstrators. Stew Albert helped me inside a first-aid tent. "My God, you're a bloody mess," he said. People were digging trenches for latrines and huddling against the chain-link fences. It was Stalag 17, it was. A fellow prisoner, Dr. Spock, came over and stitched me up. "Hi, Doc, I didn't know you made house calls," I mumbled, managing to get off one last grin.

"It's broken pretty bad, you know," he said.

Camouflaged in the white coat of a medical orderly, I was secreted out of the compound. I called Anita from a phone booth. "I'll be home late from work, babes."

Well, the feds weren't so happy I escaped. They were still watching last year's movie. I was charged once more with conspiracy to incite a riot, and they put out the alarm. It took some twenty-odd agents to bring me in. Face bandaged. Arm in a sling. Anita now seven months pregnant. Jumping out of the dark hallway in our building, they took me at night. "Get him!" yelled an agent, gun flying in my face. Anita got shoved to the floor. I was cuffed and dragged off to jail.

america Is Born

The cops in Washington really had worked me over. I received a bonus felony charge for assaulting an officer, which the authorities later canceled when they saw my scrambled puss. Doctors at Albert Einstein built a reasonable facsimile of the old schnozzola and sent me back to the streets with the warning, "One more time and you'll be sneezing out your ear." I resolved to hang up my Ho Chi Minh jogging shoes, shook their hands, and took the subway back to the Lower East Side.

Anita was just about ready to pop now. We had loved the baby before he was born. He was our way of saying relationships counted. Ours was a marriage with great tenderness and precious little tedium. We did not work hard at it because there just didn't seem to be that much friction to resolve. Something enjoyable passed between us. "Smash Monogamy" was one of those hard-edge movement slogans that left us with a bad chill. It smacked of Stalin abolishing Valentine's Day and stern lectures to the relatives about how they were all living in bondage. Neither of us ever went in for that brand of generational arrogance. The child would be an expression of our curiosity toward life and commitment to the future. The baby was not something separate from our politics. He was a reaffirmation. Like our books, we began with a catchy title—america. Boy or girl, we would call the child "america," insisting it be spelled with lower case. (It's written on the birth certificate that way.) Reporters reacted in chorus, "Is that America with a *kkk*?" I couldn't believe how many times that question was asked. It underscored, to me anyway, just how often the press was missing the point. A fascist baby?? Grace and Paul of the Jefferson Airplane had named their baby china, and if we had a boy we figured Henry Kissinger, as Protestant rabbi, could marry them, out near the Continental Divide. "Now, let's see," Anita fantasized, "we'll serve hash brownies and get the Mormon Tabernacle Choir to sing."

"I couldn't agree more. That china'll come with a helluva dowry!" I nodded, passing the joint. We brought our infantile reveries right into the delivery room—just as we took them most other places.

For months we had attended Lamaze classes. "One-two-three—Push! One-two-three—Push!" I repeated in the labor room, clocking the intervals.

"Eeeyow!" she screamed. "That's easy for you to say. It hurts like a fucker!"

I held Anita real tight while keeping a sharp eye out for the emerging baby. And then it happened. "A boy!" someone said. Six and a half pounds of squirming human. I swear I saw a tiny clenched fist shaking in triumph just as he hit the wide-open spaces. The kid wanted to be born. I don't believe birth trauma theories anymore.

He did not come into the world unnoticed. The hospital room was crammed with floral displays, bunting, and baby garments sent by friends. All, of course, in the family colors—red, white, and blue. WBAI heralded the event. Radio Bob played "God Bless America" throughout the night. In time we had our own record of Kate Smith singing what we now regarded as the kid's theme song. I had added a special yippie touch. Down in Washington, politicians send out congratulation cards on cue if you notify them about things like babies, weddings, promotions, or house warmings. Just before Anita went into the hospital, I bought the most Lawrence Welkian announcement I could find and sent it off to the White House. I sent the announcement from Mr. & Mrs. A. H. Hoffman. Sure enough, back came an embossed card saying "President and Pat Nixon wish to congratulate you on the birth of your new baby." So naturally when the family scribe, Associated Press, came to visit, I proudly announced that the Nixons had just sent us best wishes. After the story hit, White House press secretary Ron Ziegler claimed it was not true. "Not true?" I responded, waving the card and envelope under reporters' noses. "This is not the first time that bastard's told a lie." Yes sir, even before he could talk the little tyke had his finger in the political pablum. A chip off the old block, little america. God shed his grace on thee.

Anita Hoffman.

america, one month old,
practicing guerrilla
maneuvers.

Andy, Amy, Abbie
among the sunflowers,
September 1971.
Anita Hoffman.

The Haircut That Ended the Era

Probably the most blatant media distortion I was ever victim to happened right after america was born. I was giving a speech at a school over in New Jersey. During one long tirade against the co-optation of the counterculture I exclaimed, "Long hair don't mean shit no more." Yanking out a switchblade, I hacked off a lock of my curly mop and threw it to the audience. Flash bulbs lit up as reporters scribbled away. Finally, one of the last holdouts was throwing in the towel. "The sixties are over! The sixties are over!" (It was such a good decade it stole two extra years.) Of course, that wasn't what I said, but I don't want to argue content. The next evening, like thirty or forty million other Americans, I switched on the evening news. For some reason I began with NBC. On came a photo of me with a lengthy commentary about how the era was over. I wish I had the entire text of that news item, because just about everything in it was inaccurate. John Chancellor "moved" the speech to Wisconsin and made it seem that I had actually gotten a real "all-American" haircut in some barbershop. The photo was two years old! The Cook County jail mug shot. Quickly I switched channels. "Come on Walter, baby, bail me out!" CBS also had the item. Cronkite reported the story accurately, but the CBS photo was a year old. It was the one taken with Gracie outside the White House. The one with the matted-down hair. Seeing is believing, of course, as I stroked my shoulder-length curls just to make certain they were real. Photos of me giving that speech had appeared correctly in most New Jersey newspapers, and at least two went out over the national wire services. So why were millions of people across the country now seeing a media Abbie shorn of his locks? Well, you see, I'm not the one to ask that question; you'll have to take it up with higher authorities.

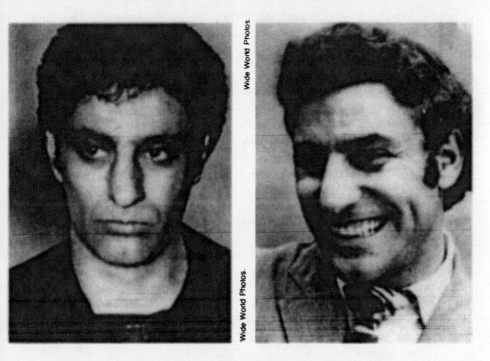

The truth behind the haircut that ended the era. The photos above were flashed to millions of TV viewers as truth. The photo below was taken the day after. (Abbie, John Lennon, Yoko Ono, Jerry Rubin.)

The following evening, I was watching CBS news, cheering the drop in the Dow Jones average, as was customary, when the telephone rang. "Hello," boomed a familiar voice, "is Abbie there?"

"Yes, this is he," I said.

"Hi Abbie, this is Walter," said the voice.

"Walter!" I responded excitedly, "but how can that be? I'm watching you right now on television."

"It's taped," said Anchorman.

"Taped?"

"Yes, I do it live from New York for the rest of the country, but it comes on a half-hour later in the city," answered Anchorman.

"But Walter, if the world ended at seven-fifteen, New York would never know," I said.

"Ho, ho, ho," he chuckled. "I guess they'd preempt. . . . By the way, I'd like to thank you for your letter . . ."

Automatically the letter flashed in my mind. A few months previous Cronkite had worn horn-rimmed glasses. After studying the effect for three days, I wrote him a letter recommending that he get contact lenses. I thought the effect of his glasses was detrimental to his image. People would say he was over the hill, couldn't see so good anymore, and would translate this into a feeling that his reporting was less accurate. I send out letters like that all the time. Dear Abbie advice. "I took your advice, you know," he offered graciously.

"We don't want to lose you, Walter," I said. "What's on your mind?"

"I'd like to interview you—live, for twenty minutes, about the collapse of the movement," he said.

"Walter, I didn't get a haircut, it's not true, that story. Those photos are years old. Besides, I don't want to talk about the end of any movement. There are ebbs and flows. It's personal, my feelings. Things get tough on the street when you're famous."

"I think I understand. It's very hard for me to walk around. I've often had the feeling I'm under house arrest."

His voice signed off exactly on cue with the television set. An experience to contemplate, talking live to Walter Cronkite while he sped home to Connecticut in his limousine, yet watching him "live" on television. It dawned on me that he was as real as the haircut. That modern society had created talking heads all mouthing lines prepared by a giant computer. A computer staffed by pale-looking technicians in long white coats. And that these heads never said anything not planned to control the people. And that nothing was real.

Bummed Out on the Movement

The movement did fall apart. For about a year, unhappy activists would call me up, baring their souls. Factional fights. Personal problems. War wounds acting up. There were objective reasons for this. The winding down of the war naturally meant a winding down of the antiwar movement. True, the bombing was still going strong, and the administration had one last invasion of Laos to launch, but it was becoming increasingly apparent that the fighting days of the U.S. military were drawing to a close. Opposition had spread to the mainstream with *The New York Times* and the *Wall Street Journal* both now calling for withdrawal. George McGovern was turning his campaign for the Democratic nomination for president into a one-issue antiwar effort. The draft was ended, and with its passing went much of the immediate self-interest that brought many young people into the streets. Idealists would remain, but idealism alone seems scarcely enough to motivate millions into opposing foreign policy.

Brezhnev had embraced Nixon and welcomed him to Moscow. Even worse, Chou En-lai toasted Nixon in Peking while at the very moment bombs were falling on North Vietnam. That was probably the saddest day for us. I remember commiserating with Irwin Silber, columnist for the Old Left weekly newspaper *The Guardian*. "You should have been around when Stalin signed the peace pact with Hitler," he said. "That was a day that really shook the faith." The comparison was justified as the crunch of global politics seemed to be foreshadowing a world more complex than that of the sixties.

Besides, internally, the movement was undergoing traumatic

divisions. Much of the reason lay in the growth of the women's movement. Sexism existed in movement offices just as it existed in corporate offices. Slightly less, perhaps, but it was undeniably there. Furthermore, it was in these movement offices and in strategy sessions that the woman question would first surface in the battle of the sexes. Resistance to internal change—the alteration of one's consciousness—is natural. Of course, we are all children of our times, and once the *idea* of women's liberation was on the table for discussion, there was no way the seating order could remain the same or be quickly rearranged. Something had to give.

There was a common movement activity appropriately called the "gut-check." Basically, it's an inhibitor to action carried out by making a fellow activist feel guilty. It happens in all relationships. It is exceptionally frequent in neurotic matings. There was a great deal of neurosis in the movement, and repeated gut-checking on the woman question drove people away. Nobody becomes liberated on a fundamental issue like sex overnight. Neither men *nor* women.

During the spring and summer of 1971, we had started a group called WPAX. Rennie Davis had worked it out with the Vietnamese that the U.S. movement would get a two to four hour daily chunk of air time from Radio Hanoi in which to broadcast to the American troops fighting in the South. Rennie handed the operation over to me, and I formed the usual open group to decide things. We attracted the standard blend of committed activists, undercover agents, and weirdos. Much of the energy, it seemed, went into attacking me because I was well known. To work out details with the Vietnamese in Paris, I was forced by the WPAX collective to take with me (at my expense) a woman who had been active about two months. Two Vietnamese officers who had come to trust me were dumbfounded when I showed up with a complete stranger. The newcomer said nothing in three days. She did, of course, get an earful. When we left the meeting, I urged we return by our separate ways. I planned to return via London to publicize the upcoming censorship trial of *Oz* magazine and to meet secretly with IRA leaders. Later, the group criticized me for not taking the woman to England. A few days later, in New York City, she met me on the street, teary-eyed, unable to understand my "elitist attitude."

"Listen, last night this gang of off-duty cops was climbing all over our roof with baseball bats," I said in exasperation. "I have a five-year prison sentence hanging over my head, I'm on probation in three states, and I'm facing another ten years in Washington. You got any real problems?" I never saw her again; her two-month fling was over. She was using the movement to work out her own neurosis and didn't care who she battled, me or the government. The nonelitist nature of the movement was admirable—but the government, if no one else, created leaders. That reality caused great friction with our "no leaders" philosophy.

The short history of WPAX was integrating. The FBI, the CIA, even the renamed HUAC recognized that broadcasting Joan Baez and Bob Dylan music along with news other than Radio Armed Forces propaganda was an effective means of undermining G.I. morale. As Hanoi Abbie, I was targeted for investigation, but the government did not have long to worry. Upon U.S. pressure, Aeroflot, the Russian airline, eventually refused to transport the tapes to Hanoi, and internal bickering in our collective made productive work impossible. The studio equipment was stolen by some jerks from Buffalo operating on a "higher revolutionary principle." WPAX disintegrated, and somehow I came to believe that my new status as "non-leader leader" made movement life impossible.

There were loads of similar incidents. I was called daily to appear at rallies and demonstrations around the country. It was impossible to honor all requests. Often when I said no, some stranger at the other end of the phone would say, "I always knew you were an elitist pig!"

Runaways would find their way to our nest hideaway and demand that we turn our small bedroom into a crash pad. I still have a strong recollection of one encounter. A street kid on the other side of the door demanded admittance and when refused started a fire and blew the smoke under the door. Anita, six months pregnant, yanked open the door and I, shotgun in hand, confronted the stranger. Some movement rival, envious of our fame, had edged him into the intrusion. He apologized and left. I shuddered, thinking I could have blown his head off.

Fame is such a strange commodity. People started wanting to just touch me, tear at my clothes, demand my autograph. One

Vietnam veteran in a wheel chair traveled 1,200 miles from Wisconsin just to meet me publicly. Desperately, in front of the press, he clutched at my legs begging that I cure him of his paralysis. I was trapped. Having been to Lourdes, to the shrine of Our Lady of Guadalupe, I understood faith healing and knew the power of hypnosis. This poor chap was ready to be cured, and if I played the role I might have made him walk. I might have tried it had not the microphones been recording the scene. While trying to sympathetically deal with the situation, my mind kept focusing on a Lenny Bruce routine and I saw myself in the future with discarded crutches and wheelchairs up to my ass. I passed on the faith healing. John Lennon told me this was an extremely common occurrence with the Beatles. The difference between us was I had no protection, no privacy, no press agent. Unlike other famous people, when the camera lights turned off, I went back to the streets.

When the false reports of my East Side "penthouse," my "theft" of *Steal This Book*, my "haircut," and the other stories began appearing, there was no public relations department to correct the information. I was still in the movement, but my heart was no longer in the fight. No matter what I did, someone bitched. Nothing I said came out right.

The final blow occurred one Sunday afternoon in Central Park. It was the straw that broke the yippie's back. Attica had just gone down. One comrade, Sam Melville, died there and another, Robin Palmer, was injured. For the first time in years, the personal attacks left me incapable of responding.

Anita and I were pushing the baby carriage through the park. Two police stopped to chat and play with little america. Friendly cops, they had hair slightly over their coat collars and moustaches. It was the limit the department allowed. It was a cozy scene. Out of the corner of my eye, I saw amateur paparazzi circling to take pictures. Yes, this was news: "Cops play with Abbie's little america while Attica burns," would be the general drift of the story. I had to scuttle the scene by quickly insulting the cops. They returned america to the carriage and sulked off. The public image had been saved, but inside I was shattered. The insults were not real. To protect an image, I was being forced to be something other than human. Anita chased after the police, and out of camera range she explained it all. No one but another famous person is likely to understand this. We rode home on the subway in silence. We just knew we could hack it no longer.

Hiding Out in the Colonies

"What a cruddy fugitive I'd make," I thought. I had come down to St. Thomas in the Virgin Islands to scout around for a small place Anita and I could raise baby america, for six months, away from the world of notoriety. I rented a car, toured the island and found a little house high in the hills. We thought we'd be left in peace if we lived under another name so I pulled one of the sets of phony identification stored in my getaway bag, flew down secretly, opened a bank account, and rented the house and car all under an alias.

About to leave a parking place, a petite meter maid noticed that the car was overtime, stepped up, and asked, "Pardon mun, but yur papahs, plez." She was all of four feet high and when I failed to produce a special V.I. license which the rental agency hadn't told me about, I found her clutching me tightly by the arm. "You'll half tah cum wit me sir, you undah arrest." Before I could say, "Bliminey Blintzes," she steered me across the square to the police station. "You half to be kind nuf explain it to de judge, mun!" "Bail be hundred dollar," said the man behind the desk. Naturally I had only sixty bucks, so I visited St. Thomas's fanciest jail cell. Two hours later, I was breezed into a courtroom to face someone named Judge Hoffman! He was black, but that was his name all right and since the Virgin Islands was a possession every arrest was another federal case. So there I was, on $45,000 bail, convicted felon for five, facing ten more in Washington, now traveling under an alias, facing yet another Judge Hoffman. After three or four routine cases he called the name on all my papers. I tried desperately to look six feet tall, blond, and hoped my nose wouldn't grow. Staring at my shoes, I walked to the bench. "Can

you speak up, son,'' he said without an accent. "Oh my god,'' I
thought, ''he's from the States.'' "Well sir, there's been a misun-
derstanding, sir, somewhere because the car rental agency, sir,
never said anything about a special license. I don't see how I can be
faulted, sir,'' I said. First I call one Judge Hoffman a schtunk and
now I was calling another Judge Hoffman sir. No one recognized
me, though. I paid the fine and walked out of court.

Two weeks later we sublet our apartment to a nice lady for
enough to cover both rents. She was, we were both convinced,
going to use it for mysterious commercial purposes at night but we
were ecstatic at the golden opportunity to flee New York.

No one who dips his or her toes into the Caribbean can ever be
perfectly content with another body of water. It is the world's
indoor heated swimming pool, only outdoors. Somehow the aqua
color and warm temperature make it seem artificial forever. Ex-
ploring the island, we discovered secret coves where we could
swim alone and lie on the beach. I indulged in one of my longtime
fantasies and enrolled in a Scuba Diving School. Some afternoons
we would rent a boat and go skin diving for conches and trade them
for dinner at a small restaurant. I began doing all the cooking and
Anita got into gardening. We bought a Volkswagen and I taught
her how to drive. At the end of each day we got wrecked on banana
daiquiries and grass we grew at the side of the house and watched
the sun drop like a spinning, blazing yo-yo into the bay beyond.

Aside from a few pieces for underground papers, I wrote nothing but letters to friends, especially long running correspondences
with James McCann of the IRA. I had romantic visions of joining
them. James Joyce visited my dream world.

Very few people knew we were on the island. We called each
other different names and I took to wearing dark glasses. We made
casual friendships with an ex-Peace Corps couple back from the
South Seas, the bug exterminator, an engineer and his wife, and a
few sailboat freaks. An effort was made to avoid the tourists. We
enjoyed that sweet arrogance that comes from living in a place
people fantasize about but pass through only long enough for the
flash sunburn and a nasty go-round with the sand fleas.

Dr. Spock kept a sailboat harbored at the nearby dock. We went for dinner aboard. I asked him if he'd mind taking a look at america's chest. The kid had an inverted sternum. Spock was delighted. He bounced the boy on his knee and felt his brown little body. "Oh, it's nothing," he said, lifting his own shirt. "See, it means he's going to grow up to be a baby doctor!"

Occasionally friends came down to visit. "How can you stand it?" Jerry Rubin wanted to know. "No movies, so boring, and downtown it's like Saigon—whites occupy it in the day and blacks at night."

"We have each other. We talk a lot," answered Anita.

"We talk to the sun and the ocean," I added. "Besides the kid keeps us occupied."

"I don't know, I'd go nuts here," Jerry said. Jerry was a media junkie and got nervous when not in the midst of big-city action.

One time Brad Fox dropped down, and we went off to Puerto Rico for a rock festival. The promoters were unscrupulous rodents. They had lured young people down for a week of sun and sounds, with no attention paid to safety. "Rock and Roast" it should have been called. The temperature hit one hundred degrees each day. The medical team wasn't sufficient for the crowd. No one in Puerto Rico had much experience with bad acid trips. The site, a remote beach, was beautiful but deadly. In the two days preceding the festival, three people drowned in the breakwater. "It was far-fuckin' out," some pink hippie wailed. "I got pictures of the body, all gray and his stomach caved in when they pulled him out. Whooshh!" Puerto Ricans flocked to goo-goo eye the nude bathers. Knife fights were rampant. Rapes commonplace. No attempt was made to include groups relating to Puerto Rican culture. In fact, Black Sabbath, complete in satanic garb, was to perform on Easter Sunday. Welcome to rock *imperialismo*.

We contacted Puerto Rican independence groups and held a joint press conference warning young people not to come down. As a gesture of good will toward the Puerto Ricans, we announced we were leaving before it began. After the festival, ten thousand people were stranded in the San Juan airport when charters failed to fulfill their contracts. "We've seen our Altamont," remarked Brad dejectedly.

Back on St. Thomas, Anita and I took long walks imagining a life of beachcombing for the three of us in some even more remote place. Much of our cover had already been blown. The FBI had been to the house on the island questioning us about Ron Kaufman. Ron, my bodyguard in Chicago, had mysteriously dropped out of sight after the trial. As *Time* magazine told the story, he had reenlisted in the service for the express purpose of learning explosives. Alone he had planted nine bombs in bank deposit boxes, each in a different city. On the eve of destruction, so to speak, he had second thoughts and sent each bank a letter stating the location of the bombs. Ron was really too gentle to even hurt a deposit box. Just after the feds left, we scampered around to the side of the house and tore up all the marijuana plants.

One day over on St. Croix some black leaders recognized me and asked if I would speak at the local college. I begged off. The local police began to take an interest in our presence. So did the local paper. I promised I would talk to a reporter just before we departed if the paper would not print that I was there. Teeny-boppers started climbing the hill to the house. They would open the door and walk right in. Anita belted two with a broom.

Funds were running out, and I had a Washington court appearance coming up soon. We dreaded the return to city life and had, as they say, "mellowed out." Perhaps all island departures are tinged with sadness—ours was.

Six days after we got back to New York, we journeyed out to the Brooklyn docks to pick up the car. "Bill of lading for one blue Volkswagen, port of departure, St. Thomas. Just have a seat, will you," said the Customs man.

After two hours, we were finally directed to the pier area, where we spotted our little Volks sitting on the dock. Two longshoremen with long hair ambled over. "Hey mack, you gotta be somebody heavy, they just pulled a 'French connection' on your car over there," one said.

"No shit," said Anita. "You see it?"

"Un-huh, first time, too. They took every fuckin' thing apart. Tires, doors, seats—the works. There musta been ten guys doing it—and look at it now, you'd never know."

We knew though.

McGovern and Miami

Once back in town, the first order of business was the pretrial hearing down in Washington on the conspiracy-to-riot charges. I was, it seemed, a conspiracy of one as Lefcourt and I flew down to the capital to begin yet another go around with federal prosecutors and judges. Richard Kleindienst was now acting attorney general, as John Mitchell turned his attention to managing Nixon's reelection campaign and directing a secret army of dirty tricksters. During one of the lengthy arguments, FBI agents entered the court and whispered in the prosecutor's ear. The lawyers huddled at the bench, and moments later it was announced that all charges had been dropped. The Justice Department preferred to keep hidden all the wiretapping on me. It was illegal and voluminous. Years later, in a suit still being processed in the federal courts, no fewer than 144 illegal wiretaps with me as subject would be revealed by the government.

What is strange, looking back on the spring of 1972, was the way in which the government perceived us. The conventions were approaching, and Nixon feared we would do to the Republicans what we had done four years before to the Democrats. Believing we could bring up to forty thousand protesters to San Diego, they began a systematic campaign to harass and intimidate local activists in southern California. At the same time they increased surveillance of known national figures. All this was happening without apparent notice of the movement's internal difficulties. There appeared to be an enormous lag between the government's intelligence gathering at the bottom and decision making at the top. Obviously the government credited us with power that had by now for the most part dissipated. They even went so far as to have Gordon Liddy draw up a plan to kidnap Jerry Rubin and me and squirrel us away in Mexico until after the convention. Eventually they convinced themselves (unprodded by us) that the disruption would be impossible to contain. At a loss of millions of dollars, they moved the convention to Miami Beach.

Jerry and I both would have welcomed the kidnapping. We were in a difficult bind. Yippie had developed its own generational schism. Younger "zippies" had been dreaming of Chicago for four years as the confrontation highlight of the sixties. To them not much else had changed. The two-party system was a two-headed pig. They wanted to go to Miami Beach and demonstrate at both conventions. The older yippies who had organized in Chicago felt the times were different. "History doesn't repeat," argued Jerry. "Everything has changed." True, the war rolled on, but now a major opposition candidate, George McGovern, advocated complete and immediate withdrawal from Vietnam. This was a significant departure from any candidate's position back in '68. Before, the most outspoken critic within the two major parties would go only so far as calling for a negotiated settlement. The antiwar movement had, since '66, insisted that the U.S. had no right to negotiate an internal war and should just get out.

I supported McGovern. I also supported the Youth International Party as a "correction" for support of a major candidate because I agreed only with McGovern's Vietnam policy. This was pretty much the position of all older yips, and in early summer we sent a delegation to Washington to meet with McGovern's campaign staff. If they had said our support would be the "kiss of death" we would have toned it down. They did not, and we promised to do nothing that would embarrass him (although many party faithfuls said our existence was embarrassing enough).

Jerry, Ed Sanders, and I contracted to work on a book about the conventions. The bulk of any profit would be used to finance organizing activities for demonstrations organized by other yippies who felt a presence in the streets was necessary. People needed to be reminded that the war and the protest movement were still going on. Being bummed out on the movement did *not* mean I was disillusioned. In spite of all the difficulties my basic political beliefs remained the same. (Still do.) I just was uncertain about how to translate those views into meaningful action.

When we arrived in Miami, Nixon announced the bombing of Laos. It was almost a last reminder to the Vietnamese that his finger still controlled the war button. A warning to their negotiators in Paris not to place false hopes in any "peace candidate" such as McGovern. We immediately organized a large rally at the University of Miami. Needing celebrities, I asked Donald Sutherland, who was one of the Hollywood crowd willing to go out of his way, to help. One of the well-meaning handful who made time and was not afraid to express his opinions. I also asked Candy Bergen. Candy had never really spoken in public. She spoke for one minute and got stage fright! Later I coached her on how to perform. "Candy, speak from the heart, tell about your background, growing up in America, what you thought governments were supposed to be about, your disappointment."

It came as a mild shock to discover that actors and actresses so often got tongue-tied speaking publicly about politics. Somehow I had attributed to them magical powers which, given a few lines, allowed them to "fake" any position. Several came to the Chicago trial to give support and the same thing happened. After I saw Jane Fonda deliver one of her first speeches I coached her, too, by telling her not to use notes and to speak more personally. She is a very unusual woman and never fails to impress me. (Though her taste in men left something to be desired.) Coming from her background, she ought to have been some flaky broad out on a do-gooder crusade. As someone famous, she had to deal with many of the same problems I was having vis-à-vis the movement. Not exactly, of course, because she was rich and a woman (both of which being an advantage). Often I would see her in semi-disguise maintaining a low profile at conferences or workshops and taking notes at rallies where few would know she was present. She became an activist because simply being a famous actress was not emotionally gratifying. I always liked Jane and tried to relate to her as a fellow activist, not as a movie star, because that's what she became.

Walking the floors of the Democratic convention was quite a trip. Four years before we were being gassed and beaten in Chicago; now as we walked about, delegates would shake our hands and embrace us. The McGovern movement had a strong grassroots component. There was, as Nixon was quick to point out, a real difference. A group of young bloods actually escorted Jerry and me to the Illinois delegation, where we ceremoniously sat in "Mayor Daley's chair." Cathy Macklin, the first woman correspondent to cover a convention, interviewed us there. *New York* magazine wrote that that interview cost McGovern two hundred and fifty thousand votes. Republicans made ample opportunity of our presence, but I doubt that McGovern could have been elected under any circumstances, even if Watergate had been more fully known by the public. He had not figured out how this new consciousness (black power, women's rights, antiwar, legalizing grass) was to merge with that of the traditional white, working-class, rank-and-file Democrat. McGovern's brief effort offered a working social experiment. We found a way to stay active; to measure our options.

The zippies made it tough on us, interpreting every zig as a sell-out, every zag as proof we were over the hill. They mocked Jerry when he turned thirty by presenting him with a "media cake." We fought them because we disagreed with their brand of humor just as we disagreed with their inflexible political tactics. People can have as many disagreements about satire as they can about any other political weapon. Zippies practiced street comedy that I thought was sick. For example, when George Wallace was shot and paralyzed, they celebrated with a "Free Arthur Bremer" rally. No matter how distasteful Wallace's politics, once paralyzed he was somewhat off-limits. A middle-aged-man slipping on a banana peel is funny. A woman is less funny. A child even less. If it happens to a handicapped person, any ridicule is simply cruelty. The zippies failed on several occasions to understand these subtleties. Their act got heavy-handed. They made an enemy of anyone (including me) who did not see things their way. They were too quick to isolate themselves from other groups and the general population. Too willing to accept the smug arrogance provided by a closed cult. Jerry and I fought throughout those months for control of the party image—even while we wanted to move on to something else. We felt it was something we owed our grandchildren.

The zippies later evolved into yippies. Their political style has also evolved and today they are one of the few sixties groups still active. Somewhere along the way the hatchet was buried, and we're on friendly terms. Aron, A. J., Alice, and Dana form the

New York core, and there are scores of chapters around the country. You can subscribe to the party newspaper, *Overthrow*, by writing YIP, 9 Bleecker Street, New York, N.Y. 10012.

In the fall of '72, I traveled giving speeches explaining, with some difficulty, why I supported McGovern. He and I bumped into each other in Minneapolis, but I was careful to stay out of camera range, not wanting to taint him. From the convention to the election it was pretty much the down-hill slalom as McGovern botched one decision after another. Sometimes I think American politicians are chosen to disappoint us. A direct result of the "lesser of two evils" selection pattern.

That winter Anita and I gave up living in the city. Our brief fling in the Virgin Islands had given us a lust for privacy and natural beauty. When her mother bought a house out on Long Island we moved there. I worked on the sequel to *Steal This Book*. The only regular political activity I was involved in was the case of Tommy Trantino.

A reporter friend, Jay Levin, had turned me on to Trantino. A poet-writer who had spent ten years on death row (twenty years total in prison), Tommy had been convicted of killing two New Jersey policemen. I read his soon-to-be-published book, *Lock-the-Lock*, and pretty soon found myself visiting him regularly in Rahway Penitentiary once a week as his "editor." We set up a defense committee and gathered support for him. Tommy reminded me a lot of Jimmy McCann, the Irish provo. One of those romantic types who spend their lives dodging Doom's sword. Tommy had done wrong I suppose, but people change, times change, and twenty years locked in a cage seemed long enough, no matter what the verdict, no matter what the crime. If New Jersey wants, they could parole him today in my custody. He has a contribution to make on the outside.

Sex, Women, Getting a Vasectomy, and All That Sticky Stuff

One day Anita returned from seeing the gynecologist. She was crying. "The IUD," she blurted out, "it slipped through my uterine wall. The doctor says I need an operation to remove it." Somehow this whole contraception business just didn't seem fair. Why should it be the woman's responsibility? From my experience with Sheila, every combination seemed to have its complications. Anita had been on the pill, but studies had convinced us extended use was ill-advised. Now this! I decided to get a vasectomy. Not only would I get a vasectomy, I would make a movie of the operation explaining all my reasons. It would be a political/cultural act. I would be putting my balls where my mouth was.

Larry Rivers filmed the entire sequence of events. The film shows me speaking of the reasons. It shows me playing with my children and "climaxes" with the actual operation. Interesting and compelling theater, it fails on a propaganda level. Guys instinctively grab their nuts when they see it. In time there will be better solutions, but looking back I have no regrets and men contemplating the operation should be reassured that it has absolutely no effect on your sex life.

The IUD incident wasn't the only reason for the vasectomy. Sometimes women balled me less for kicks than to get pregnant. One story came back that out there in the universe somewhere I had unknowingly sired a little yippela. I hated the idea. Sure I enjoyed sex. I have more fun in bed than anywhere else, and I just love all that touching, fondling, squeezing, sucking, and fucking.

My marriage to Sheila was monogamous. Anita and I had an open-ended relationship, with my end considerably more open than hers. (Much more!) For a short period we experimented with every kind of sex. Well, not every kind! None of that whips-and-chains stuff. Anita marveled at my sexual appetite. She often saw me as a reincarnation of Pan, the seducer. I think you would expect a double Sagittarius to be a little lusty. I always thought the idea of postponing pleasure was something Wasps dreamed up to keep Jews out of the country clubs and fancier restaurants. When I heard that Hemingway believed screwing sapped his creative energy and that Muhammad Ali wouldn't fuck while in training, I knew right off I never wanted to be a writer or a boxer. Whenever I look at one of those charts surveying how often men do it I end up falling off the right end of the bell-shaped curve. In other words, a lot. Ed Sanders opened his novel *Shards of God* with me out-fucking a machine in front of the Pentagon. Whereas Jerry Rubin's published sexual history consisted of trouble getting it up, my problem is keeping it in my pants. (For some reason thinking about baseball and saying the word over and over like a mantra—Baseball-Baseball-Baseball—makes the flag go down.) You know, admitting all this, today, I'm not sure whether I'm bragging or confessing a weakness. I consider myself a macho-feminist. Which means I completely reject Midge Decter's conservatism and, in general, feel the only thing good about the good old days is that we survived and outgrew them. Guys and gals that cling to the old roles, I see as "sissies" afraid to meet the challenge and adventure of a new attitude. When it comes time to clear away the dishes only cowards stay seated at the table.

I'm not ashamed to say I jerk-off. Some critics have said I masturbate in public, and my hunch is that no one under thirty-five would even consider that an insult anymore. Tuli Kupferberg once wrote: "To masturbate is human, to fuck divine." I never liked that distinction. Norman Mailer considers it a sin, but I have trouble accepting most of his frontier views on sex. I found his book *The Prisoner of Sex* to be a brave, honest description of the sexual tensions and conflicts experienced by the typical American male who reached adolescence before the pill came into general usage. It's my story all right. I do tend to see women as sex objects first. But, the first duty of a prisoner is to escape, and I think the book implies more determinism than warranted. Equality between the sexes implies working out sexual relationships with a good deal of creativity and love. The more discussion the better. This has been hard for both males and females, but I think the women's movement is a healthy step up the human ladder. Biology should never be accepted as a political argument. Evolution promises equality, and revolution is the individual commitment to that process. There will *not* always be societies in which the strong eat the weak. The division of labor which insists that men hunt, that women nurse and cook, will fade into the past. Eventually even our unconscious mythology will evolve. Sex is politics and as such revolutionary sex demands justice. Sex is play and as such seeks enjoyment. It's fair to say I balled my way through the movement, but in your standard double-standard way was faithful to Anita. I never stood her up. Hedonistic communism seems to me not a bad program for bedrooms or, for that matter, for governments.

We lived as a couple. We talked intellectually about the advantages of communal living but somehow just never met the right commune. New York City didn't seem to allow for extended-family living arrangements. That seemed to work better in the country where larger dwellings were available. Besides, communes seemed to fall apart quicker than couples. Our relationship outlasted almost all our friends, we never fought and, romantically, believed it would go on forever.

The movement, coming in the sixties as it did, was simultaneous with the sexual revolution. Because of increased mobility, greater exchange of information, and changing work patterns, the nuclear family did break down. There was a lot of sex in the movement but only in contrast to the repression that had been the history of sex. A new morality began to evolve as a result of the cultural break-up. There was a certain excitement to all the fresh air. Like the Kennedys following the Eisenhowers. Then came women's liberation, which moved the discussion to an even higher level of honesty. Sex is pretty much a mysterious adventure. In about thirty or forty years maybe I'll have something to say on the subject. Right now I enjoy it too much for extended dissection.

You Can't Have Your Coke and Eat It, Too

I can't tell you all the details of the coke bust because someday all this might end up in court. I'm not even that sure myself of what happened; for instance, I never met one of the other people arrested. There were undercover cops on both sides. I helped bring people together, but it wasn't my coke. According to neutral witnesses at a later court hearing, the police who busted me posed as telephone men and worked on the basement terminal box in my mother-in-law's apartment. I lived there when in town. They also reportedly asked the assistant super for a key to enter her premises. It's not that ridiculous to assume they bugged the joint. I was interviewing several dealers there and on the phone in connection with the *Steal This Book* sequel, and they probably figured a way to get me cornered in a deal. There was plenty of reason: just two weeks before, I had been involved in a lawsuit that resulted in forcing the New York City Police Department to destroy intelligence files on a million people. Mine was the only individual name involved, and I was a persistent thorn in their side.

Of course, all these behind-the-scenes shenanigans don't excuse the fact, and I shouldn't have been there. I was just curious, that's all. Probably everyone reading this book except my mother has snorted coke. The only reason it's illegal is that some southern politicians, a long time ago, convinced Congress it made black people lust for white flesh and unafraid of bullets. Then came Harry Anslinger and his FDA bureaucracy, and the penalties for coke possession kept getting stiffer. Everyone misequated cocaine with heroin. Now you can't find a single pharmacologist who will say cocaine is a narcotic. But what the first judge in my case stated is true: "If the legislature wants to define milk as a narcotic, it can." I was busted on the eve the Rockefeller Drug Laws went into effect. I face a mandatory fifteen-year-to-life sentence. General drug hysteria was sweeping the city and there were great misconceptions about coke. The prosecutor demanded five hundred thousand dollars in bail and deemed what had happened "a crime more heinous than murder." Now the prosecutor works as a partner with one of my lawyers, defending folks busted for dope. Today in court he argues that coke is harmless.

When I first entered the Tombs waiting for the appeals court to lower the bail I had no intention of splitting. The Tombs probably has another more formal name but everyone calls it that. There's good reason. Each floor had its own category. Top floor got your "coconuts." Next down, "ad segs"—administrative segregation. Murder and up goes there. Then your homos; two floors of general population; one floor of trusties, prisoners who keep the joint running, buying time with labor. The ground floor is bright, exceptionally clean, and is used to see lawyers and visitors. It hides the horror above from the outer world. I was caged in administrative segregation with the other prisoners facing life sentences. The general atmosphere is very well captured in the movie *Short Eyes*. New York was experiencing its worst heat wave in sixty years when they locked me up. It was stifling. The windows had been welded shut; dirt and grime had long ago blocked out any possible view of the sky. Inmates were locked in their cells all the time except for meals, visits, and a weekly shower. There was no air conditioning and to get relief from the unbearable heat, everyone stayed naked wrapped in a wet sheet.

It seemed even the giant cockroaches sweated. I was almost raped in the shower by a guy named Candy. Candy did a thousand pushups a day. He was once cornered by a cop with a police dog. He broke the dog's neck, grabbed the cop's gun and blew his head off. Five cells down an inmate hanged himself with a sheet one morning. There was a lot of suspicion about it being a suicide. The food was almost inedible and heavy on the starches. The two trusties who brought it up apologized one day because there wasn't enough bread. They said the rats had gotten it. Late at night you could hear the rats scratching in the ventilator shaft. The bright, bare light bulb burned the nights away, making time seem like an unending pressure in your brain.

Out of a population of thirty-five men, three of us were white, the other two being Mafiosi. The blacks formed into two gangs—Muslims and non-Muslims. There were several bloody fights. Below my cell, one bunch gang-jumped two guys suspected of snitching and beat them unconscious. One of the victims was hit in the face with a heavy metal wringer used to squeeze out mops. I saw an eye ripped out of his head, dangling on nerve strings. The other guy, bleeding badly, was dragged off the floor feet first by the guards, who seemed to enjoy it all.

I spent six weeks in my cage, staring out through the bars wondering if I could do fifteen or twenty years like this up in Attica. I had never been a well-adjusted prisoner, and more often than not ended up in solitary confinement. There was a good chance of beating the case, but as the days wore on the depression increased. One day I made up my mind that if I ever got out I'd just keep going.

Anita came to visit a lot. She'd hold the kid up to the thick, stained window and we'd talk through a telephone. "Gee honey, if I ever get free I'd like to go swimming." I said.

"Yes, I know," she said putting a finger to her lips. "Swimming" was one of our code words for living underground. Living under surveillance for so long we had a well-developed code we used to discuss things not meant for federal ears.

Eventually the bail came down, and I was back on the streets. I had maybe two months to map my escape. What were the options? Exile? Yes, that had to be considered. I asked two friends if they would go to Europe and track down all the latest on each country's attitude toward my moving there. All this required the utmost security, because if anything leaked bail could be terminated. Surprisingly the courts even let me travel abroad. I went to Europe and then flew to Mexico to meet secretly with a group of left-wing lawyers. Customs-men always used to say, "Hey Abbie, we didn't expect you back!" I spent long nights plowing through extradition treaties and became, I was told, something of an expert on the field. In general, few countries will accept exiles on a "what-if" basis. There was good indication Sweden would take me in since many artists and intellectuals there knew me and lawyers felt enough support existed to successfully fight extradition. Israel, of course, has a law of the returned stating all Jews no matter what the crime can seek refuge there, but politics takes precedence over all such laws and fugitives from the U.S. are sent back. Months later word came that I could go to Cuba to live. And from several countries came news that there were contacts ready and willing to help secure working papers and a new identity.

In January I let out word that I wanted to meet with Weatherpeople living underground in the U.S. That was the route I had pretty much decided to take and I wanted to hear what it was like firsthand. It took a week to arrange the meeting. Several conduits shuttled me from subway to taxi to elevator to taxi until everyone was convinced the coast was clear. Finally I was instructed to go into a movie theater and sit in the third row. We were somewhere in Brooklyn. Ironically, the movie playing was *The Way We Were*. Half an hour later Delgado sat down next to me. He had been under four years by then. We had not seen each other for over a year. His hair was a new color. He was twenty pounds lighter. He was far sadder than that night in Death Valley we got stoned and talked of revolution forever.

"This will be very hard for you, you know that," he said.

"I talked with Robin, who is just back from Attica and my mind's made up," I replied. "I'll take my chances on the street."

"Can you win the trial?" he asked.

"Probably. It's really the cop's word against mine. It's just the atmosphere, and the penalty's so high if I lose. I'm sick of trials."

"Anita going?"

"No. We talked it over. It's too hard on the kid. She's tired of doing my thing. We'll try a year apart and see."

"That's tough. Alone is very tough. None of our people make it alone. The change is very drastic. You're older than us. So well known. Concentrate on your walk and your voice. You must become very conscious of how you project yourself in the world. You really have to do this by yourself, Abbie."

"Delgado, I'm leaving next month. I'd like these letters sent from the cities indicated. They're to Anita, my lawyer, friends being watched. A false trail. Like they do in the movies."

"Do you know where you're going?"

"Not really—but I'll tell you one thing—it's gonna be warmer than Brooklyn. I'll send you a postcard."

Gateway to the Underground

Delgado was right about Anita. We had gone through it all together, and now there would be no one. As the day grew closer, I'd sit near the foot of the bed watching her sleep. Inside I begged she would change her mind.

It was February and the snows came. Anita had moved to a tiny place in the warehouse district south of Canal Street. Ever since america had been born I had done all the cooking, so I prepared a feast for our last meal. We made love through the night. One long tantric screw I hoped would never end. In the morning we bundled the kid up and drove him to the daycare center. For days now, I had been putting him to sleep with a bedtime story about the bunny rabbit who hid in the forest from the bad hunters. When I was gone Anita would translate the story, and rather quickly he would come to understand why Daddy was gone.

On the way to the airport we blew a tire and a policeman stopped to help me change it. We chatted about the weather. "Don't I know you?" he asked.

"Doubt it, just visiting my sister here," I said, stretching the Boston accent. He nodded.

The plane was on time. I was flying to Richmond, Virginia, for a speech and then would disappear. We embraced one last time. "Let's promise each other never to smoke cigarettes again," she said. We had quit together on the moment four years previous. It was our private victory. She turned and walked away. Black boots. Bell-bottom jeans. Cowgirl shirt. The black leather jacket with fur collar. The sexy red spot in her eye. With her went the best years of my life.

I was alone. Almost immediately, survival instincts took over. Depression seemed to roll away like midmorning fog. The speech went well. No one seemed to understand it when I closed saying,   .

"So long, if you see ol' Rockefeller lookin' for me, tell him I went thataway" (pointing to heaven). Next stop Atlanta. Gladys Knight and the Pips echoed in my ears: "He's leavin', he's leavin', on the midnight train to Georgia. . . . goin' back to a life he used to know. . . ."

Already I could feel the changes. Stiff shoes. Sport jacket. Black horn-rimmed glasses matching the photo on the license I now carried.

"Hey buddy," I called, hailing a cab.

"You's new in town, Speedy."

"Sho-nuff, up from Jacksonville," I ad-libbed. "Headed for Boston. I'm a stage-actor. Got this two-bit part in a new musical called *Atlantis*. Gotta get my head conked. Screwy director says all the people lived in Atlantis had straight hair."

"Lloyd Sheffield in Jonesboro, out in Clayton County's ya bess bet. Day say der he's dah bess," answered the cabbie.

"Eyow!" I screamed. "That stuff burns like a bitch!"

"Gets the job done," replied the barber. "We used to use hot irons—but didn't last but a month or so. Dis here stuff's good for six months if you rub it in good. Won make it fall out none, either."

"You Italian or somethin?" he added.

"How'd you guess?" I responded, figuring everybody was helping me develop a new identity.

"Oh, you look Italian. Some of my best friends' Italians," he agreed. "I always wanted to be Italian," I thought.

In the hotel bathroom I laid out the Clairol bottles and reread the instructions. Shampoo. Rinse. Rub in bottle A. Rinse. Rub in bottle B. Let sit for forty minutes. I could feel the thick gray lather oozing down my face. "Mirror, mirror on the wall. Who's the fairest blond at the Holiday Inn tonight?" I opened my eyes.

"It ain't you, Frankie," replied the mirror. Ah rats! I do the entire treatment again, finally settling for near-blond. My hair's so soft and fluffy, just like on television. I get all dressed up again. "Your name is Frank. Your name is Frank," I keep repeating, staring at the stranger in the mirror. The rest of the night I spent memorizing every number on my identification papers. On a yellow legal pad I wrote the autobiography of my new life. Italian. Aquarius. Mother and father killed in an automobile accident. That will stop folks from asking about my past. Recently divorced. That will explain any sadness.

Next stop Los Angeles. Half my five-thousand-dollar getaway stash is going for the operation. There's just no way to guess how hard they'll look. Everything has to change.

"Oh, you're Lance's friend, Sam, from Canada," says the doctor. I had already arranged things with him. Lance Reventlow, the racing car driver, once told me this doctor was the best plastic surgeon in the country. Lance was dead. Dead men don't gossip. The doctor had no idea about me except that I was a Canadian TV personality getting on in years who needed a new face.

The Demerol was beginning to take effect. I barely had time to hypnotize myself. Time circled my head like the rings of Saturn. I transformed myself into an astronaut as they wheeled me into the operating room. I was in the last reel of Kubrick's *2001*.

"She's from Ireland," nodded the doctor in the direction of another form.

Both were wearing surgical masks.

"Ireland. Free Ireland . . . Erin go . . . Green . . . green . . . green . . ." I murmured half-conscious.

I was running through the streets of Belfast now. I could hear the women banging on the garbage cans calling the families to battle.

I felt the cold steel of a chisel press against my nose.

"This might hurt a little," mumbled the voice behind the mask.

I was in Grand Central Station now and waves of bodies were flowing as the police held a kid face down to the floor and smashed.

"Bradley, watch out!"

I was in Mississippi, marching on the dirt roads. "Oh freedom," sang the marchers, "oh freedom, before I be a slave, I'll be buried in my grave . . . goin' home to my land to be FREE."

I was breathing deeply now as the doctor raised the mallet in the air.

"Suzie. Suzie, let's go steady . . . But Ma, I don't wanna be a doctor . . . Tell him I don't wanna be a doctor."

I became little again. I was in a playground. All my kids and I

held hands and circled. Laughing. Giggling. Faster and faster . . .

"Run, run, run, fast as you can. You can't catch me, I'm the
gingerbread man . . ."

We collapsed near the sandbox, happy but exhausted. Andy
hugged little america. Amy started to sing softly . . .

Row, row, row your boat
Gently down the stream
Merrily, merrily,
Merrily, merrily,
Life is but a dream.

Epilogue

We have come to the end of my story. Of course, in this case the
end is also the beginning. I dropped out of sight in late February
1974 and for the past six years have lived on the lam. It would be
impossible, without jeopardizing my security, to write about my
underground life with the same candor as in the preceding pages.

During the incubation period I worked diligently to develop a
new identity. I learned to live with the terror of unfamiliar sounds
in the night, anxiety about being recognized in the streets, the pain
of separation from friends and loved ones, and abrupt changes in
class, culture, and appearance. The universe still went Boo! But I
disciplined myself and survived. Smart money was laying eight to
five that the house dicks would nail me in six months. Not even I
would have taken the bet.

In the first year I was really buried away. I lived mostly alone in
a small boarding house, taught school, and took classes at night. I
really doubt any of the people in my new world would have known
who I was even if I had told them. There were persistent nightmares, but slowly I became accustomed to being hunted. And
hunted I was. Weekly there were raids on communes and visits to

friends and relatives by the body snatchers. When my father died the FBI sent several agents to infiltrate the crowd hoping to grab me.

I learned of all these things by mail, through an elaborate network I had put together before splitting. But no one from my past world, not even those who volunteered to forward mail, knew my whereabouts. Patiently, I dug in for the long haul.

Then came word that the charges might be dropped. Independent witnesses were turning up who identified the police who trapped me. Seems that on several occasions they had posed as telephone repairmen and had worked on the junction box in the basement of my mother-in-law's apartment building where I lived when in New York. They also had entered the apartment with a janitor's pass key. Similar incidents took place at a friend's house where they were also identified by the superintendent. Despite these revelations the charges stayed fixed.

Along about this time, I met Angel and we decided to pool our talents. We managed to get by on our wits and occasional odd jobs. An offer came for a TV interview and I accepted. I felt the most shocking character I could play—and at the same time the safest—was the media image of myself. We went to the Max Factor School for Make-up in Hollywood, where we picked up enough tricks to re-create the old me. It was probably the most difficult interview I ever gave. I had to be able to say things I honestly felt, while at the same time blurring the truth when it came to specific questions about life underground. I had to recall each story I told in my cover life, continuously and rapidly. My passing comments about society, even my political arguments, had to be scrutinized for tell-tale clues. It was an ordeal to be so on guard. To top off the strain, we were stopped for speeding and an identification problem led to a tough grilling by the California Highway Patrol.

During this same period, friends smuggled my youngest son cross-country for an emotional rendezvous. We ran around to tourist spots, with my underground running mate snapping photos. After carefully avoiding the telephone for a year, I exploded with a burst of hundreds of calls. I startled friends in the night, titillated reporters, and defied the authorities. I called the New York City Police Department and reported myself a missing person. A large party was organized. Everyone knew who I was. If something went wrong, all I had to do was scale a wall and pilot the escape car to freedom. Some meetings with old friends were arranged with elaborate security precautions. And throughout this period: little sleep and constant speeding from hideout to pay phone to parking lot to hidden farmhouse to Mexico and back. On top of this, I underwent a difficult operation. Just before the operation, the anesthesiologist asked what drug had been used on me in past operations. "Demerol," I replied, for a reason. Demerol does not render the patient unconscious. Lying unconscious on an operating table surrounded by complete strangers is the type of situation fugitives try to avoid. Without telling me, they used a drug that knocked me out. Hours later I was smuggled out of the hospital. During the recovery I had to treat myself. Sometimes the pain was so great that I had to bite on a towel to stifle screams. All this combined to produce my first crack-up.

I am sitting in the middle of insanity on the floor of a Las Vegas hotel room. We have been racing madly for days, a step or two ahead of the body snatchers. Angel is trying to figure out what preparations are needed for what seems like inevitable capture. She's exhausted from watching the man she loves turn into a monster. My lips are cracked from hours of talk binge. I think that the doctors inserted a transmitting device during the operation. I'm trying to decode the beeps. I crawl rather than walk, avoiding the gaze of the people behind the two-way mirror.

The TV set is talking to me. Everything is code. Saigon is being liberated. Dominoes are falling in my head. Soon Las Vegas will fall. I wander about, mumbling incoherent phrases, engaging people in dialogue, playing strange roles. Lucky for me it's Las Vegas. Temporary insanity is more commonplace than the cold.

We drive through the desert. C.B.'ers broadcast contradictory directions. The ashtray and the doorknob pick up signals. It hurts inside. I know I've gone crazy. Finally we arrive at a friendly house isolated in the mountains. I am quieter and accept food and medication.

Slowly sanity returns. We begin re-establishing our former underground lives. We return to where we were living and get jobs as caretakers of a large house managing smaller units. We live very cheaply. Friends help occasionally. We survive. More than that, we frolic and enjoy life. We let new people share our guarded secret. We broaden the network of underground communication and survival. We owe so much to those who've kept their mouths shut avoiding the temptation to idle gossip.

Another year passed. Each month brought new revelations of government schemes to get me. In the spring of 1975 the CIA stated in court that it had no files on me, but several months later the National Security Agency admitted to intercepting calls, telegrams, and letters of mine. In a congressional hearing, the National Security Agency said it turned over all this data to the CIA. An intelligence officer who used to work for the Defense Department told lawyers that he saw a Pentagon plan to set me up on a dope bust. Anita's and my correspondence, *To america With Love: Letters from the Underground*, was about to be published. She was now living on welfare, but energetically involved in organizing other welfare mothers in an advocacy group. She had been constantly under FBI surveillance.

A reporter from *Playboy* and I worked out arrangements for an interview. He violated our trust agreement. Sure enough, when Angel and I read it, we realized that our cover would be blown as soon as the magazine hit the streets. I went into a rage, and again, exploded with a maniacal burst of energy. Beneath the surface, though, I was terror stricken. In hours we had to uproot, separate, and disappear. I fled alone to Canada. Then to Chicago, of all places. Once even to New York, where I walked into the Phil Ochs memorial concert. Lonely for my friends who would be there, wanting to pay some extra tribute to my old trail buddy, ready to defy those who hunted me, I took a dangerous chance.

Scampering through New York, the flashing lights triggered electronic impulses in my brain. I weirded-out on the phone system—calling at times a hundred people a night, reciting poems, singing songs, talking about current events. Startled voices reacted to my laughter and screams. I walked into people's apartments unannounced and got kicks out of asking cops for information. I took so many needless chances that I must have desired to be caught or killed. Finally I was talked into leaving New York.

Alone, in a strange city, the whirly-wheels in my brain took off. I pictured myself growing old. I became old. I experienced false heart attacks. I talked to machines, people on the other side of the

world, and finally to the dead. I became obsessed with visions of
my father, the grief over his death finally came pouring out. Often
I would get lost in the streets. A fugitive's brain is filled with a
mass of data—social security numbers, job histories, birthdates,
coded contacts, even different birth signs. There are at least two
dozen names I use. If I examine the problem of who I am,
something everyone does in introspective periods, the problem
only gets magnified. A simple "What's your name?" can produce
insane giggles.

At the height of this hysterical episode, I was thrown in jail. My
credentials were carefully checked. My cover story, concocted on
the spot, was so overblown that the cops weren't sure if I should be
locked up or given the keys to the city. At one point I was locked in
a cell. The click of the door was one of the loudest sounds I've ever
heard. I was certain the police suspected who I was. I picked up
some wax paper and rubbed the wax into the whorls of my
fingertips. Sometimes you can alter your prints with wax. I put my
address book in a sandwich and ate it. If I go down, I thought, I
want it to be just me they get. A few hours later I was released. An
old friend had driven non-stop for nine hours with the bail money
he took out of his kid's bar mitzvah fund. It turned out the alias I
was using was that of some other outlaw who had passed that way
before. What was equally coincidental was that at the time of my
brief incarceration someone named Albert Hoffman had been
apprehended by the FBI in New Orleans, and the wire services
started putting out reports that he was me.

Instead of shaking me out of the psychotic state, the trip to the
slam made it worse. Now I felt I was invulnerable. I scorned sleep.
Extra energy went into exercises. I wrote half a dozen articles,
some songs, poems, scores of letters. I started practicing with
weapons, convinced I was becoming a criminal.

Finally, alone and broke, I crashed out of my manic cycle. I
cried uncontrollably, realizing that I had chased away everyone I
loved and had prepared for self-annihilation. I craved death but
lacked the energy or initiative to do the deed. Instead I lay in bed
and waited. Terror crept through my bones and I was afraid.
Ashamed and afraid. I could barely write my name, *any* name; and
scores of ideas died in the blur of my depression. Some studies
have linked manic cycles with creativity and through the years, I

had come to believe this. I had always found it impossible to write when down in the dumps; now I realized that I had to learn how to harness misery as well as euphoria. The realization was hard to translate into action. Mind and body fatigue seemed to overwhelm any effort I made to pull myself together. Every day began with thoughts of suicide and turning myself in; I was convinced that I had failed all those real and imaginary people cheering for me to go the distance. On more than one occasion I made plans to return to New York defeated.

I tried to help myself. I even checked into a psychiatric clinic, but left before seeing a therapist. The effort itself had a beneficial effect. Convinced that the authorities had plentiful leads on me (I couldn't pay the phone bill, anyway) I decided to move again— this time to a large city in the Northeast. The landlord drove me and my two suitcases to the bus stop; we went into a restaurant and I told him I was a fugitive. We had become close in a short time and something told me I could trust this man. He sat in silence, listening to my story. Soon he was talking of his own life—how he had been in jail, how he had lost his business and was tired of life, how his brother had been killed in Korea. I never mentioned my real name, but later I sent him an autographed book. When we parted friends he pressed some bills into my hand.

Wandering the new city, I searched for a cheap room. The only place I could afford was a broken-down rat trap in the slums. Twenty-five dollars a week got me a hole in the wall. Give the inmate a key to his own cell. Winos crowded the stoop. Prostitutes clicked their heels in the hall. A pimp dragged one by the hair out of the elevator. Saturday night brought the shoes; I.D. checks and illegal room searches. Everyone lived in fear, shaking in his withered skin.

After four days I met a guy in the street who saw me reading the classifieds and asked if I was looking for a place to rent. I followed him to his apartment. Piles of left-wing literature were scattered about. I noticed *Steal This Book* on a shelf. I took a deep breath and collapsed into a chair. I told him who I was and what had been happening during the past months. He listened quietly. The picture in the book and my face bore some similarity. We agreed to meet the following day. He said he would help, but he wanted me to meet a friend of his.

The next day we met in a cafe. His friend was a Marxist psychiatrist who had once heard me speak. It was not long before they believed me and offered help. My new friend John let me have his apartment and he moved in with his girlfriend. The psychiatrist agreed to hang out with me for a few days. I found a job. Manual labor proved to be the best therapy. It felt good to make something happen through physical work. The work ran out and I decided it was again time to move on. On to another town, another job.

Angel and I reunited. She got a job as a waitress, I as a cook. The mental wounds began to heal. I began to learn how to live as a controlled schizophrenic. Not only had I picked up a new identity, but occasionally I bumped into people I had met from the time I was a teacher or on the road. I had several different lives by now. At night I would work on various articles for magazines. About twenty have been published so far. Four years ago, we more or less settled in a peaceful valley, a heartland paradise. Our town has less than a thousand people. For a long time I didn't even have a last name. I learned a bunch of new rural skills. My accent even changed and the locals started to accept me. Angel and I kept "Abbie" in a box under lock and key and when I could handle it, I'd pull down the box, get out the notes and work on this book. Talk about being reborn! I never was quite sure I was writing an autobiography or a biography. The movie "The Big Fix" guessed at what my life was like. They tried to hang the sixties-turned-seventies myth of disillusioned assimilation on me. It was way off the mark, but it pushed me into completing this book.

A year before the near-disaster at Three Mile Island, our valley was selected as the site for a series of nuclear reactors. The place Angel and I had come, in our rootless existence, to call home was being invaded by outside bureaucrats. I decided to take them on and plunged into round-the-clock community organizing. I didn't seek the issue, but once engaged I found the energy that got me through Mississippi and Chicago returning. This struggle was different, though; it was *our* home, *our* land under attack. My handicap caused me to cautiously think through every move. I play it much more deliberate. Somehow I'm getting away with it. The local paper once had a story about "me" and another about "Abbie" in the same edition! I've spoken at universities, churches, high schools, and have even been on radio and television. At one early meeting, a fellow activist remarked, "I wish we had Rennie Davis here." The committee is a genuine American coalition. Once an active woman, a conservative in her fifties, told me, "You know that anti-nuke group in ———————— County didn't win because they had professional radicals come in and try to organize them." I had to muffle a giggle when I argued there was no such animal as a "professional radical." Even without Three Mile Island we won our battle—for the time being, anyway. Someday I suppose I'll be free to tell the whole story. I'm not your most silent fugitive. I often wonder if the folks round these parts could accept Abbie as much as they do the other guy.

Our local victory has drawn national attention. There are at least two mass publications that have unknowingly in the past year written about both people. A year ago I planned to join other anti-nuke activists and fight as the other person. I puzzled for months about which person should meet Jackson Browne and Bonnie Raitt to discuss rallies and benefits. I still haven't decided. Then Three Mile Island hit, and overnight the anti-nuke movement came under too close scrutiny for me to go national. I withdrew to the valley. Once we thought my cover there had been blown, within an hour I was out on the highway hitchhiking out of the state, while Angel wiped away the fingerprints in our nest. Somehow we managed to shut down the rumor and I returned. I plan to see this through, no matter what the risks, no matter the consequences. It is probably the best organizing I have ever done, and I have never seen myself as anything more than a good community organizer. It was just the Vietnam war that made the community bigger, that's all. Eventually I know I'll get caught, but there's no doubt in my mind, what I'm doing and learning is worth the effort and the risk.

There is absolutely no greater high than challenging the power structure as a nobody, giving it your all, and winning. I think I've learned that lesson twice now. The essence of successful revolution, be it for an individual, a community of individuals, or a nation, depends on accepting that challenge. Revolution is not something fixed in ideology, nor is it something fashioned to a particular decade. It is a perpetual process imbedded in the human spirit. When all today's *isms* have become yesterday's ancient philosophy, there will still be reactionaries and there will still be revolutionaries. No amount of rationalization can avoid the moment of choice each of us brings to our situation here on the planet. I still believe in the fundamental injustice of the profit system and do not accept the proposition there will be rich and poor for all eternity.

I've had some good times, had some bad. Took some lumps. Scored some points. Half-way through life, at 43, I still say, "go for broke." No government, no FBI, no judge, no jailer is ever gonna make me say "uncle." Now, as then, let the game continue. I bet my stake on freedom's call; I'll play these cards with no regrets.

> Abbie Hoffman
> Underground, USA
> In the Autumn of the Seventies

Epilogue

P.S. On second thoughts. . . . .

Maybe I was wrong.

You know, I'm really sorry and I wanna come home. I love the flag. Blue for truth. White for right. Red for blood our boys shed in war. I love my mother. I was wrong to tell kids to kill their parents. It was the children's fault. Spoiled, selfish brats made the sixties. We encouraged kids to leave home. Forgive me, Mother. I love Jesus, the smooth arch of his back, his long blond curls. Jesus died for us all, even us Jews. Thank you, Lord. Pat and Debbie Boone introduced me to Jesus in their swimming pool. Thanks, Pat. Thanks, Debbie. Thanks, Jesus. I love Israel as protector of Western civilization. Most of my thinking was the result of brainwashing by KGB agents. The FBI was right; the KGB gave us money and dope as well as training. We met regularly at the Cuban mission to the U.N.

I hate drugs. They are bad for you. Marijuana has a terrible effect on the brain. It makes you forget everything you learned in school. When you smoke it's hard to work. I only used it to lure young virgins into bed. I'm very ashamed of this. Cocaine is murderous. It makes you sex crazy and gets uneducated people all worked up. Friends are kidding themselves when they say it's nonaddictive. The nose knows, and the nose says no. More people should listen to their noses and not to rich rock-n-roll singers and white house officials. LSD is the work of the Devil. I know many crippled babies whose thoughtless mothers were hooked on LSD. Laughing gas is no laughing matter. When it comes to drugs, only your doctor knows for sure. Take his advice and pay him for his service. Stealing is a crime.

Once I burned money at the stock exchange. This was way out of line. People work hard to make money. Even stockbrokers work hard. No one works hard in Bangladesh—that's why they are starving today and we are not. With inflation, everyone works extra hard for their money. It's not our fault or the fault of our government. If anyone's to blame it's the Arabs and those knee-jerking Europeans who cozy up to them by paying their price for oil. We have no choice but to go along. We should starve the world to get our way. If we got our priorities straightened out, we wouldn't have to change the meters on the gas pumps.

Long ago I worked for the Negro cause. It was fashionable. We meant well but got carried away. They just wanted to be left alone anyway. They love their neighborhoods so much there are crowds waiting to get in. Buses are an affront to all people, no matter what the color of their skin. If blacks don't love America their ancestors shouldn't have been so anxious to come here. It's not our fault they chained themselves to ships and ended up in America. No matter how we came to the free world, we are all equal: black and white, male and female, rich and poor, healthy and sick. Free choice is fundamental to our Way of Life. I was wrong to try and upset that delicate balance. Communism is evil incarnate. You can see it in Karl Marx's beady eyes, long nose, and the sneering smile behind his beard. One-and-a-half billion people now live in forced slavery. The only good thing you can observe in communist countries is the art. When their artists paint pictures of people, you see two eyes, two ears, and one mouth. Our artists are all perverts except, of course, for the late Norman Rockwell. And another thing about communistic pictures: the people have their clothes on. I'm not against nudity, but there's nothing artistic about naked bodies. Anatomy should be something doctors study. Keep it away from our children and womenfolk. Hippies kept taking off their clothes and that's the real reason there are no more hippies. They all got pneumonia and died. Good riddance to bad rubbish!! At least you can walk down the street without tripping over them.

Freedom is a precious right, not to be abused, but violence does not belong on television unless it's the news. Murders and rapes should be reported so people will know just what's happening downtown and will be more careful when they go out. People who commit serious crimes should not be coddled—the death penalty is too good for them.

The anti-nuke people I've met are just kidding themselves. They're nothing but a bunch of lonely neurotics looking for free sex. If we took them seriously we'd be sticking our heads in the sand. America would be reduced to a second-rate power. Our country stands for progress. Nuclear energy is clean and it's fun! Besides if these misfits irritate the utility companies, some officials might decide to pull the plug just to teach them a lesson. You'll see how fast those picket signs come down when they can't hear their punk music or watch themselves on *60 Minutes*.

Our system of democracy is the best in the world. I don't know much about other systems, but if you pick up the newspaper or turn on the TV, all the others seem to be falling apart. Good governments don't fall apart so easily. South Africa has been there for three hundred years. Don't get me wrong, they're not perfect down there. They work hard enough, but they should be nicer to their blacks, especially those who behave. I believe what Henry Ford said there recently: "Change takes time." Another three hundred years is not too long to wait for peaceful change.

Homosexuals live in sin. It says so in the Bible. Anyone who ever took the time to have a heart-to-heart talk with one of these sorry victims of our permissive society has heard the pain they've been trying to express. What every homo needs is a good shoulder to cry on. In the meantime, they should be kept away from children too easily influenced by homosexuals from New York. I love New York as much as anybody. I certainly admire the ambition that got those big buildings off the ground, but they do have strange notions. That's because the U.N. is in New York and the good people there are subjected to foreign ideas. If the U.N. was in Salt Lake City, if Puerto Ricans flooded Utah to get rich quick on welfare schemes, and if homos owned all the movie theaters and barbershops there, you couldn't expect anything different. I believe in women's rights, but it should be done outside the family. Family is the essence of democracy—destroy one and you destroy the other.

It's mind-boggling, but being a fugitive I've seen the way normal people live and it's made me realize just how wrong I was in the past. I've grown up, too. You know how it is when you're young and not in control. I'd like to go back to school and learn how to be a credit to the community. I've always had an itch to become a certified public accountant and work with a group like the boat people. Maybe I could sponsor some disease that needs a

personality, something like hemorrhoids. If a judge sentenced
Keith Richards to sing for the blind, because he fooled with coke,
I'm willing to sing for the deaf as punishment. If a judge sentenced
Linda Blair to speak out against drug abuse, I'd be more than
willing to do that. If the charges against me were dropped, I
promise to never put anything in my nose again. Not even my
finger. I'd teach drug abuse at Sunday Bible classes, supermarket
check-out lines and outside Studio 54.

Of course, there's the upcoming operation. The doctors are not
saying if the tumor is or isn't cancer, but they can't look me in the
eye. How could I have said all those terrible things about Hubert
Humphrey, rest his soul? Age takes its toll, but it teaches wisdom.
When you're in the foxhole of life, you see things clearer than
when the bands are playing and the crowds are cheering. I realize I
can't repair all the damage to our system I feel responsible for, but
I'm willing to roll up my sleeves and give it a try. It's damp
underground.

Now can I come back?

Aiding and Abetting

"I get by with a little help from my friends."

—The Beatles

Thanks to my publisher for having more brains and guts
than the other twenty antique dealers who turned down this book;
to my editor, Fred Jordan—this work was as much his as mine; to
Heather Martin and Barbara Lagowski for not fearing tapped
phones; to Secret Agents Elaine and Sheryl for relating to me as
one of the gals, and an extra star for nailing down the toilet seat; to
Secret Agent Ron who gives some of the best phone in the East; to
book therapists Cathy and John who helped me unblock and tuck
my dangling participle back in. Because the book was literally
written on the run, special gratitude goes to Judy, the Martins, the

outlaw brothers of Humbolt County, Lafayette, David, Dan and Pat, Paulie, Mister J. R., Jason, Pam and Reggie, Jane, Howard, and, of course, america, who read parts of the manuscript and offered advice; to Stew Albert for letting me wake him with late night calls to check assorted facts and factoids; to anthropologist Samuel Leff, Ph.D., for access to the famed Yippie Archives; to Norman Mailer for an assist to a fellow Jewish outlaw—a man, in my estimation, who is America's greatest journalist, a real, honest-to-goodness truth seeker.

Short Changed: Dave Dellinger, on second reading, deserves more credit. He was our anchorman, steady-eddy. His contribution to making America live up to its dreams is invaluable. Huey Newton was a true hero of the sixties and in my brief encounter with him I found him to be a gentleman and a scholar. I could, if pushed hard enough, find something good (the Port Huron Statement) to say about Uncle Tom Hayden, but his measure of accomplishment does not counterbalance my constructive criticism of his trip down. Thanks to Ron Kaufman, wherever you are—the wrong power trail; Danny Schecter was an early movement buddy in need of mention; Ron Kovics, whom I embrace as a fellow antiwar veteran, and to all the soldiers, sailors and civilians who lost something more than pride in Vietnam; to those who marched and trashed to convince the U.S. powers that they were battling on the wrong team over there in Asia. A special hero of labor award to Uncle B. who, in this writer's humble estimation, had the best combination of heart and mind of any sixties hero I encountered.

I only survive as a hunted outlaw because I have the kind of friends money can't buy. A,D,E,B,B,A,F,M,J,H,R,P,W,S,T, and the Mayor all performed brilliantly. A word to Carol Ramer—your tears were mine. A word of caution to all readers: Fugitives do not like being pointed at. Never come up to say hello. We have great vision and see you first. You say hello to a fugitive by winking or smiling. Also, it is blasphemy to gossip about Angels. We need all the help we can get and loose lips sink ships.

Finally, to my family: To my father for teaching me there is no contradiction between being a good businessman, a good guy, and a good revolutionary; to my mother for the gift of humor, and the chicken soup; to the women in my life, especially Sheila, who taught me to aim for nothing short of the best, and encouraged my movement career. Through the catharsis of this book I have once again learned to love her. To my dearest wife, Anita, whose smile and courage will join us till death and beyond; to Angel for everything, and to her father for teaching me to stick to strong ideals and basic values, and to her mother for teaching me manners and how to become a better writer and husband. In closing, a word to my three children: Papa misses you Andy, Amy, and america. He loves you very much and won't say nothin' if you steal this book.

A. H., November 8, 1979

Afterword:
Remembering Abbie
by Howard Zinn

Recently, I told Kurt Vonnegut about a man I know named Bill Breeden, a minister and truckdriver who lives in the woods of Indiana with his wife and children. When his tiny hometown of Odon named a street after John Poindexter, Reagan's associate in the Iran-Contra scandal, Breeden stole the street sign and announced he was holding it for $30 million ransom, the amount involved in the scandal.

That man, Vonnegut said, is "a holy clown." He added: "So was Joe Heller. And Abbie Hoffman."

Abbie Hoffman holds a unique place in the history of our time. There was no one quite like him, no one who so combined brilliant, zany wit with serious political purpose. There also was no one who so brought together—as with a clash of cymbals—the cultural revolution of the sixties with the tumultuous protests for racial justice and against the war in Vietnam, and very few who carried over the energy and commitment of those years into the seventies and eighties, without a pause and without any twinge of uncertainty.

Abbie's comic adventures were educational in the best sense of the word, in which a master teacher uses the arts of humor and drama to make a profound commentary on the world in which we live. He joined that honorable group of artists who have always given their talents to the struggle for peace and justice, whether through music, as with Bob Dylan, Woody Guthrie, Paul Robeson, Joan Baez, Pete Seeger; or with humor, as with Mark Twain, Lenny Bruce, Dick Gregory; or in literature, as with John Steinbeck, Theodore Dreiser, Arthur Miller, James Baldwin.

A political movement needs more than astute analysis, efficient organization, and inspiring speeches. It needs heart and soul, which

Abbie had in abundance. It needs passion and excitement, which flowed out of Abbie and enveloped the people he touched. For him to describe himself as "a community organizer" (understanding that his was a community extended to the entire nation) was true enough, but it omits what was most striking about his contribution to the movements of the sixties: he helped turn the antiauthoritarian instincts of the younger generation into political resistance to racism and war. He spoke to the gentleness, the longing for a nonviolent world, of the flower children, but said, "I always held my flower in a clenched fist."

At the conclusion of *Soon to Be a Major Motion Picture*, Abbie is going underground—"going swimming" as he put it in code language. There were those who were not at all in Abbie's dangerous situation, yet dropped out of the movement. But Abbie, facing life in prison and the possibility of detection every hour he was on the lam, refused to remain silent. He underwent plastic surgery, cut and dyed his hair, and moved around the country with an audacity that would have been astonishing for anyone else, but was to be expected from Abbie Hoffman.

While underground, Abbie made speeches, appeared on television, wrote at least forty articles, and spoke on the radio. He even went on a visitors' tour of the FBI building in Washington.

But Abbie was not totally alone. Early in his underground days, having gone through a painful good-bye from his wife, Anita, and his three children, he found a companion while spending some time in Mexico. Johanna Lawrenson became his "running mate," for his years underground and thereafter, until his death in 1989.

Abbie and Johanna did some Abbie-type escapades together. They went on a European tour for six months, eating marvelous meals at fifty-four of the world's best restaurants—not paying of course, because Abbie had a fake letter introducing them to the chefs as journalists on assignment for *Playboy* to do an article on the new French cuisine.

More important, they moved to Johanna's cottage in the Thousand Islands on the St. Lawrence River, certainly one of the most beautiful places on the continent. The St. Lawrence Seaway, connecting the Great Lakes with the Atlantic Ocean, was one of the great engineering feats of the century, an enormous complex of water basins, earth dikes, power plants, dams, bridges, highways, and new communities. Environmentally, however, there had been disastrous results, with whole islands demolished and ten thousand people forced off the land.

As Abbie and Johanna settled in, the Army Corps of Engineers proposed a plan to make the river navigable in the winter by a combination of icebreakers and log booms. Abbie studied the proposal and soon realized that it would destroy watering pools for the endangered bald eagle, disturb the aquatic life chain, and eliminate wetlands. There would be serious erosion and flooding. Chemical wastes would be released into the drinking water. There was also the prospect of oil spills.

Abbie and Johanna cofounded Save the River! with neighbors and friends, and Abbie's organizing experience went to work. He spoke endlessly on the radio and television, held press conferences, mobilized experts. When the Army Corps of Engineers held a hearing on their plan, there was an overflow crowd of more than six hundred. U.S. Senator Daniel Patrick Moynihan held a Senate Field Hearing and nine hundred people packed the hall. Abbie held forth eloquently. Moynihan praised him as Barry Freed, the fighter for environmental rights. In the spring of 1980, Congress refused to reauthorize funding for the Corps of Engineers' plan. It was an extraordinary victory for the people.

Shortly afterward, Abbie decided he would no longer be a fugitive. An arrangement was made for him to return to New York City and serve what turned out to be a year in prison. When he was free again, he was unstoppable, speaking on campuses all over the country. In 1987 he participated in civil disobedience at the University of Massachusetts in Amherst, blocking the passage of recruiters for the CIA.

I had known Abbie from the days of the southern civil rights movement, and our paths crossed a number of times after that. I was now called on to be one of the "expert witnesses" in the trial of Abbie and his fellow protesters. My assignment was to do what I had done many times during the political trials of the Vietnam era—to talk about the necessity of civil disobedience in the face of dangerous governmental policies. There was also testimony about the CIA, from former agents who told of its murderous and illegal activities all over the world.

But the highlight of the trial was Abbie's closing remarks to the jury. Anyone familiar with his antics at the 1969 Chicago trial would have been awed by his dress, his manner, his language—sober, thoughtful, reasoned, persuasive. In the end, the jury acquitted the defendants. The county district attorney prosecuting the case concluded: "If there is a message, it was that . . . Middle America doesn't want the CIA doing what they are doing."

I encountered Abbie once more after that, when he and I spoke at a student rally for academic freedom on the campus of Boston University. He would die in April of 1989, from what appeared to be a massive dose of phenobarbitol and alcohol, taken in the midst of a deep depression.

After his death I spoke one night about Abbie in a jammed tavern in downtown Manhattan, along with Norman Mailer, Allen Ginsberg, Barbara Ehrenreich, and others. He had touched all of us, in different ways. We all felt it was profoundly important for the future of our country that his legacy of fun and rebellion, of indomitable spirit, of passionate concern for justice, live on.

Boston, Massachusetts
January 2000

Abbie Hoffman's 1975 California driver's license.

While underground, Abbie Hoffman and Johanna Lawrenson (aka Angel) traveled across the United States., as well as to Mexico, Guatemala, Canada, Holland, and France. Abbie is pictured here in disguise as Mark Samuels, food critic for *Playboy* magazine, sampling the cuisine of French chef Paul Bocuse. Lyon, France, fall 1977. Photograph by Johanna Lawrenson.

Abbie as Barry Freed with photographer Johanna Lawrenson—wife, companion, and running mate. Abbie and Johanna got together in Mexico in spring 1974. Here they are hiding in the locks on the Rideau Canal, Ontario, Canada, August 1978. At the same time, a "Bring Abbie Home" event is taking place at the Felt Forum, New York City. Photograph by America Hoffman. Courtesy of Johanna Lawrenson.

Underground in the 1000 Islands in summer 1978, Barry Freed and Johanna Lawrenson helped create Save The River! to stop the Army Corps of Engineers' plan for winter navigation on the St. Lawrence River. Organizing house to house by boat across the islands, a committed, binational group of citizen activists emerged victorious in their battle against the Army Corps. Senator Daniel Patrick Moynihan announces that we all owe Barry Freed a debt of gratitude for his important work. U.S. Senate Field Hearing, Alexandria Bay, August 27, 1979. Photograph by Johanna Lawrenson.

Barry in an outboard with his three children—Andrew, Ilya (aka Amy) and America (aka Alan). St. Lawrence River, summer 1979. Photograph by Johanna Lawrenson.

Barry Freed moderates a Meet the Candidates Forum in July 1980, asking candidates for U.S. Congress for New York's 30th District to "Stand Up For The River." Photograph by Johanna Lawrenson.

Abbie's dedication to political organizing never wavered. After coming aboveground, Abbie founded Citizens Against Nuclear Trucking (CANT) to stop the trucking of nuclear waste across New York City. Here's Abbie at the historic June 12, 1982, antinuke march in Central Park. Photograph by Johanna Lawrenson.

Abbie and Johanna led tours to Nicaragua during the mid-1980s to see the country under the new Sandinista government. Here is Abbie in Managua with Fernando Cardinal and Betty Friedan, New Year's, 1985. Photograph by Johanna Lawrenson.

Abbie protesting U.S. aid to the Contras at a demonstration in front of the U.S. Embassy, Managua, Nicaragua, January 1985. Abbie told the crowd, "No quiero viver en el mundo sin Nicaragua Libre!" Photograph by Johanna Lawrenson.

One of Abbie's passions in the 1980s was passing along his organizing skills and experience to young organizers. He spoke on campuses throughout the United States and Canada, and served as adviser to a host of student activist projects including National Student Convention '88 (at Rutgers University) and Student Action Union. Here are Abbie and Johanna flying back from Nicaragua with young activists Al Giordano and Lisa Fithian, 1985. Courtesy of Johanna Lawrenson.

Abbie and Johanna with Randy Gorman on Rio Aqua Rico, Headwaters of the Amazon, Ecuador, January 1986. Courtesy of Johanna Lawrenson.

At the University of Massachusetts, Amherst, Abbie joined students, including Amy Carter, in a sit-in protesting CIA recruitment on campus. In court, the defendants argued the necessity defense, contending that their minor act of trespassing was necessary to stop larger crimes of CIA covert actions in Central America and elsewhere. In a landmark decision, a jury found the protesters not guilty, in effect finding the CIA guilty of international crimes. Here, outside the Northampton courthouse, the defendants celebrate their victory. Amy Carter is at the megaphone. Standing next to Abbie is lawyer Len Weinglass, April 15, 1987. Photograph by Johanna Lawrenson.

Abbie in conversation with poet Allen Ginsberg during a Washington, D.C., "National March Against U.S. Intervention in Central America and Southern Africa," April 1987. Photograph by Johanna Lawrenson.

Daniel Ellsberg, Allen Ginsberg, Betsy Tomlinson, and two fellow demonstrators with Abbie and Johanna at a Washington, D.C., rally, April 1987. Courtesy of Johanna Lawrenson.

Abbie with Dave Dellinger and Bobby Seale in Chicago twenty years after the Chicago Conspiracy Trial, Chicago, 1988. Photograph by Johanna Lawrenson.